3rd Edition

Intermediate

MARKET LEADER

Business English Teacher's Resource Book

Bill Mascull

PEARSON

Longman

FINANCIAL
TIMES

Pearson Education Limited
Edinburgh Gate, Harlow, Essex CM20 2JE, England
and Associated Companies throughout the world.

www.pearsonlongman.com
© Pearson Education Limited 2010

First published 2000
Third edition 2010
ISBN: 978 1 4082 4949 9
Set in: MetaPlus 9.5/12
Printed by Graficas Estella, Bilboa, Spain

We are grateful to the following for permission to reproduce copyright material:
The Financial Times
Extract 1. from "Real chief says own brand is the way ahead", *The Financial Times*,
22 December 2008 (Wiesmann, G.), copyright © The Financial Times Ltd; Extract 1.
from "Chinese shoppers focus more on prices", *The Financial Times*, 15 September
2008 (Waldmeir, P.), copyright © The Financial Times Ltd; Extract 2. adapted from
"Hotel changes the landscape of building", *The Financial Times*, 22 January 2009
(Cookson, R.), copyright © The Financial Times Ltd; Extract 2. adapted from "IT Going
Green: Reluctant users hamper take-up of videoconferencing", *The Financial Times*,
20 November 2007 (Bradbury, D.), copyright © The Financial Times Ltd; Extract 3.
adapted from "An enduring sermon", *The Financial Times*, 21 January 2009 (Witzel, M.),
copyright © The Financial Times Ltd; Extract 3. adapted from "Structural engineering",
The Financial Times, 17 October 2008 (Empson, L.), copyright © The Financial Times
Ltd; Extract 4. from "Looking to Wikipedia for answers", *The Financial Times*, 5
November 2008 (Malone, T.), copyright © The Financial Times Ltd; Extract 4. adapted
from "Corporate management: Creating a breadth of development", *The Financial
Times*, 14 October 2005 (Overell, S.), copyright © The Financial Times Ltd; Extract 5.
adapted from "Advertisers try the soft sell as TV drifts online", *The Financial Times*, 27
March 2008 (Chaffin, J.), copyright © The Financial Times Ltd; Extract 5. from "Pfizer
uses big screen to fight counterfeit", *The Financial Times*, 15 January 2009 (Jack, A.),
copyright © The Financial Times Ltd; Extract 6. adapted from "Wal-Mart profits reach
$13bn", *The Financial Times*, 18 February 2009 (Birchall, J.), copyright © The Financial
Times Ltd; Extract 6. adapted from "Beware men in white hats", *The Financial Times*,
27 September 2008 (Leith, W.), copyright © The Financial Times Ltd; Extract 7. adapted
from "Tricky feats of cross-cultural communication", *The Financial Times*, 7 August
2008 (Barnes, W.), copyright © The Financial Times Ltd; Extract 8. adapted from
"Helping workers manage bad news", *The Financial Times*, 9 November 2008 (Jacobs,
E.), copyright © The Financial Times Ltd; Extract 8. adapted from "The right people
for the right jobs", *The Financial Times*, 11 March 2009 (Witzel, M.), copyright © The
Financial Times Ltd; Extract 9. from "Panasonic enters European white goods market",
The Financial Times, 24 February 2009 (Harding, R.), copyright © The Financial
Times Ltd; Extract 10. adapted from "Beware the risky business of résumé fraud",
The Financial Times, 4 March 2009 (Guthrie, J.), copyright © The Financial Times Ltd;
Extract 10. adapted from "What would-be whistleblowers should know", *The Financial
Times*, 16 February 2009 (Skapinker, M.), copyright © The Financial Times Ltd; Extract
12. from "Best Buy highlights competitive threat to rivals", *The Financial Times*, 8
May 2008 (Braithwaite, T.), copyright © The Financial Times Ltd; Extract 12. from
"Competition: Tide slowly begins to turn against private monopolies", *The Financial
Times*, 14 November 2008 (ThomsonA.), copyright © The Financial Times Ltd

In some instances we have been unable to trace the owners of copyright material, and
we would appreciate any information that would enable us to do so.

Front cover image: Fotolia: SuzyM
Project managed by Chris Hartley

Introduction

Market Leader Third Edition reflects the fast-changing world of business with thoroughly updated material from authentic sources such as the *Financial Times*. The Third Edition retains the dynamic and effective approach that has made this course so successful in business English classes worldwide. In addition to new authentic reading texts and listening material, the Third Edition features a number of exciting new resources:

- specially filmed interviews with business practitioners for each unit
- *Case study commentaries* on DVD-ROM, with expert views on each case
- *Working across cultures* – regular input and tasks to develop students' intercultural awareness and skills
- four Revision units, one after every three main units
- an interactive i-Glossary on DVD-ROM
- additional photocopiable tasks in this Teacher's Resource Book

1 Course aims

Market Leader is an extensive business English course designed to bring the real world of international business into the language-teaching classroom. It has been developed in association with the *Financial Times*, one of the world's leading sources of professional information, to ensure the maximum range and authenticity of international business content.

The course is intended for use by either students preparing for a career in business or those already working who want to improve their English communication skills. *Market Leader* combines some of the most stimulating recent ideas from the world of business with a strongly task-based approach. Role plays and case studies are regular features of each unit. Throughout the course, students are encouraged to use their own experience and opinions in order to maximise involvement and learning.

An essential requirement of business English materials is that they cater for the wide range of needs which students have, including different areas of interest and specialisation, different skills needs and varying amounts of time available to study. *Market Leader* offers teachers and course planners a unique range of flexible materials to help meet these needs. There are suggestions in this book on how to use the unit material extensively or intensively and how the material in the Practice File integrates with the Course Book. There are optional extra components, including a Business Grammar and Usage book, a DVD-ROM and a series of special subject books to develop vocabulary and reading skills. This book contains extensive extra photocopiable material in the Text bank and Resource bank sections.

2 The main course components

Course Book

This provides the main part of the teaching material, divided into 12 topic-based units. The topics have been chosen following research among teachers to establish the areas of widest possible interest to the majority of their students. The Course Book provides input in reading, speaking and listening, with guidance for writing tasks too. Every unit contains vocabulary-development activities and a rapid review of essential grammar. There is a regular focus on key business functions, and each unit ends with a motivating case study to allow students to practise language they have worked on during the unit. For more details on the Course Book units, see *Overview of a Course Book unit* below.

After every three units is a spread called *Working across cultures*. Here, students are introduced to key intercultural concepts, developing their awareness and skills in order to function effectively in international business situations.

There are also four Revision units in the Course Book that revise and consolidate the work done in the main units and culture spreads.

Practice File

This gives extra practice in the areas of grammar and vocabulary, together with a complete syllabus in business writing. In each unit, students work with text models and useful language, then do a writing task to consolidate the learning. Additionally, the Practice File provides regular self-study pronunciation work (with an audio CD and exercises) and a valuable survival language section for students when travelling.

Audio and DVD-ROM materials

All the listening material from the Course Book is available on audio CD. Additionally, the Course Book interviews (together with *Case study commentaries*) can be viewed on DVD-ROM with the option of sub-titles, depending on users' preference. The DVD-ROM also contains all the listening material from the Course Book.

The Practice File pronunciation exercises are on the accompanying audio CD.

Teacher's Resource Book

This book provides teachers with an overview of the whole course, together with detailed teaching notes, background briefings on business content, the Text bank (24 optional extra reading texts) and the Resource bank (photocopiable worksheets practising speaking, listening and writing skills).

Test File

Six photocopiable tests are available to teachers and course planners to monitor students' progress during the course. There is an entry test, four progress tests and an exit test, which reviews the work done throughout the course.

3 Overview of a Course Book unit

A typical unit consists of the following sections:

Starting up

Students have the opportunity to think about the unit topic and to exchange ideas and opinions with each other and with the teacher. There is a variety of stimulating activities such as answering quiz questions, reflecting on difficult decisions, prioritising options and completing charts. Throughout, students are encouraged to draw upon their life and business experience as appropriate.

Vocabulary

Essential business vocabulary is presented and practised through a wide variety of creative and engaging exercises. Students learn new words, phrases and collocations and are given tasks which help to activate the vocabulary they already know or have just learnt.

There is further vocabulary practice in the Practice File.

There are a number of discussion activities in the book. Their main purpose is to build up students' confidence in expressing their views in English and to improve their fluency.

Reading

Students read interesting and relevant authentic texts from the *Financial Times* and other business sources. They develop their reading skills and acquire essential business vocabulary. The texts provide a context for language work and discussion later in the unit.

Listening

The authentic listening texts are based on interviews with businesspeople and experts in their field. Students develop listening skills such as prediction, listening for specific information and note-taking. They can, if they prefer, watch the interviews on the DVD-ROM.

Language review

These sections develop students' awareness of the common problem areas at intermediate level. They focus on accuracy and knowledge of key areas of grammar. If students already know the grammar point, this section works as a quick check for them and the teacher. If they need more explanation, they are referred to the Grammar reference at the back of the Course Book.

There is further grammar practice in the Practice File and in the Business Grammar and Usage book (see *Extending the course* below).

Skills

This section helps learners to develop their communication skills in the key business areas of presentations, meetings, negotiations, telephoning and social English. Each section contains a *Useful language* box which provides students with the phrases they need to carry out the business tasks in the regular role-play activities.

Case studies

Each unit ends with a case study linked to the unit's business topic. The case studies are based on realistic business problems or situations and are designed to motivate and actively engage students. Students use the language and communication skills which they have acquired while working through the unit. Typically, students will be involved in discussing business problems and recommending solutions through active group work.

All of the case studies have been developed and tested with students in class and are designed to be easy to present and use. No special knowledge or extra materials are required. For teaching tips on making the best use of the case studies, see *Case studies that work* on page 5.

Each case study ends with a realistic writing task. These tasks reflect the real world of business correspondence and will also help those students preparing for business English exams. Models of writing text types are given in the Writing file at the end of the Course Book.

After students have completed each case study, they can watch the *Case study commentaries* on the DVD-ROM. Here, a consultant talks about the business issues raised by each case. This may in turn lead to further discussion of the case in class.

4 Using the course

Accessibility for teachers

Less-experienced teachers can sometimes find teaching business English a daunting experience. They may be anxious about their lack of knowledge of the business world and of the topics covered in the course. *Market Leader* sets out to provide the maximum support for teachers. The *Business brief* section at the beginning of each unit in the Teacher's Resource Book gives an overview of the business topic, covering key terms (given in bold, and which can be checked in the *Longman Dictionary of Business English*) and suggesting a list of titles for further reading and information.

Authenticity of content

One of the principles of the course is that students should deal with as much authentic content as their language level allows. Authentic reading and listening texts are motivating for students and bring the real world of business into the classroom, increasing students' knowledge of business practice and concepts. Due to its international coverage, the *Financial Times* has been a rich source of text, video and business information for the course.

The case studies present realistic business situations and problems, and the communication activities based on them – group discussions, simulations and role plays – serve to enhance the authenticity of the course.

Flexibility of use

Demands of business English courses vary greatly, and materials accordingly need to be flexible and adaptable. *Market Leader* has been designed to give teachers and course planners the maximum flexibility. The course can be used either extensively or intensively. At the beginning of each unit in the Teacher's Resource Book are suggestions for a fast route through the unit if time is short. This intensive route focuses mainly on speaking and listening skills. If the teacher wants to extend this concentration on particular skills, optional components are available in the course (see *Extending the course* on page 5).

5 Case studies that work

The following teaching tips will help when using case studies.

1 Involve all the students at every stage of the lesson. Encourage everyone to participate.
2 Draw on the students' knowledge of business and the world.
3 Be very careful how you present the case study at the beginning. Make sure your instructions are clear and that the task is understood. (See individual units in the Teacher's Resource Book for detailed suggestions on introducing the case study.)
4 Ensure that all students have understood the case and the key vocabulary.
5 Encourage the students to use the language and communication skills they have acquired in the rest of the unit. A short review of the key language will help.
6 Focus on communication and fluency during the case-study activities. Language errors can be dealt with at the end. Make a record of important errors and give students feedback at the end in a sympathetic and constructive way.
7 If the activity is developing slowly or you have a group of students who are a little reticent, you could intervene by asking questions or making helpful suggestions.
8 Allow students to reach their own conclusions. Many students expect there to be a correct answer. The teacher can give their own opinion but should stress that there is usually no single 'right' answer.
9 Encourage creative and imaginative solutions to the problems expressed.
10 Encourage students to use people-management skills such as working in teams, leading teams, delegating and interacting effectively with each other.
11 Allocate sufficient time for the major tasks such as negotiating. At the same time, do not allow activities to drag on too long. You want the students to have enough time to perform the task and yet the lesson needs to have pace.
12 Students should identify the key issues of the case and discuss all the options before reaching a decision.
13 Encourage students to actively listen to each other. This is essential for both language practice and effective teamwork!

6 Extending the course

Some students will require more input or practice in certain areas, either in terms of subject matter or skills, than is provided in the Course Book. In order to meet their needs, *Market Leader* provides a wide range of optional extra materials and components to choose from.

Teacher's Resource Book

The Text bank: two extra reading texts per unit, together with comprehension and vocabulary exercises

The Resource bank: photocopiable worksheet-based communication activities linked to particular sections of the Course Book units

- Listening: extra activities based on each Course Book Listening interview
- Speaking: extra activities based on each Skills section
- Writing: a model answer to the Course Book Writing task, together with an additional writing exercise

Business Grammar and Usage New Edition

For students needing more work on their grammar, this book provides reference and practice in all the most important areas of business English usage. It is organised into structural and functional sections. The book has been revised and updated for the Third Edition.

DVD-ROM

The DVD-ROM contains a great deal of optional extra material:

All audiovisual content relating to the Course Book (Listening interviews and *Case study commentaries*). Sub-titles are available if students working on their own need them.

The i-Glossary, an interactive mini-dictionary which provides definitions and pronunciation of all the key vocabulary listed at the back of the Course Book.

Special subject series

Many students will need to learn the language of more specialised areas of business English. To provide them with authentic and engaging material, *Market Leader* includes a range of special subject books which focus on reading skills and vocabulary development.

The first books in the series are *Accounting and Finance*, *Business Law*, *Human Resources*, *Logistics Management*, *Marketing* and *Working Across Cultures*. This series will expand to cover the most common areas of business specialisation. Each book includes two tests and a glossary of specialised language.

Longman Dictionary of Business English New Edition

This is the most up-to-date source of reference in business English today. Compiled from a wide range of text sources, it allows students and teachers rapid access to clear, straightforward definitions of the latest international business terminology. The fully updated New Edition includes an interactive CD-ROM with 35,000 key words pronounced in both British and American English, together with practice material for both the BEC and BULATS exams.

Market Leader website

http://www.market-leader.net

The *Market Leader* companion website provides up-to-date information about the Course Books and specialist titles and offers a wide range of materials teachers can use to supplement and enrich their lessons. Resources include free writing and listening tests for each level, links to websites relevant to units and topics in the Course Books and downloadable glossaries of business terms.

The Premier Lessons subscription area of the website has a bank of ready-made lessons with authentic texts from the *FT* that have student worksheets and answers. These lessons are regularly updated and can be searched in order to find relevant texts for the unit, topic and level that students are studying. Premier Lessons can be used in the classroom or for self-study.

Contents

CONTENTS

Resource bank

UNIT 1 Brands

AT A GLANCE

	Classwork – Course Book	Further work
Lesson 1 *Each lesson (excluding case studies) is about 45 to 60 minutes. This does not include time spent going through homework.*	<u>**Starting up**</u> Students' attitudes to brands **Vocabulary: Brand management** Students look at word partnerships with *brand*, *product* and *market*. **Listening: Successful brands** A brands specialist talks about the function of brands and work he has done to help develop a particular brand.	**Practice File** Vocabulary (page 4) **i-Glossary** (DVD-ROM) **Resource bank: Listening** (page 188) **Course Book Listening** (DVD-ROM)
Lesson 2	**Reading: Building luxury brands** Students read an article about Dior and its plans for moving into new markets. **Language review: Present simple and present continuous** Students look at the differences between these two tenses.	**Text bank** (pages 114–117) **ML Grammar and Usage** **Practice File** Language review (page 5)
Lesson 3	<u>**Skills: Taking part in meetings**</u> Students listen to a meeting where there is a difference of opinion and learn key language for participating in meetings.	**Resource bank: Speaking** (page 174) **Practice File** Making suggestions (page 55)
Lesson 4 *Each case study is about 1½ to 2 hours.*	<u>**Case study: Hudson Corporation**</u> A US company is facing a strategic choice for its marketing in Europe. Students discuss the alternatives and make a recommendation.	**Resource bank: Writing** (page 204) **Practice File** Writing (pages 6–7) **Case study commentary** (DVD-ROM)

For a fast route through the unit focusing mainly on speaking skills, just use the underlined sections.

For one-to-one situations, most parts of the unit lend themselves, with minimal adaptation, to use with individual students. Where this is not the case, alternative procedures are given.

BUSINESS BRIEF

As the marketing expert Philip Kotler has said, 'The most distinctive skill of professional marketers is their ability to **create, maintain, protect** and **enhance brands**.' But, despite the best efforts of professional marketers, the list of top brands of today is not so different from that of 30 or 40 years ago: Coca-Cola, IBM, Ford and Hoover are all still there. A brand is a **set of associations** in the mind of the consumer. Consumers tend to form **emotional attachments** to foods and household goods they grow up with. These brands gain **mind share** in consumers at an early age, and **new brands** find it hard to compete with the **established brands**.

One area where new brands can appear is in **new categories**. For example, the names Amazon, Google and Facebook have emerged as extremely **strong brands** on the Internet in e-commerce, search and social networking respectively.

We tend to think of brands in relation to **consumer marketing** and **packaged goods**, and consumer goods companies will often employ **brand managers** to develop their brands. But the use of brands and branding is also important in **industrial** or **business-to-business (B2B) marketing**, where companies are selling to other companies rather than to consumers. In business-to-business marketing, substitute **'buyer'** for 'consumer' and there will be similar issues of **brand awareness**, **brand image** and **brand equity**: the value to a company of the brands that it owns.

In business-to-business marketing, the company name itself is often its most important brand. A company's **image** and **reputation** will clearly be key to its success.

Brands and your students

Both pre-work and in-work students should have lots to say about their own **brand preferences** as consumers.

In-work students not involved in sales or marketing may say that brands do not directly concern them, but they should be able to discuss their organisation's reputation relative to its competitors. This is **brand positioning**: the way that a brand is perceived in relation to other brands.

Read on

Thomas Gad: *4D Branding*, FT Prentice Hall, 2000

David A. Aaker: *Building Strong Brands*, Simon & Schuster, 2002

Andy Milligan: *Brand it like Beckham*, Cyan, 2005

Philip Kotler and Kevin Keller: *Marketing Management*, Pearson, 2008

LESSON NOTES

LESSON NOTES

Warmer

- Write two headings on the board: *Types of product* and *Brands*. Under the first heading, write some product types that you think your students will be interested in, for example *Cars*, *Clothes*, *Electrical goods*, *Soft drinks*, *Foods*.

- Then get students to suggest one or two brands for each category and write them up on the right-hand side of the board.

- Ask students to work in small groups and think of some more brands for each category. Go round the room to help where necessary.

- After a few minutes, ask each group for their ideas and add them to the right-hand column.

- Ask students why they chose the brands they did and if they have bought any of them recently. Anticipate but do not pre-empt the activities in the rest of the unit.

Overview

- Tell students that they will be looking at brands, one of the key parts of marketing.

- Ask students to look at the Overview panel at the beginning of the unit, pointing out the sections that you will be covering.

Quotation

- Ask one student to read the quotation at the head of the page. Ask other students if they agree with it and if so, why, and if not, why not. (If students are interested, you can tell them to look at www.landor.com after the class, to get information about the consultancy that still bears his name. This Walter Landor is not to be confused, by the way, with the nineteenth-century English poet of the same name.)

- A discussion may develop. Remember any points that may be relevant to later parts of the lesson, and tell students you will come back to them.

Starting up

This section introduces the main themes of the unit and provides speaking practice.

A

- Tell students to work in simultaneous pairs and make lists of their favourite brands and then answer the five questions.

- Go round the room and help where necessary, especially with the vocabulary in question 3.

- When they have finished, get two or three pairs to summarise their answers and discuss them with the whole group.

- In relation to question 2, get students to look at the rankings on page 134. Ask the whole group if they are surprised by any of the answers. AT&T, a US telecoms group, and Marlboro have gone; new entries are Mercedes-Benz (perhaps surprisingly as it has been around for so long) and Nokia.

- Ask if they are surprised by the absence of any brands from the 2007 list (perhaps Google).

- Do a final check on the vocabulary in question 3 by giving definitions of the expressions and getting students to find the corresponding answers.

- Write up these expressions in a column for vocabulary on one side of the board. During the rest of the lesson, go on adding key vocabulary to this 'permanent' list, especially vocabulary relating to brands.

B 🔊 CD1.1

- Tell students they are going to listen to two speakers talking about brands.

- Play the recording once right through and ask which speaker is in favour of brands and which against.

- Play each speaker's response again, explaining vocabulary that students find difficult and writing up key words in the list on the board.

- Go round the class and ask three or four students to say which speaker they agree with and why.

Vocabulary: Brand management

Students look at word partnerships with *brand*, *product* and *market*.

A

- If this is your first lesson with the students, tell or remind them about the idea of word partnerships, the idea that there are words that usually go with other words to form typical partnerships or combinations.

- Check students can pronounce the expressions with the correct stress. Get individual students to repeat difficult ones, e.g. 'brand aWAREness'.

- Get students to work on the exercise in pairs. Go round the class and assist where necessary.

- Then ask the whole class for the answers.

1 d	2 c	3 b	4 e	5 a	6 i	7 j	8 f	9 h
10 g	11 m	12 n	13 k	14 o	15 l

B

- Still in pairs, get students to work on the exercise. Go round the class and assist where necessary.

- Then ask the whole class for the answers and work on any remaining difficulties.

brand

1 awareness   **2** loyalty   **3** stretching   **4** image

(You could point out that 'raise awareness' is another form of word partnership, this time between a verb an a noun.)

product

5 endorsement   **6** lifecycle   **7** range   **8** placement

market

9 leader   **10** segment   **11** challenger   **12** research

C

- Put students into pairs. Go round the class and assist where necessary. (If this is the first lesson, point out the existence of the i-Glossary, which is on the DVD-ROM supplied with the Course Book.)

- If there is interest and time, there could be class discussion of some of the issues raised, for example, the use of celebrities to endorse products and the products that they endorse.

 i-Glossary

Listening: Successful brands

Students listen to Chris Cleaver, Managing Director, Business Brands at Dragon Brands, a London-based consultancy. In the first two parts of the interview, he talks about the function of brands. In the third, he talks about work that he did for Nokia, to illustrate a particular point about brands.

A 🔊 CD1.2

- Explain to students who Chris Cleaver is and where he works. If necessary, explain *consultancy*, an organisation that sells expertise and advice in particular areas to other companies.

- Play the recording once through.

- Then play it again, stopping after each sentence to explain any difficulties (e.g. *manifestation*, *recognition*, *perception*), but without giving away the answers.

- Then play it a third time, stopping after each sentence so that students can complete the exercise.

- With the whole class, ask individual students for the answers. Explain any remaining difficulties.

A brand:

1 helps people to become familiar with a product.

2 gives a product an identity. ✓

3 increases the sales of a product or service.

4 enables the target consumer to decide if they want the product or not. ✓

B 🔊 CD1.3

- Depending on level, play the recording two or three times, explaining any difficulties as above. Here, *raft of important information* may cause problems.

- On the last play-through, get students to give the answer:

A brand's main function is 'to enable you to choose one thing from another – often in markets where there is very little actual difference between, you know, the product'.

- Encourage students to give answers in their own words, paraphrasing this.

C 🔊 CD1.4

- Again depending on level, play the recording two or three times, explaining any difficulties as above.

- On the last play-through, get students to give their answers.

Chris Cleaver's company has helped Nokia:

- with the question of what the Nokia brand represents and how customers relate to it – to get them to think of it as the 'master brand'.

- to develop parts of their offer (point out this specialised use of *offer*) and keeping the brand fresh with multimedia devices, not just 'phones'.

(Point out Chris's use of *Firstly* and *And* to signpost these two main ideas.)

- For lower-level classes, you may at this point want to play the whole interview again while students look at the script on page 152.

- If there is time and interest, discuss with students the brands that cause them real excitement and passion, in similar ways to Nokia (e.g. Apple and its iPod and iPhone). If relevant, go back to some of the examples they gave in the Warmer section.

D

- Divide the class into groups of three and get them to discuss the question.

- Go round the class to assist where necessary.

- Bring the whole class to order and get a member of each group to give its 'findings'. Encourage discussion with the whole class.

➡ Resource bank: Listening (page 188).

◎ Students can watch the interview with Chris Cleaver on the DVD-ROM.

Reading: Building luxury brands

Students read an article about a luxury-goods company and its efforts to get into new markets.

 A

- Ask students what sort of products have a 'luxury' category and what luxury brands they can think of for each product. Which are related mainly to cars, which to clothes, which to cosmetics, etc.? For example, Rolls Royce (still the epitome of luxury cars, even if the brand is used mainly in connection with aircraft engines now), Gucci, Hermes, Burberry (clothes) and, hopefully, Dior… (perfumes/cosmetics).

- Then ask the pre-question in the Course Book: What is the brand image of Dior? (Elicit or explain words such as *luxurious*, *exclusive*, *sophisticated*.)

B

- Draw attention to the four points and then get students to skim the article individually or in pairs to look for them. Go round and assist where necessary with language problems.

- Bring the class to order and elicit and discuss the answers.

The only point specifically mentioned is:

2 Investing in markets that may take some time to grow: 'You have to look for newness, look for what is happening next. Forget the calculator. Understand the people from different countries and what they want.' (lines 24–28)

'… a brand should go to its customers but that it should anticipate their needs and invest early in markets that may not show real growth for up to six years.' (lines 67–71)

C

- Get students to read the article individually or in pairs in order to fill in the maps. Go round and help with any difficulties.

- Bring the class to order and elicit answers to complete the maps.

1	demands	**5**	understand
2	label	**6**	forget
3	exclusivity	**7**	double
4	look for	**8**	of luxury

- Then elicit the ten mistakes in the maps.

1 Bernard Arnault is Sydney Toledano's boss, not his assistant. (line 11)

2, 3 Galliano and de Castellane need to be swapped round in relation to clothes and jewellery. (lines 14–16)

4, 5 Swap round two pieces of advice: 'when times are bad, you need to get out of the office; when things are good, you can spend time on the organisation'. (lines 18–21)

6, 7 In the Dior map, swap round: 'we have to develop our network and perfect our supply chain'. (lines 60–61)

8, 9, 10 Russia is correct, but the other three markets are not. They are, in fact, the Middle East, Hong Kong and Korea. (lines 64–65)

- If there is time and interest, get students to talk about their own companies (or ones they would like to work for) and how their markets will develop over the next few years, using some of the language from the article, e.g. *We have to develop our … and perfect our … in … .*

⟹ Text bank (pages 114–117)

Language review: Present simple and present continuous

Students look at the (sometimes tricky) differences between these two tenses. They will have met these tenses before, of course, but choosing the correct one will probably go on causing problems even when your students become more advanced speakers. Here, students have a chance to revise and consolidate their knowledge.

- With the whole class, go through the commentary and examples in the panel. Point out that present continuous is used for temporary activities, even if they are not going on right now. For example, you can say, *Dior is currently looking to recruit a marketing director for the UK and Ireland*, even if it's late at night and no one is doing any looking at the time you're speaking.

- If necessary, depending on the level of the group, quickly revise the formation of affirmatives, negatives and questions in each tense by writing examples of each on the board.

- Point out the existence of the Grammar reference section at the end of the Course Book, especially if you have not done this before. If time permits, go through the information on page 146 or ask students to do this for homework.

A

- With the whole class, go through the list, explaining where necessary. (Only *currently* and *nowadays* are likely cause problems at this level.)

- Get students to say which expressions are used with each tense, reminding them of the difference: present simple (PS) for general facts and routines and present continuous (PC) for temporary situations.

usually (PS)	this year (PC)
every day (PS)	now (PC)
often (PS)	nowadays (PC)
once a month (PS)	currently (PS and PC)
at the moment (PS and PC)	these days (PS and PC)

B

- Get students to work on the exercise in pairs. Go round the room and give assistance where necessary.

- With the whole class, go through the exercise, asking for answers.

1 a) is working
  b) spends (or *spend*) (Explain that you can treat a company as singular or plural.)
2 a) sells (In this case, the singular must be used to agree with *its products*.)
  b) is negotiating (or *are negotiating* but this wouldn't be consistent with the previous sentence)
3 a) are launching
  b) have (because *have* is not used in the continuous in this context; *are having* would be very strange here)

C

- Still in pairs, get students to work on the exercise. Again, go round the room and give assistance where necessary.

- Go through the answers with the whole class, explaining any difficulties.

1	is growing	7	see
2	holds	8	are beginning
3	dominates	9	are becoming
4	operates	10	generate
5	generates	11	holds
6	focuses	12	is growing

Skills: Taking part in meetings

In this section, students listen to a meeting where there are differences of opinion and learn key language for participating in meetings.

A ◀)) CD1.5

- Play the recording once. Ask students what it's about. (Four marketing executives at a sports sponsorship agency are talking about finding a new sponsor for their client, a well-known media company. They look at various sports, choose one and agree to contact their client about it, before contacting an advertising agency that one of the executives has in mind.)

- Get students to look at the four questions, explain any difficulties and play the recording again, stopping after they hear the answer to each question and elicit the answer. (With lower-level groups, you may have to play the recording several times.)

1 The football club that the client currently sponsors is asking for too much money, and the client is looking for a sport with more excitement and a bigger effect.
2 Ice hockey, baseball, tennis, Formula One motor racing
3 Motor racing because it is fast, exciting and has good TV coverage, which means that the client would get a lot of exposure (explain this word). It would strengthen their image. (Explain, if necessary, by pointing out the connection between *strengthen* and *strong*.)
4 He must contact the client to see if they are happy with the choice. (Point out the use of the expression *happy with*.)

B ◀)) CD1.5

- Get students to look through the items with the missing expressions.

- Then play the recording again, stopping after each item to elicit the answer.

1 How about
2 What do you think
3 I'm not so sure
4 That's true
5 how do you feel about this
6 In my opinion
7 Why don't we

- Get students to read the conversation in simultaneous groups of four. Then ask one group to read it for the whole class.

C

- Ask the whole class quickly for their answers to the four questions.

1 Asking for opinions: What do you think, How do you feel about this
2 Giving opinions: In my opinion ...
3 Agreeing or disagreeing: I'm not so sure, That's true
4 Making suggestions: How about ..., Why don't we ...

- Point out to students that this opinion language is very important and that it's worth learning these expressions by heart. Bring their attention to the Useful language box and get individual students to read out the different expressions. Help with pronunciation where necessary.

D

- Get students to look at the general role-play information. Ensure that they understand the situation.

- Get students to work in threes. Tell students who is A, B and C in each three. (Do not let students choose, as this wastes time.)

- Go round the room and help students to prepare their roles where necessary.

- When students are ready, tell them to start their 'meetings'. Go round and monitor good performance and common mistakes, especially in opinions language, e.g. *I am agree with you*.

- When students have finished, point out five good performance points and five key mistakes, quickly writing up correct versions on the board.

- Then get one of the threes to repeat their meeting for the whole class, paying attention to the key points you have covered.

- At this point, round off the activity by getting the whole class to look at the Useful language box, checking understanding and pronunciation of expressions, especially ones that have not come up so far.

> **One-to-one**
> - Role-play the discussion with the student taking one of the roles and you taking another.
> - Don't dominate the discussion, but say enough to keep it going and allow your student to make their points.
> - At the same time, monitor the language that your student is using. Note down strong points and points that need correction or improvement. Come back to these after the discussion.
> - If there is time and interest, do the role play again with you and the student taking other roles and getting your student to integrate the corrections that you made in the first role play.

 Resource bank: Speaking (page 174)

CASE STUDY

Hudson Corporation

In this case study, a luxury luggage manufacturer is facing increased competition from cheaper imports. It must decide how to protect its brand and create new markets for its products. Students analyse the situation, suggest solutions and make a final decision.

If this is the first case study you have done with the group, be sure to prepare it carefully before the class. Read the information in the introduction of this Teacher's Resource Book on *Case studies that work* (page 5).

In the class, pay particular attention to breaking the case study clearly into its component parts and making sure that students understand and follow the structure of what you are doing. Clear and timely instructions are key to this.

Background

- Read aloud, or get a student to read aloud, the background information. Explain any difficulties. Write the headings on the left-hand side of the table and elicit information from students to complete the right-hand side of the table.

Company	Hudson Corporation
Brand name	Well-known, associated with high quality, traditional design and craftsmanship (teach this last word if necessary)
Market share	Declining in the USA because of increased competition from Asia
Competitors	Asian competitors offer similar products at lower prices
Recent developments	Entered Europe a year ago – Switzerland, Germany, France and Italy. Office and warehouse in Zurich used as a base for expansion.

- Get students to discuss the possible problems in pairs.
- Bring students to order and discuss as a class.

For example:
- The company doesn't know the European market as well as the US one
- Its products may not match European tastes
- It may face new and different competitors
- It may experience distribution problems

Market research

- Tell students that one of them will be giving a mini-presentation of the information from the focus groups. (Explain *focus groups* – small groups of typical consumers who are asked to discuss and give their opinions about products.) Then divide students into groups of four to study the information. (Tell students who is in each group to avoid wasting time.)
- In each group, one of the students then has to present the information to the other three, using

appropriate language, e.g. *Nearly three-quarters of the people in the focus groups thought that Hudson products were expensive, but only 56 per cent considered that they were exclusive.* ... Go round and assist with any difficulties.

- Call the class to order, and choose one presenter to do the presentation again for the whole class. Underline the importance of the correct use of the language mentioned above.

Listening 🔊 CD1.6

- Explain who the speakers are (Hudson executives: Cornelius, Diana, Ruth and Tom) and play the recording right through once or twice. Explain any difficulties.
- Get students to say what it's about by writing the names on the left-hand side of the table in the order shown and eliciting information from students about each speaker's views to complete the table as follows.

Diana	Hudson will have to do a lot of advertising. May need to adapt their products for European markets.
Ruth	Have to get pricing right. Can charge high prices if we position (teach this use of the word) the brand as one for luxury goods, justifying high price. Europeans less price-conscious than Americans.
Tom	Go downmarket (explain this), reduce prices and increase volumes (explain).
Cornelius	Increase range and stretch brand (explain).

Marketing strategies for Europe

- Tell students they will be studying the information here in relation to what they have just heard. They will have to match each strategy with one of the speakers above. (Some of the strategies here were not mentioned by any of the speakers – point this out.)
- Divide students into the same groups of four and get them to study the information. Go round the class to explain any difficulties and get students to do the matching task.
- Bring the class to order and get a student from one of the groups to explain the matches. (You may have to play the recording again to confirm the answers to the students.)

- Reposition the brand, sell product in medium price range – Tom
- Develop the Hudson brand – Ruth
- Hire a top designer – not mentioned
- Develop a wider product range – Cornelius
- Stretch the Hudson brand – Cornelius
- Develop sales using e-commerce – not mentioned

Task

- Explain the task to the whole class. They will be role-playing a meeting between the four Hudson executives, who have to consider the advantages and disadvantages of each option and choose two of the marketing strategies they will use to expand sales in Europe.

- Get students to work in the same groups of four as above. Appoint a chair for each group to open the meeting, invite contributions and summarise the discussion at the end. (Go round the room and explain this to the chairs.)

- Tell chairs to start their meetings. Go round the room and monitor the language being used. Note down strong points and points that need correction or improvement.

- When each meeting has finished with the chair summarising the discussion, bring the whole class to order.

- Get the chairs to say what happened in their groups, which two strategies they chose and why.

- Then discuss the strategies with the whole class meeting as one group.

Feedback

- Praise the strong language points that you heard and work on five or six key points that need improvement, especially in relation to the language of opinion and discussion.

One-to-one

Go through the information in the Course Book with your student. Explain any difficulties. In the task, you and your student are Hudson executives. Discuss the advantages and disadvantages of the different solutions. Don't dominate the discussion, but say enough to keep it going and allow your student to make their points.

At the same time, monitor the language that your student is using. Note down strong points and points that need correction or improvement. Come back to these in order to work on them after the student has said which two strategies are best.

⊙ You can also refer to the *Case study commentary* section of the DVD-ROM, where students can watch an interview with a consultant discussing the key issues raised by the case study.

Writing

- Set the writing task for homework or get students

to do it in pairs in class. Give a rough maximum number of words for the e-mail – perhaps 150 words, depending on the level of class.

⇨ Writing file, Course Book page 127
⇨ Resource bank: Writing (page 204)

Travel

AT A GLANCE

	Classwork – Course Book	Further work
Lesson 1 *Each lesson (excluding case studies) is about 45 to 60 minutes. This does not include time spent going through homework.*	**Starting up** Students talk about some travel issues and listen to people discussing travel problems. **Vocabulary: British and American English** Students look at the differences in travel terminology between the two varieties of English. **Listening: Hyatt Hotels** Sholto Smith, Area Sales Director for a hotel group, talks about developments in the industry.	**Practice File** Vocabulary (pages 8–9) **i-Glossary** (DVD-ROM) **Resource bank: Listening** (page 189) **Course Book Listening** (DVD-ROM)
Lesson 2	**Reading: What business travellers want** Students compare articles about business travel: one about a businessman who travels a lot and one about travelling on a budget. **Language review: Talking about the future** Students work on tenses used to talk about the future and how they differ in their uses.	**Text bank** (pages 118–121) **Practice File** Language review (page 10) **ML Grammar and Usage**
Lesson 3	**Skills: Telephoning: making arrangements** Students listen to phone calls where people make arrangements and then role-play conversations.	**Resource bank: Speaking** (pages 175–176) **Practice File** Getting the message right (page 57)
Lesson 4 *Each case study is about 1½ to 2 hours.*	**Case study: BTS** Students suggest solutions to problems that the client of a business travel agency has had when using the services the agency has arranged.	**Resource bank: Writing** (page 205) **Practice File** Writing (page 11) **Case study commentary** (DVD-ROM)

For a fast route through the unit focusing mainly on speaking skills, just use the underlined sections.

For one-to-one situations, most parts of the unit lend themselves, with minimal adaptation, to use with individual students. Where this is not the case, alternative procedures are given.

BUSINESS BRIEF

Air travel in Europe has been shaken up by **low-cost airlines** offering spartan **in-flight service** and selling tickets direct over the Internet. **National flag carriers** (government-owned airlines) continue to go bust, partly as a result of the success of the low-cost carriers. **Deregulation** and **liberalisation**, driven by the competition laws of the European Union, mean that governments are no longer allowed to **bail out** their airlines.

Low-cost airlines are increasingly attractive to businesses watching their costs. Many business travellers are now using them, saying that there is no point in paying more for a flight just to get a badly cooked breakfast. The established players reply that, especially on **long-haul routes**, there will always be a place for **full-service airlines** with ground staff, city-centre ticket offices and so on. However, all this **infrastructure** means that traditional airlines have very high **fixed costs**: it costs almost as much to fly a plane three-quarters empty as full and the main aim is to get as many passengers on seats as possible, paying as much as possible to maximise the revenues, or **yield**, from each flight.

The relative fragility of individual airlines all over the world has led to the growth of **global alliances**. Most national European airlines are now members of either Oneworld or Star Alliance, and Air France and KLM have opted for a full merger. On transatlantic routes, British Airways has long been in alliance with American Airlines. Co-operation means that airlines can feed passengers into each others' **hubs** for onward journeys and costs of marketing and logistics are not duplicated.

In the USA, there have been a number of airline mergers, for example between Delta and Northwest, resulting in bigger airlines with lower **cost bases** per passenger. However, airlines are among the first to suffer during economic downturns, and the USA has been accused of unfairly protecting its airlines with laws on bankruptcy protection that give airlines time to reorganise and restructure when in other countries they would go out of business.

Fuel costs have been another factor in the fragility of airlines' finances. They can to an extent buy fuel into the future at prices fixed with suppliers today, but the wild swings in fuel prices of recent years have made budget planning very difficult.

Another aspect of travel is, of course, the **hotel industry**. Here, there are similar issues of high fixed costs that have led to the development of **hotel chains** able to share them. Each chain is a **brand** and, wherever you go, you should know exactly what you are going to find when you get there.

However, business travellers are beginning to question the sense of travelling at all. Some argue that after the first face-to-face meeting between customer and supplier, further discussions can take place using purpose-built **video-conferencing suites**, **webcams** combined with PCs on the Internet and so on. Costs of video-conferencing are coming down, but it is probably more suitable for internal company communication, with colleagues who already know each other well.

Travel and your students

Everyone loves to tell their travel horror stories, so you should have no trouble getting your students to relate to the subject.

Some senior managers, especially in hi-tech industries, may have personal experience of video-conferencing: it will be interesting to see what they think about it.

Read on

Rigas Doganis: *The Airline Business in the 21st Century*, Routledge, 2nd edition, 2006

The *Economist* (www.economist.com) and the *Financial Times* (www.ft.com) are both excellent for the latest developments in the airline industry.

Janelle Barlow, et al: *Smart Videoconferencing: New Habits for Virtual Meetings*, Berrett-Koehler, 2002

LESSON NOTES

Warmer

- Write the following questions on the board:
What was your best travel experience?
What was your worst?

- Put students into pairs. Get them to discuss the two questions and make brief notes about their partner's answers. Go round the room and help where necessary, for example with vocabulary.

- Then get individual students to tell the class about their partner's experience, rather than their own.

- Note key travel vocabulary in a 'permanent' list to keep to the end of the lesson on one side of the board.

Overview

- Tell students they will be looking at language and issues (teach this word) related to travel.

- Go through the overview section at the beginning of the unit, pointing out the sections that students will be looking at.

Quotation

- Get students to look at the quotation and get them to talk briefly about lost or delayed baggage problems that they might have had. (Point out that *baggage* and *luggage* are the same thing, but be sure to correct students who talk about *baggages* and *luggages*; the correct form is *items of baggage or luggage*.)

Starting up

Students look at some of the vocabulary related to the irritations of air travel and use it in context.

A

- Put students into pairs. Get students to ask their partners questions 1 to 3.

- With the whole class, do a round-up of some students' answers to the questions.

- For question 3, you could ask students to vote on the different points in relation to one particular type of travel, for example a transatlantic flight. Work on the correct stress of *COMfort* and *reliaBILity*.

B

- Do as a quick-fire whole-class activity.

1 room
2 luggage
3 queues
4 food
5 trolleys

6 seats (Point out that this is the word used, not *chairs* or *places*.)
7 cancellations
8 jet
9 checks (not *controls*)
10 cabin

C 🔊 CD1.7

- Play each section two or three times, depending on level. Get students to note down problems they hear that are in Exercise B. (Point out that it's not words from Exercise B that they should listen for, but problems. For example, they hear the word *seats* from Traveller 1, but not in the context of overbooking of seats, which is mentioned by Traveller 3.)

Traveller 1
not enough legroom
poor-quality food and drink
Traveller 2
long queues at check-in
no baggage trolleys available
flight delays and cancellations
Traveller 3
lost or delayed luggage
overbooking of seats ('they overbook seats')
jet lag

D

- Put students into different pairs. Go round the room and help where necessary.

- With the whole class, get members of each pair to talk about their experiences.

Vocabulary: British and American English

Students look at the differences in travel terminology between the two main varieties of English.

A

- Put students into pairs. (At this point, you could change the make-up of the pairs again.) Go round the room and help where necessary.

- With the whole class, get students to call out the answers. Practise pronunciation where necessary. (*Schedule* is pronounced 'skedule' in American English, and 'shedule' in British English, but stick to the former, as students are being given it as the American English equivalent of *timetable*.)

1 m   2 k   3 n   4 f   5 j   6 l   7 c   8 b   9 e
10 d   11 o   12 a   13 h   14 i   15 g

The British English expressions are underlined below:

1 subway	a) line
2 city centre	b) lift
3 carry-on baggage	c) public toilet
4 one way	d) schedule
5 return	e) economy class
6 freeway	f) single
7 rest room	g) first floor
8 elevator	h) bill
9 coach class	i) booking
10 timetable	j) round trip
11 car park	k) downtown
12 queue	l) motorway
13 check	m) underground
14 reservation	n) hand luggage
15 ground floor	o) parking lot

B

- Put students into pairs. Go round the room and help where necessary.

2	parking lot	6	line
3	carry-on baggage	7	downtown
4	subway	8	reservation
5	schedule	9	elevator

C 🔊 CD1.8

- Play the recording and get students to check their answers. Clear up any remaining problems.

◉ i-Glossary

Listening: Hyatt Hotels

Students listen to Sholto Smith, Area Sales Director for Hyatt Hotels, talking about how the company meets the needs of business travellers, how it is adding value for them and about future developments in business travel.

A 🔊 CD1.9

- Play the recording twice, or more often if necessary, pausing occasionally to give students time to tick the items in the list which are mentioned.

- Get students to give the answers as a quick-fire whole-class activity.

Location of hotels ✓	Good links with underground networks ✓	Close to the airport ✓
Totally non-smoking	Good restaurant	Close to client's office ✓
Technology ✓	Internet ✓	Business centre ✓
Swimming pool	Translation services ✓	Free transport to hotel

B 🔊 CD1.10

- Explain the idea of 'adding value' (in the context of hotels, getting extra services and facilities in addition to the room).

- Play the recording twice and get students to complete the notes.

- Elicit answers from the students and explain any difficulties, e.g. *shuttle*.

Breakfast[1] on a daily basis
Membership to the health club[2]
Newspapers
Transportation to and from the airport[3]
A shuttle service to:
    a) the local department store[4]
    b) the offices[5] in which the client works

C 🔊 CD1.11

- Get students to look at the rubric, then play part three of the recording two or three times.

- Elicit answers from the students and explain any difficulties. (Point out how Sholto Smith mentions technology and environmental policies, gives examples of the latter and then gives examples of the former.)

Technology: high-speed Internet, television on demand, lower cost telephone calls
Environmental policies: water conservation, low-energy lighting in bedrooms

- Work on pronunciation of *environmental* and *conservation* and explain any remaining difficulties.

D

- Get students to discuss the question in groups of three or four. Go round and assist where necessary.

- Call the class to order. Elicit the ideas and get students to comment on those of other groups.

⮕ Resource bank: Listening (page 189)

◉ Students can watch the interview with Sholto Smith on the DVD-ROM.

Reading: What business travellers want

Students compare articles about business travel, one about a businessman who travels a lot and one about travelling on a budget.

A

- Get students to discuss this as a quick-fire whole-class activity. Things that might be mentioned include fares, reputation of service and food, safety record, age of planes, schedules, convenience of airports used. Teach any vocabulary that students are unfamiliar with.

B

- Explain what they will have to do – each reads an article then explains information from it to their partner in order to complete the table. Make sure that the Student Bs turn to the correct page.

- Get students to read their article individually and complete the relevant part of the table. Go round the room and help where necessary.

	Edmond Moutran	**John Cox**
job	Chairman of Memac Ogilvy & Mather	runs a publishing consultancy
nationality	Lebanese	British
travel destinations	Dubai, Bahrain, UK, Cairo, Jordan, Jeddah, Riyadh, Kuwait, Tunis, Algeria, South Africa, Barcelona, Paris	mainly the US
amount of air travel	60% of working week	80,000 to 100,000 miles per year
choice of class	first class or business class	economy class
choice of airline	Middle East Airlines (MEA), followed by Gulf Air, Emirates, British Airways, Air France	United and Star Alliance airlines
likes	new aircraft and equipment; well-trained, fresh, energetic staff; airline lounges (good chairs, plenty of newspapers and TV); extra-special treatment at airport	cheap fares, frequent-flyer points to get upgrades
dislikes	attitude of crew and staff; problems with ground staff; lack of openness by airlines when there are problems and delays	expensive fares, taxis
travel to airport	car to airport provided by airline	public transport
hotel requirements	not mentioned	wireless Internet access, good laundry service

C

- Now in their pairs, students exchange information to complete the table. Also get them to discuss the question. Go round and assist where necessary, for example with vocabulary and pronunciation.

- Bring the class to order and elicit the views of one or two pairs. Work on travel-related vocabulary and pronunciation points that have caused difficulty but don't pre-empt the next exercise.

D

- Do as a quick-fire whole-class activity. Point out the grammatical and other clues that help to find the right answers. You could try getting students to cover the right-hand column and get them to suggest what might follow on from the expressions on the left before they do the exercise.

> **1** f　**2** g　**3** e　**4** a　**5** b　**6** c　**7** d

- Work on stress and pronunciation of difficult words e.g. *awarded* (not *rewarded*) and *lounge*. (Get students to distinguish the latter from *lunch*!)

E

- Again, do as a quick-fire whole-class activity, getting students to suggest answers.

> **1** peak travel　　　　**5** boarding pass
> **2** frequent-flyer points　**6** check in
> **3** upgrade　　　　　　**7** lounge
> **4** ground staff

➡ Text bank (pages 118–121)

Language review: Talking about the future

Students work on tenses used to talk about the future and how they differ in their uses.

A

- Talk students through the commentary and examples in the panel.

- Do the exercise as a whole-class activity and answer any questions. Remind students of the *reason* for each answer whilst working through the exercise.

1	're going to	4	'll
2	'll	5	'll
3	're going to		

- Get individual pairs to read the exchanges for the whole class.

B

- With the whole class, ask for the answers. Again, work on the reason for each answer.

1 are staying

2 departs

3 does the conference begin

4 are you doing

5 does this train get

6 am travelling

C

- Put students into pairs. Go round the room and help where necessary. Encourage creativity, as long as the grammar rules are followed.

- With the whole class, get suggestions for possible answers and discuss why they are possible, referring back to the information in the panel.

Sample answers

1 The flight's delayed, so I'm going to wait in the lounge.

2 OK, I've decided. I'm going to book the next flight to New York.

3 Let's check the timetable. The flight leaves at 18:30.

4 It's OK, I don't need a lift. I'm taking a taxi to the airport.

5 Friday afternoon? I'll just check my diary. I'm not doing anything special.

6 There are two flights to Hong Kong on Friday. I'll catch the later one.

7 It's all arranged, we're meeting at five in reception.

8 Next week, we're flying to Munich for the conference.

Skills: Telephoning: making arrangements

Students listen to phone calls where people make and then have to change arrangements. Students then use these calls as models for role-play conversations.

A 🔊 CD1.12, 1.13

- Describe the situation and bring students' attention to the information they are listening for.

- Play the first recording two or three times, explain any difficulties and ask for the answers.

- Then do the same for the second recording.

1 a) To arrange a meeting for the following week
   b) The meeting is arranged for Wednesday at 2 p.m.
2 a) To advise Cristina of a delay and rearrange the meeting
   b) A message is left for Cristina to call her back.

B 🔊 CD1.12

- Play the first call again and get students to complete the extract.

1 I'd like to make an appointment

2 day would suit you

3 How about Wednesday

4 you make it

5 me check the diary

6 What about

- Recap the complete expressions that contain the missing words above with the whole class, working on natural intonation.

- Get students to read the complete conversation in pairs. Go round the room and help where necessary.

- Get one or two pairs to read the conversation for the whole class.

C 🔊 CD1.13

- Follow the above procedure again.

1	Will you hold	4	preferably
2	but something's come up	5	Could she call me back
3	I'd like to meet her	6	020 7855 3814

D

- With the whole class, explain the two situations.

- Put students into pairs. Tell students they can refer to the key expressions in the Useful language box. Go round the room and help where necessary.

- Work with the whole class on common problems.

- Get two or three pairs to role-play the situation again for the whole class.

➡ Resource bank: Speaking (page 177)

CASE STUDY

Business Travel Services

Students suggest solutions to problems that the client of a business travel agency has had when using the services the agency has arranged.

Background

- Get students to focus on the case study by asking them about the services that a business travel agency typically provides to companies (flights, hotels, car rental, conference bookings, etc., perhaps with discounted prices).

- Write the headings on the left-hand side of the table and elicit information from students to complete the right-hand side.

Company	BTS
Based in	Philadelphia
Services	Flights, hotels, car rental, conference bookings, insurance
Clients	Multinational companies, some of which are household names
Criteria for selection of partners and service providers	High standards of service, attention to detail, quality of 'product'
Prices	Additional discounts (i.e. in relation to the usual discounts)
Issues	NeoTech's senior executives have had problems on business trips organised by BTS

- Explain vocabulary where necessary, e.g. *household name*. Point out that *product* can also mean *service* in contexts like this.

Stage 1

- Ensure students understand the situation. Explain *account manager*, someone in a company who takes care of particular clients.

- Put students into pairs. Allocate roles and get students to turn to the page with their role.

- Go round the room and help where necessary, monitoring the way they are using the language for making arrangements by phone that they met in the Skills section.

- Bring the class to order. Praise good points, and work on any that are causing problems.

Stage 2

- Again in pairs, get students to change the date of the meeting.

- Go round the room and monitor the way they are using the language for changing arrangements by phone that they saw in the Skills section.

- With the whole class, check again on the language for changing arrangements. Praise good points and work on things that need improvement.

Stage 3

- Put students into fours – BTS's account manager and the three travel consultants. Allocate each problem to one member of each group of four. Explain that he/she has to read it and will then have to explain it to other members of the group. The group will then discuss the problem in order to try to resolve it.

- Go round the room. Monitor and help where necessary, checking they are doing the task correctly.

- After the first problem, bring the class to order. Explain anything that still presents problems.

- Then get students to explain and discuss the other three problems in the same way.

- Bring the class to order. Get one or two of the groups to summarise what they said in their group about some of the problems.

- Praise five or six relevant language points and work on five or six others that need correction or improvement, especially ones relating to travel, accommodation, etc.

> **One-to-one**
>
> Go through the information in the introduction with your student. Explain any difficulties.
>
> In the task, get your student to read the first problem, making notes so as to be able to summarise it in their own words.
>
> Take the role of Account Manager and get your student to take the role of Travel Consultant. Discuss possible solutions.
>
> At the same time, monitor the language that your student is using. After the activity, underline some of the language that you chose to use and some that your student used correctly and work on five or six points from what they said that need improving.
>
> Then get your student to read and summarise the second problem, swapping roles. Discuss the problem, getting your student to pay particular attention to the corrections you made. Go through the remaining problems in the same way.

- You can also refer to the *Case study commentary* section of the DVD-ROM, where students can watch an interview with a consultant discussing the key issues raised by the case study.

Writing

- Set the task for homework or get students to do it in pairs in class. Give an approximate number of words for the e-mail, perhaps 200–250 words, depending on the level of the class.

➡ Writing file, page 127

➡ Resource bank: Writing (page 205)

UNIT 3 Change

AT A GLANCE

	Classwork – Course Book	Further work
Lesson 1 *Each lesson (excluding case studies) is about 45 to 60 minutes. This does not include time spent going through homework.*	<u>**Starting up**</u> This section gets students to focus on change in their personal lives. **Vocabulary: Describing change** Students look at the prefixes used in many verbs relating to change and at how these verbs are used. **Reading: Mercedes, shining star** Students read about problems at Mercedes and how its Chief Executive turned the company round.	**Practice File** Vocabulary (page 12) **i-Glossary** (DVD-ROM) **Text bank** (pages 122–125)
Lesson 2	**Listening: Helping companies to change** Students listen to a consultant talking about ways of bringing about change in organisations. **Language review: Past simple and present perfect** Students compare and contrast these two tenses and develop their awareness in a sequence of exercises.	**Resource bank: Listening** (page 192) **Course Book Listening** (DVD-ROM) **Practice File** Language review (pages 13–14) **ML Grammar and Usage**
Lesson 3	<u>**Skills: Managing meetings**</u> This section looks at the language of managing (chairing) meetings.	**Resource bank: Speaking** (page 177)
Lesson 4 *Each case study is about 1½ to 2 hours.*	<u>**Case study: Acquiring Asia Entertainment**</u> An international media group has to find ways to integrate the new Hong Kong-based company it has recently merged with.	**Resource bank: Writing** (page 206) **Practice File** Writing (pages 14–15) **Case study commentary** (DVD-ROM)

For a fast route through the unit focusing mainly on speaking skills, just use the underlined sections.

For one-to-one situations, most parts of the unit lend themselves, with minimal adaptation, to use with individual students. Where this is not the case, alternative procedures are given.

BUSINESS BRIEF

If a successful organisation is to continue to succeed, it will need to change. A large part of **leadership** is to do with bringing about change. But the arrival of consultants to look at an organisation and suggest ways of **restructuring** it can make employees extremely nervous if there is not proper **consultation** with them: explanation and discussion of what the company is trying to achieve by this change. Much of the work of executives is taken up with **change management**.

Companies may **downsize** and **de-layer**, eliminating levels of **middle management** in order to become **leaner, flatter,** supposedly more efficient organisations. Often the reasoning was that computer networks allow top managers instant access to information that was previously gathered and transmitted upwards by middle managers, whose other main function was to communicate executives' key messages downwards to the workforce. In doing the latter, they were sometimes accused of diluting or confusing the messages, or worse. With fewer organisational layers, top managers say they can communicate more directly with **front-line** employees, the people who actually produce the goods or services and deal with customers. With less direct supervision, employees have often been encouraged to make more decisions for themselves in a process of **empowerment**.

Change and restructuring will also occur when a company is bought by another as an **acquisition** or **takeover**, or when two companies join as equals in a **merger**. It may be difficult to combine the **cultures** (ways of doing things) of the two companies.

Companies may also have to **shed staff** in periods of economic difficulty: **economic downturns**.

In all these scenarios, there will be **redundancies**. The people remaining might feel demoralised, wondering when the next wave of change is going to come and whether it would be their turn to lose their jobs.

There has been a realisation that, beyond the sloganeering, an organisation's most precious asset may well be its people and, above all, what they *know*. A company's accumulated knowledge and experience is part of **company culture** and is increasingly seen as a key to success. The collective knowledge of the **core competents** (the people with the key skills) is something to cultivate and develop. It is beginning to be seen that it may be a good idea to have people around with their accumulated years of experience. Some companies have appointed a **chief knowledge officer** to create systems to make this **intellectual capital** available to all employees via the company **intranet** (an Internet-type system available only to company employees). **Knowledge management** is a new business skill, essential if an organisation is to achieve **knowledge capitalisation** – the most profitable application of the knowledge available to it.

Change and your students

It will be interesting to see how your students react. Pre-work students will perhaps have difficulty relating to the upheavals that can occur when organisations restructure and/or are acquired by others.

There will be few in-work students who have not seen change in their organisations at first hand. Some people like change, almost to the point of restlessness; others prefer long-term stability. Be tactful when discussing this sensitive issue.

Read on

John Hayes: *Theory and Practice of Change Management*, Palgrave Macmillan; 2nd revised edition, 2006

John P. Kotter, Dan S. Cohen: *The Heart of Change: Real life stories of how people change their organizations*, Harvard Business School Press, 2002

Jonas Ridderstråle, Mark Wilcox: *Re-energizing the Corporation: How Leaders Make Change Happen*, Wiley, 2008

LESSON NOTES

Warmer

- Get students to look at a good dictionary, for example *Longman Dictionary of Contemporary English*. (It doesn't matter if students don't all look at the same dictionary. They can even look in bilingual dictionaries.)

- Ask them to look through the entry/ies for *change*. Then get them to tell you everything they have found about the word. For example:
  - it's a noun and a verb
  - as a noun, it can mean when something becomes something else, the money you get back when pay for something, etc.
  - as a noun, it can be both countable and uncountable
  - as a verb, it can be used in expressions like *change clothes*, *change gear*, etc.

Overview

- Tell students they will be looking at different aspects of change, in people and in organisations.

- Go through the overview section at the beginning of the unit, pointing out the sections that students will be looking at.

Quotation

- Ask students what they understand from the quotation. (They might mention that people, organisations, etc. have to adapt if they are to survive. This quote comes from the novel *Il Gattopardo* (*The Leopard*), about the nineteenth-century Italian aristocracy having to adapt to new political circumstances. If appropriate, ask students if they have seen the film with Burt Lancaster and Claudia Cardinale.)

Starting up

This section gets students to focus on change in their personal lives.

A

- Explain that this activity is related to stress: which of these things is most stressful? You could get students to rate these things on a scale of 1 to 10.

- Put students into pairs. Go round the room and help where necessary.

- With the whole class, compare notes on students' findings. If the class is not too big, you could write up each pair's score on the board and then work out the average. The main thing is to stimulate discussion.

B

- Do as a quick-fire whole-class activity.

C

- Explain that the idea here is to find the most worrying experience.

- Put students into pairs again. Go round the room and help where necessary, explaining any difficulties.

- With the whole class, discuss findings. (The answer may be *It depends*, e.g., on the nature of the acquiring company, as to whether the merger is unwelcome or not.)

Vocabulary: Describing change

Students look at the prefixes used in many verbs relating to change and at how these verbs are used.

A

- Tell students that they are going to look at some key vocabulary relating to change.

- With the whole class, put one or two words under their correct headings in a table on the board and explain their meanings.

- Then get students to do the others in pairs. Go round the room and help where necessary.

- With the whole class, complete the table on the board. Explain any difficulties and practise stress and pronunciation (e.g. *deCENTralise*).

down-	de-	up-	re-
grade	centralise	date	assess
size	regulate	grade	develop
			launch
			locate
			organise
			structure
			train

B – **C**

- Still in their pairs, get students to work on sentences using a good dictionary such as the *Longman Dictionary of Contemporary English*.

- Go through the answers with the whole class, getting students to call out the answers and explaining any difficulties.

Exercise B

1	reorganised	7	upgrade
2	restructure	8	decentralise
3	relocating	9	redevelop
4	downsized	10	update
5	retrain	11	deregulate
6	relaunch	12	reassess

Exercise C

1 the <u>office layout</u> was reorganised
2 restructure the <u>company</u>
3 relocating their <u>operations</u>
4 downsized its <u>workforce</u>
5 retrain all <u>sales staff</u>
6 relaunch (the <u>product</u>)
7 upgrade the <u>computer system</u>
8 decentralise the <u>decision-making process</u>
9 redevelop the disused <u>car-park site</u>
10 update the <u>whole image</u>
11 deregulate the <u>industry</u>
12 reassess the <u>situation</u>

D

- Put students into pairs. If possible, get them to work with someone from another organisation. Students explain to each other a change that has happened in their particular organisation.
- Go round the room and help where necessary. Check that students are using change vocabulary correctly.
- Bring the class to order and get one or two pairs to talk about the changes they discussed. Again, work on the correct use of change vocabulary.

◎ i-Glossary

Reading: Mercedes, shining star

Students read about problems at Mercedes and how its chief executive has turned the company round.

A

- Introduce the subject by asking students about their perceptions (teach this word) of the Mercedes brand. Some may mention the quality problems that it suffered about eight to ten years ago.
- Put students into pairs. Get them to read the first two paragraphs quickly and decide if the statements are true or false.

1 False
2 False
3 False
4 True

B

- Do this as a quick-fire whole-class activity.

1 dramatic (line 2)
2 decade (line 5)
3 breaking down (line 8)
4 trailblazer (line 22)
5 rival (line 23)
6 enviously (line 24)
7 turnaround (line 29)
8 the bottom line (line 47)

- Work on pronunciation and stress (e.g. *TRAILblazer*, *TURNaround*).

C

- Get students to cover the article with a piece of paper. Then get them to do the exercise, calling out the answers as a quick-fire whole-class activity.

1 e   2 a   3 d   4 h   5 f   6 b   7 g   8 c

- Again, work on pronunciation and stress (e.g. *fuel-eFFICient*).

D

- Get students to look at the task and get them to read the article again in pairs to find the answers.

3, 6, 7, 10, 11, 12

E

- Do as a whole-class activity. Students might mention some of the things that the leaders of their own organisations have done to increase productivity and profitability.

⇒ Text bank (pages 122–125)

Listening: Helping companies to change

Students listen to Anne Deering, Head of Transformation Practice at international management consultants AT Kearney, talking about ways of bringing about change, and an example of this from two organisations that she has worked with – Nokia and Siemens.

A ◀)) CD1.14

- Get students to focus on the person they are going to listen to by asking what consultants do. (They go into companies and give advice on how to improve performance in specific areas.)
- Get students to read the short text before playing the recording. Explain any difficulties (without giving away the answers, of course).
- Play the recording in chunks, stopping at key points to allow students to complete the gaps.

LESSON NOTES

- Play the recording two or three times in this way if necessary. Then get students to call out the answers.

1	going to change	4	fully engaged
2	measure that change	5	themselves
3	been successful	6	to them

B 🔊 CD1.15

- Play the second part of the recording, stopping at key points as above.
- Elicit the answers and explain any difficulties (e.g. *fatigue*, *aligned*).

1 change fatigue
2 getting leaders engaged and aligned around the change

C 🔊 CD1.16

- Play the final part of the recording a couple of times, again stopping at key points so that students can answer the questions.
- Elicit the answers.

1 to create better value / a future for the organisation
2 a) the number of people involved in the development stage of the project
   b) the number of hours over which this 'conversation' took place

- If there is time and interest, get students to talk about the 'values for the future' they would like to see in their own organisation or school.

➡ Resource bank: Listening (page 190)

◎ Students can watch the interview with Anne Deering on the DVD-ROM.

Language review: Past simple and present perfect

Students compare and contrast these two tenses and develop their awareness in a sequence of exercises.

- Write up the two example sentences on the board and comment on the difference between them. Tell them that the giveaway in each case is the expression that they are used with: *In 2002* and *Since 2005* respectively.

A

- Do as a quick-fire whole-class activity.

Past simple: in 2010, yesterday, last year, six months ago
Present perfect: since 2009, yet*, ever
Both: this week, recently

* Unless you are teaching an American English class, don't get bogged down in differences between British English and American English. It's true that in American English the past simple can be used with *yet*, as in *Did you eat yet?*, but only confirm this if a student mentions it.

B

- Get students to work on the exercise in pairs. Go round the room and help where necessary.
- With the whole class, elicit the answers and discuss with students why each answer is the correct one.

1 has been/gone
2 has experienced
3 introduced
4 permitted
5 abolished
6 has recently become/recently became
7 has shown
8 declared
9 has also made
10 became
11 have appeared
12 was
13 have changed

C

- Tell students to discuss the question in pairs and then report back. Go round the room and help where necessary. Insist on the use of the correct tense.
- With the whole class, get some examples from two or three pairs and write them up on the board, getting students to explain the tenses they use.

Skills: Managing meetings

This section looks at the language of managing (chairing) meetings.

A

- Tell students that they are going to work on the language of managing or chairing meetings.
- Ask them about their experiences of successful and unsuccessful meetings. Be tactful, especially if managers and the people who work under them are present in the same class!

B 🔊 CD1.17

- Get students to look through the questions and clear up any difficulties.
- Play the recording two or three times and get students either to note down the answers or to call them out orally.

1 Smokers have been leaving cigarette ends outside the building.
2 To allow smokers to smoke on the balcony outside the restaurant.
3 Because non-smokers like to use the balcony to relax.
4 To allow smokers to have a longer break in the morning so that they can go to the park for a cigarette.
5 No. The decision is postponed.

- Work on any remaining difficulties (e.g. *postponed*).

C 🔊 CD1.17

- Go through the expressions in the Useful language box.

- Then play the recording again once or twice and get students to tick the expressions that they hear.

> The purpose of this meeting is …
>
> How do you feel about …?
>
> What do you think?
>
> Could you let [Mitsuko] finish, please?
>
> I think we should move on now.
>
> To sum up, then …

- Work on pronunciation and intonation of key expressions.

D

- Go through the role-play situation and explain any difficulties. Explain that students will be using the language of managing meetings to discuss the problems faced by the managers of a chain of clothing stores.

- Put students into threes or fours and get them to discuss the problems. (If there is not much time, allocate just a couple of problems to each group.)

- Go round the room and monitor the language being used. Note down strong points and points that need correction or improvement, especially in relation to the language used to manage meetings.

- When students have discussed the items, bring the class to order. Ask some of the groups to say briefly what their group decided in relation to the issues.

- Then praise the strong points that you heard and work on points that need correction or improvement, getting individual students to say the correct thing. Write up key points in your 'permanent' list at the side of the board.

➡ Resource bank: Speaking (page 177)

CASE STUDY

Acquiring Asia Entertainment

An international media group has to find ways to integrate the new Hong Kong-based company it has recently merged with. Students role-play managers from both companies who discuss the problems and propose solutions.

Background

- Get students to focus on the case study by looking through the information in the company profile.

- Write the headings on the left-hand side of this table and elicit information from students to complete the right-hand side.

Company	Decker Group
Based in	Sydney, Australia
Workforce	35,000
Turnover (= sales)	A$4.6bn
Activities	Diversified media group with interests in broadcasting, entertainment and Internet services
Has merged with	Asia Entertainment
Merger or takeover?	Takeover by Decker of Asia Entertainment

- Stop at this point to work on numbers, especially *four point six billion Australian dollars* and to explain *diversified* – a diversified company is one with a lot of different interests, i.e. activities.

- Write the numbers 1 to 3 on the left-hand side of the following table and continue with the next part of the information gathering, getting students to express the information in their own words.

Reasons for Decker's acquisition

1	Decker wants to expand in a fast-growing new market, China.
2	It will use Asia Entertainment so that it can enter and grow in other Asian markets such as Singapore, Malaysia and Vietnam.
3	Decker is attracted by Asia Entertainment's successful online DVD viewing service.

- Work on the meaning of *presence* in this context. Relate the word to *present* – Decker is present in particular markets.

Comment

- Get students to 'develop' the comment section, in their own words.

For example:

Asia Entertainment (AE) seems to be a suitable company for Decker to buy because it's strong in the areas that Decker wants to develop.

However, there may be a clash between Australian and Chinese ways of doing things.

Scott Henderson, though fluent in Mandarin, may be seen by AE as an assertive outsider.

Interview with Scott Henderson 🔊 CD1.18

- Reiterate that Scott Henderson is the new CEO of the combined company. Play the recording a couple of times and get students to express Scott Henderson's ideas in their own words.

For example:

The acquisition will benefit the group and boost earnings, although not immediately. Additional costs will be incurred at the beginning, but nothing's been decided about staff cuts. In the long term, they aim to expand the TV channels and import Australian films. He doesn't foresee ongoing problems with the cultural differences.

Problems

- Get students to read through the e-mail in pairs. Go round the room and help where necessary.

- With the whole class, quickly summarise the information in students' own words using the headings on the left below. (You could get individual students to come up to the board and complete different sections of the table, in note form where appropriate. Only use common abbreviations like *mgt*.)

E-mail to	Robert Crawford, a VP of Decker
E-mail from	Cindy Chow, HRD at AE
General problem	High staff turnover and low morale at AE.
Re-applying for positions	People at AE have to apply again for the jobs they already have – bad feeling between people, don't want to compete against each other.
Redundancies (= job losses)	All depts affected, but particularly HR and Sales. People there looking for new jobs. Not good for morale and performance.
Compensation	Low levels of compensation for people forced out of their jobs and no help to find new ones.
English	All staff to improve their English. No financial assistance.

Mgt style	Change too fast – new IT system, Aus films we know nothing about.
	Informal atmosphere, but we're not used to that.
	Food in restaurant too Western.
	Most of the mgt jobs have gone to Australians, not many Chinese in senior posts – unfair.
	Bad communications – no clear job descriptions or lines of responsibility.
	Loss of Chinese identity – new managers only interested in results.

● Work on any remaining difficulties.

Task

● Divide the class into fours or sixes – group A: two or three Australian managers, one of whom is Scott Henderson (tell them which one) and group B: two or three AE executives.

● Each group prepares separately for the meeting, going over the problems and thinking of solutions. Each group should make notes about what they are going to say at the meeting. Go round and assist where necessary.

● When the groups have prepared, get the two sides together. The student playing Scott Henderson should chair the meeting. Another student should take notes about the discussion. Tell students they should use as much meetings language as possible.

● Tell the groups to start their meetings. Go round the class and note down strong points and points that need correction or improvement. Make sure that the chair is including everyone in the discussion.

● Bring the class to order. Ask the note-taker in each group to report on what happened in their group and what they decided about each point.

● Praise some of the good language points that you heard, and work on half a dozen others that need improvement, getting individual students to say the correct thing.

● If there is time and interest, have a general class discussion about the issues. You could talk about the cultural and practical issues involved when a company is taken over by an overseas company. Point out that this sort of merger often fails, sometimes for the reasons your students have discussed in the case study.

One-to-one

Work on the background to bring out the key points in the tables.

Get the student to prepare one of the roles in Group A or Group B. You take the other.

Run the task. Monitor the language that you both use. After the activity, underline some of the key meetings language that you chose to use and that your student used correctly, and work on five or six points from what they said that needs improving.

If there is time and interest, do the role play again, swapping roles. Ask your student to pay particular attention to the corrections you made.

◎ You can also refer to the *Case study commentary* section of the DVD-ROM, where students can watch an interview with a consultant discussing the key issues raised by the case study.

Writing

● Get your students to write the action minutes from the meeting (about 150–200 words). Students could do this for homework or in pairs in class. (Make sure students understand these should be action minutes, not just minutes.)

➡ Resource bank: Writing (page 206)

➡ Writing file, page 129

WORKING ACROSS CULTURES 1 Socialising

Introduction

As this is probably the first Working across cultures unit that you are doing with students, explain what cultural awareness is – the idea that people should be aware of different attitudes, ways of behaving, taking decisions, using time, etc. that other cultures may have. See the Business brief on page 64 of this Teacher's Resource Book for some key cultural issues.

This cultural awareness unit focuses on the language of social English and how to talk to people, especially people from other cultures, that you haven't met before.

A

- Go through the questions quickly with the whole class and get students to discuss them in groups of four.
- Go round the class and assist where necessary. Make sure that every group member is participating actively.
- Bring the class to order. Get a student from each group to say what their 'findings' were. (Be tactful – students may well say that all of these things are difficult.)

B

- Again, go through the questions quickly with the whole class and get students to discuss them in groups of four, ranking the points from 1 to 6.
- Bring the class to order. Get a student from each group to say what their rankings were and what else came out of the discussion. (For example, they may say that there is a limit to the number of times one can ask *Are you saying ...?* during a conversation without the other person getting irritated!)
- Ask individual students for their own preferences. For example, what do they think of watching English-language DVDs with the English subtitles switched on and then watching again with them switched off?

C

- Do this as a quick-fire whole-class activity. Students might suggest talking about which companies they come from, how they travelled to the conference, the speakers at the conference, the hotels they are staying in, etc. You could introduce the idea of 'small talk' – things that are easy to talk about, often in order to get to know people better. (It might be interesting to ask students if they think that the weather is a worthy subject of conversation in this context!)

D ◀)) CD1.19

- Get students to look through the questions.
- Play the recording once or twice, depending on the general level of the class, and elicit the answers.

> 1   Antonio Silva, from Belo Horizonte, Brazil, and James Whitfield, from Atlanta, Georgia, US.
>
> 2   a, b, c, d, e, g

E ◀)) CD1.19

- Get students to look at the questions and then listen to the recording again.
- With the whole class, elicit the answers.

> 1   Nice to meet you.
>
> 2

	Antonio	James
Type of company	office equipment	
Job title	Sales Manager	Systems Analyst
Company performance	not too good, redundancies and cost-cutting	sales up last quarter, but worried about the future
Flight	exhausting, stopped over in Los Angeles	long, turbulent, but food and service OK
Accommodation	in cheap hotel a few blocks away; not many facilities, couldn't use business centre	staying with daughter downtown

- If necessary, explain and practise the pronunciation of *exhausting* and *turbulent*.

F 🔊 CD1.20

- Get students to look at the questions and then listen to the recording once or twice.
- With the whole class, elicit the answers.

> 1 **a)** Nancy Chen
>   **b)** Ludmila Poigina
>   **c)** Klaus Liebermann
> 2 Whether they've visited Seattle at all and which speakers are worth seeing.

G 🔊 CD1.20

- Get students to look through the extract and suggest what might go in the gaps before they hear the recording again.
- Play the recording, stopping at convenient points so that students can note the missing words.
- With the whole class, elicit the answers.

> 1 systems analyst
> 2 This is
> 3 sales manager
> 4 How do you do
> 5 Pleased to meet you
> 6 Managing Director
> 7 Frankfurt subsidiary
> 8 St Petersburg

- Point out that *How do you do?* is not a question (the expression in response to this is *How do you do* or *Pleased to meet you*) and in any case is now considered rather old-fashioned, especially among younger people.

H – **I**

- Do as a quick-fire whole-class activity, playing the recording again if necessary. Elicit the answers.

> **Exercise H**
>
> **a)** Nancy   **b)** Ludmila   **c)** James
>
> **Exercise I**
>
> David Broadus: has written a lot of books on information systems; a very stimulating speaker; obviously knowledgable about his topic
>
> Jerry Chin: expert on management software; shouldn't be missed

Task

- Go through the task with the whole class and make sure they understand it.
- Get each student to choose a role, without saying what it is. (It doesn't matter if two students in the same group have the same job – it might end up being one of the things they find they have in common!)

- Get students individually to prepare notes, as in section 3 of the task.
- Put students into groups of four. Get them to imagine that they are sitting round a table in a conference hotel bar or restaurant. Get them to talk to one of the other members of the group one-to-one and then, after a few minutes, get them to change, so they talk to a different person one-to-one.
- Go round the class to assist if necessary. Monitor the language being used but monitor also the cultural 'appropriateness' of the subjects that students are talking about.
- Bring the class to order. Ask some of the students what they found they had in common, if anything, with each of the two people that they spoke to.
- Praise five or six good language points that you heard. Then work on some language points that need correction or improvement. However, pay as much attention to issues of cultural appropriateness as to language – perhaps you heard things that might not have been appropriate at this 'small talk' stage of people getting to know each other.

UNIT A Revision

This unit revises and reinforces some of the key language points from Units 1–3 and from *Working across cultures* 1. Links with those units are clearly shown. You can point out these links to your students.

1 Brands

Vocabulary

● This exercise recycles the vocabulary relating to brands.

1 b **2** a **3** c **4** c **5** c **6** a **7** b **8** a
9 b **10** b

Present simple and present continuous

● Students get further practice in the use of these two tenses.

1	loves	**7**	are trying
2	does	**8**	are not working
3	works	**9**	are attending
4	is gaining	**10**	knows
5	know	**11**	want
6	is spreading	**12**	believes

Skills

● This exercise recycles the vocabulary used for taking part in meetings.

1	views	**5**	How
2	opinion	**6**	see
3	Why	**7**	so
4	afraid	**8**	Perhaps

2 Travel

Talking about the future

● This exercise gives practice in the use of *will* and *going to*.

1	'll	**3**	're going to
2	's going to	**4**	'll

Skills

● Students get more practice of the language used to make arrangements over the telephone.

1	How	**5**	up
2	like	**6**	back
3	leave	**7**	sure
4	reason	**8**	Thanks

Writing

● This task gives practice in the writing of messages following telephone conversations.

3 Change

Vocabulary

● This exercise gives more practice in using vocabulary for describing change.

1	reassess (all three)
2	downsizes, downsizes, has downsized
3	update (all three)
4	deregulate (all three)
5	retrain (all three)

Past simple and present perfect

● Students get further practice in the use of these two tenses.

1 have your offices been		**2** were you		**3** was	
4 decided	**5** have you ever regretted			**6** were	
7 soon realised	**8** has developed		**9** have had		
10 stood	**11** have already increased				
12 has remained	**13** Have you had to				
14 have not been					

Cultures: Socialising

● These exercises provide further practice in small talk.

Exercise 1

1	Nice	**5**	journey
2	I'm	**6**	tiring
3	Where	**7**	staying
4	How	**8**	like

Exercise 2

1 How's business? / How's your business doing?
2 What do you do? / What's your job?
3 Have you seen / visited any of the city (yet)?
4 How did you come / travel / get to the conference?
5 Did you have any problems / difficulty finding the (conference) centre?
6 Where are you staying? / Which hotel are you staying at?
7 What's your room like?
8 Are there any talks you (particularly) want to go to? / Which speakers are you interested in?

UNIT 4 Organisation

AT A GLANCE

	Classwork – Course Book	Further work
Lesson 1 *Each lesson (excluding case studies) is about 45 to 60 minutes. This does not include time spent going through homework.*	**Starting up** Students discuss some issues of status in organisations. **Vocabulary: Company structure** Students learn key vocabulary used in talking about companies and the ways they are organised.	**Practice File** Vocabulary (page 16) **i-Glossary** (DVD-ROM)
Lesson 2	**Reading: A successful organisation** Students read about the benefits of working for Google and think about whether other organisations could be modelled on it. **Language review: Noun combinations** Students look at this key language feature and develop their knowledge through a variety of exercises.	**Text bank** (pages 126–129) **Practice File** Language review (page 17–18) **ML Grammar and Usage**
Lesson 3	**Listening: Analysing company organisation** Students listen to a management consultant who advises companies on how they should be organised. **Skills: Socialising: introductions and networking** Students look at the language of networking and have the chance to apply it themselves.	**Resource bank: Listening** (page 191) **Course Book Listening** (DVD-ROM) **Resource bank: Speaking** (page 178–179)
Lesson 4 *Each case study is about 1½ to 2 hours.*	**Case study: InStep's relocation** Students make a decision about a company considering the relocation of its offices from the capital to a small town.	**Resource bank: Writing** (page 207) **Practice File** Writing (pages 18–19) **Case study commentary** (DVD-ROM)

For a fast route through the unit focusing mainly on speaking skills, just use the underlined sections.

For one-to-one situations, most parts of the unit lend themselves, with minimal adaptation, to use with individual students. Where this is not the case, alternative procedures are given.

BUSINESS BRIEF

Businesses come in many guises, from the lonely sounding **self-employed** person and **sole trader**, through the **SME** – the **small to medium-sized enterprise** – to the **multinational** with its **hierarchy** and tens of thousands of employees. But the questions about what motivates people in work are basically the same everywhere. The first question that self-employed people get asked is how they find the self-discipline to work alone and **motivate** themselves when there is no one telling them what to do. Some companies are also looking for this: job advertisements often talk about the need for recruits to be **self-starters**. Some organisations (like advertising agencies) want to find ways of motivating their people to be ever more **productive** and **creative**. Employees and their managers in this type of organisation are relatively **autonomous** – they aren't given exact procedures on how to meet objectives.

But others (like banks) need people who can follow rules and apply procedures. (You do not want too much creativity when cashiers are counting banknotes!) These tend to be organisations with **centralised cultures** – exact procedures that must be followed are imposed from above.

In organisations of all kinds, the tendency is towards relatively **flat structures,** with only a few levels of **hierarchy** – this way, the senior management is relatively close to people dealing with clients.

The current buzzword is **flexibility**. This has a number of related meanings. One type of flexibility has existed for some time in the form of **flexitime** or **flextime**, where people can choose when they work, within certain limits. Then there is **flexible working** with some staff **hot-desking,** particularly those who are **homeworking, teleworking** or **telecommuting** and only need to come into the office occasionally. The number of **teleworkers** is rising rapidly, thanks partly to the decreasing cost and increasing availability of fast **broadband Internet connections** and **mobile Internet**.

A third type of flexibility is where employees are recruited on short contracts to work on specific projects, maybe part time. Perhaps the organisation only has a **core staff** and **outsources** or **contracts out** work to external people or companies as and when required. Some management experts say that this is the future, with self-employment as the norm and **portfolio workers** who have a number of different clients.

Organisation and your students

In-work students by definition work in organisations. You obviously have to be tactful when you ask your students what type of organisation it is in terms of creativity, following procedures, etc.

You can ask pre-work students to look at their institution in similar terms: how much student autonomy is there? Is creativity encouraged? How much time are students expected to spend on the premises? Ask them also what sort of organisation they would like to work for – one where creativity is encouraged or one where there are well-established procedures.

Read on

D. S. Pugh and D. J. Hickson: *Great Writers on Organizations*, Ashgate, 2nd omnibus edition, 2000

Charles Handy: *Understanding Organisations,* Penguin, 4th edition, 2005

LESSON NOTES

Warmer

- Tell students they will be looking at the subject of organisation (and organisations).

- Remind them that organisations come in all shapes and sizes. Ask them to brainstorm as many different examples of *types* (not just *size*) of organisation that they can think of. You could start by writing up some examples of very different organisations:

  - a corner shop run by an old couple
  - the Chinese army
  - the BBC
  - a barber working with two assistants
  - a multinational with operations in 120 countries

- With the whole class, get students to call out different organisations to add to the list. The idea is to make students aware of the variety of organisations that exist.

Overview

- Go through the overview section at the beginning of the unit, pointing out the sections that students will be looking at.

Quotation

- Get the students to look at and comment on the quotation, asking if they agree with it. Explain *constructive* if necessary and ask students if they can think of any examples of constructive conflict they have known.

Starting up

Students discuss some issues of status in organisations.

A

- With the whole class, explain any difficulties. Practise stress and pronunciation of *seniORity* and *confidentiALity*.

- Then have a class discussion. If students come from more than one organisation, compare and contrast them.

B

- Put students into pairs. Get students to discuss and allocate scores. Go round the room and help where necessary.

- Then have a class discussion about the issue. Again, be tactful about the status symbols in their organisations.

Vocabulary: Company structure

Students learn key vocabulary used in talking about companies and the ways they are organised.

A

- With the whole class, explain any difficulties. (*Subsidiary* and *outlet* might need explaining. A subsidiary is a company that is owned in whole or in part by another company, the parent company.)

- Put students into pairs. Get students to discuss and do the matching exercise.

- Go through the answers as a quick-fire whole-class activity.

1 e	2 h	3 a	4 d	5 f	6 b	7 g	8 c

B 🔊 CD1.21

- Get students to listen to the recording two or three times, depending on level. Stop during and after each comment at appropriate points to allow students time to write down what they hear. Go round the class and assist where necessary.

- Then ask for answers. Play the recording once more if necessary.

1	warehouse	5	factory/plant
2	subsidiary	6	headquarters
3	call centre	7	outlet
4	distribution centre	8	service centre

C – D

- Do this as a quick-fire whole-class activity. Students may suggest these things and others.

Exercise C – sample answers

2 Answer calls from customers

3 Recruit staff

4 Sell products or services

5 Make products

6 Find the money to invest in new activities

7 Do paperwork (teach this word)

8 Deal with contracts, regulations and any disputes involving the company

9 Manage incoming supplies, warehouse stocks and the way products are moved around

10 Deal with journalists' enquiries and the public

11 Information technology: run computer systems

- Move on fairly quickly to Exercise D. Get students to suggest answers, again as a quick-fire whole-class activity.

Exercise D
a 2   b 8   c 1   d 3   e 4   f 10   g 5   h 6
i 7   j 9   k 11

- Point out that some of the functions might be dealt with by more than one department, e.g. *draw up contracts* could also be a function of HR.

- Ask students about an organisation they know (for example, their company or institution). How is it organised? What departments does it have?

E 🔊 CD1.22

- Play the recording once. Explain any difficulties, but don't give the answers away.

- Play the recording again. Stop after each speaker and get students to say which department the speaker works in.

1 Administration   2 Public Relations
3 Human Resources

F – **G** 🔊 CD1.23

- Play the recording (or read out the words yourself) and get students to say which syllable is stressed in each case.

- Get individual students to repeat the words.

Exercises F and G

1 bureau<u>cra</u>tic – b	7 <u>cen</u>tralised – a or b
2 de<u>cen</u>tralised – a or b	8 dy<u>na</u>mic – a
3 im<u>per</u>sonal – b	9 pro<u>fess</u>ional – a
4 <u>car</u>ing – a	10 con<u>ser</u>vative – a or b
5 demo<u>cra</u>tic – a	11 hier<u>ar</u>chical – b
6 <u>mar</u>ket-<u>dri</u>ven – a	12 pro<u>gress</u>ive – a

- Get students to say which are 'good' (a) and which are 'bad' (b) qualities.

- The ostensible answers as to good and bad qualities are given above, but your students may point out that the answer is sometimes *It depends*. For example, most of us prefer our banks to be reasonably conservative, for example by not lending to people who can't repay, discouraging new-fangled practices in counting cash, etc.

- Invite students to add any other words which describe organisations they know.

 i-Glossary

Reading: A successful organisation

Students read about the benefits of working for Google and think about whether other organisations could be modelled on it.

A

- Tell students that they are going to read about an unusual company.

- Get students to read the first paragraph. Go round the room and help where necessary. (Explain, if necessary, that 15 pounds is about 7 kilos.)

- Get students to answer the question.

b

B

- Describe the task and explain any difficulties in the paragraph headings, e.g. that *celebratory* is related to *celebration*.

- Put students into pairs. Get students to read the rest of the article in pairs. Go round the room and help where necessary.

- With the whole class, go over expressions that have caused particular difficulty.

- Then get students to suggest answers.

Sample answers
4   Making offices interesting places to be
5   Intellectually challenging work
6   A culture of autonomy and empowerment
7   Learning and development programme

C

- Again in pairs, get students to work out the answers. Go round the room and help where necessary.

- With the whole class, get students to call out the answers.

1   True
2   True
3   False. One hundred per cent of Google Italy workers thought it was a friendly place to work.
4   True
5   False. There is no mention of the qualifications needed to work there.
6   True
7   True

D

- With the whole class, get students to look at the items 1–5 in the context of the article. Work on pronunciation and stress, e.g. *acCOMplishments*.

- Get students to call out the answers.

1 b   2 a   3 e   4 c   5 d

E

- Get students to discuss the questions in pairs.

- After a few minutes, get pairs to report on their findings and discuss with the whole class. Be tactful. (For question 2, most students will probably say not, if only for cost reasons. It is important to get students to say why each approach would or wouldn't work.)

- Work on any remaining difficulties of vocabulary or pronunciation.

➡️ Text bank (pages 126–129)

Language review: Noun combinations

Students look at this key language feature and develop their knowledge through a variety of exercises.

- Tell students that they are going to look at a common feature of English – noun combinations.

- Go through the information in the panel and bring students' attention to the information on page 147 in the grammar reference section. Tell students to look at this for homework.

- Get students to call out the answers to the matching exercise.

---

1 c　**2** a　**3** b　**4** d

A

- Explain the task and get students to work on the exercise in pairs. Get different groups of pairs to work on the four different compound types: allocate a type to each pair.

- Go round the room and help where necessary.

- With the whole class, ask students for answers.

---

1 company's university programmes manager

2 side effects, Internet company, skiing trips, games rooms, office decorating, team feeling, massage chairs, table-tennis tables, video games, lava lamps, Google offices, university faculty, lunchtime talks

3 number of pounds, business of work, type of people, degree of independence, culture of autonomy

4 teamwork, workplace, beanbags, lunchtime

B – **C**

- Do as whole-class activities. Get students to call out the most likely combinations in Exercise B. Tell them that there are no rules – the best thing is to learn each combination as a whole.

- For Exercise C, write up the answers on the board, clearly pointing out the absence of plural -s.

Exercise B

1 b　**2** a　**3** a　**4** c

Exercise C

2 a five-star hotel

3 a three-million-dollar budget

4 a 20-minute presentation

5 a 200,000-dollar contract

6 a 150-year-old industrial empire

D

- Put students into pairs. Explain the task then go round the room helping where necessary.

- Check the answers with the whole class.

---

1 b, c　**2** a, c　**3** a, b　**4** a, c　**5** b, c　**6** b, c
7 a, c　**8** a, b　**9** a, c　**10** b, c

E

- Do this exercise with the whole class by giving them the beginning of a statement and getting them to complete it using a noun combination. For example, *Is a business idea useful by itself? – No, you need a business plan to support it*. Tell them that in some cases, they will need to use the plural form of the compound – make sure they get these right.

- Do the others in a similar way.

- When you think students have got the idea, tell them to do the activity in pairs.

- Go round the room and help. In this exercise, students may need quite a lot of assistance, as thinking up sentences from scratch is difficult.

- With the whole class, get students from different pairs to call out possible answers and write the best two or three on the board.

Listening: Analysing company organisation

Students listen to a management consultant who advises companies on how they should be organised.

A 🔊 CD1.24

- Tell students that they are going to hear a management consultant talk about the advice that he gives to companies on how to change, and get them to read the questions

- Play the recording two or three times. Explain any difficulties and elicit the four areas that Booz & Co look at when analysing a company's organisation.

The formal organisation, the decision rights, the information flows and the incentives

---

B 🔊 CD1.25

- Play the second part of the recording.

- Elicit the answers.

1 A small number of questions about your organisation

2 Answers from about 40,000 other executives

3 Patterns that help analysts to say that one organisation is like other organisations

4 It organises both workshops with the executives and further research into particular aspects that seem to be particularly interesting.

- At this point, if you have experienced managers in your class, ask them if they agree with what the consultant has just said in relation to how decisions are taken in their own organisation(s). Treat this tactfully, of course.

- For homework and if appropriate, you could ask students to look at the website mentioned: www.orgdna.com and get them to report back on what they find there about their own organisations. (Don't forget to follow up on this in the next lesson if you ask them to do it.)

C 🔊 CD1.26

- Play the recording once or twice and get students to provide the missing items.

1 By function

2 Manufacturing had responsibility for all the plants around the world; Marketing ran all the brands in every country.

3 Responding to the local markets

4 They considered whether all business units should report to the US or regionally.

D 🔊 CD1.26

- Play the recording once or twice more and get students to provide the missing items.

1	operated	4	organised
2	made	5	regional organisations
3	shipped to	6	headquarters

- Work on any remaining difficulties from the whole interview.

E

- If there is time and interest, put students into pairs and get them to discuss this question. Otherwise do as a quick-fire whole-class activity. The important thing is to get students to give their reasons.

- Treat responses tactfully, as there may be some strong feelings about this.

➡ Resource bank: Listening (page 191)

◎ Students can watch the interview with Richard Rawlinson on the DVD-ROM.

Skills: Socialising: introductions and networking

Students look at the language of networking and have the chance to apply it themselves.

- Tell students they are going to look at some of the language associated with networking and socialising. (This is a very frequent student request, so you should have no trouble 'selling' it to them.)

A 🔊 CD1.27, 1.28, 1.29

- Explain the situation and get students to look through the different conversation types.

- Play the recording with the whole class and ask students to call out the answers.

1 d   2 c   3 b

B 🔊 CD1.27

- Play the first conversation again and get students to call out the answers.

1 b, d, e   2 Alex   3 Maria

C 🔊 CD1.28

- Play the second conversation again and elicit the answers.

name	company	activity
Bob Danvers	Clear View	outsourcing business; supplies companies and organisations with various services including IT, office equipment, travel and cleaning services
Karin Schmidt	MCB	market research

D 🔊 CD1.28

- Get students to look through the conversation outline, then play the recording again several times, stopping to allow students to fill in the gaps.

- Get students to call out the answers and then explain any difficulties, for example *outsourcing* – when a company buys in supplies of goods or services that it previously produced in-house.

1 outsourcing

2 office equipment

3 founded

4 divisions

5 employees

6 headquarters

7 offices

E 🔊 CD1.29

- Get students to look through the three questions.

- Play the recording once or twice and get individual students to answer the questions. Write the answers on the board, with students telling you exactly what to write. For example, check they hear the *'d* in *I'd* in *Christoph, I'd like you to meet Nathalie.*

1 Christoph, I'd like you to meet Nathalie.
2 She speaks fluent Spanish, so could help him deal with South American customers.
3 Sailing

F

- Explain the situation to students and ensure that they understand it: Student A is attending with his/her boss (Student B).

  Student B is attending with a junior colleague (Student A).

  Student C is a colleague of Students A and B from a subsidiary who met Student A at the same conference last year.

  Student D is attending the conference for the first time and doesn't know anyone.

- Divide the class into fours, allocating roles of Students A, B, C and D.

- Get Students A and B to prepare their roles together, with Students C and D each preparing their roles separately. Go round and assist where necessary.

- When groups are ready, get them to begin the role play. At this point, students remain seated. Go round and monitor language, noting strong points and those that need improvement, especially in relation to networking language.

- Bring the class to order. Mention some of the good points in the language you heard and work on half a dozen points that need improvement.

- Get one or two groups to repeat their 'performances', this time standing up in front of the class as if they were really at a conference.

- Go through the expressions in the Useful language box, telling students that you will 'test' them orally on it in the next lesson. (Don't forget to do this next time.)

➡ Resource bank: Speaking (pages 178–179)

CASE STUDY

InStep's relocation

Students make a decision about a company considering the relocation of its offices from the capital to a small town.

Background

● Tell students that they are going to do a case study on an organisational problem at a company that is considering relocating its offices. Get students to read through the background silently.

● Write the headings on the left-hand side of the table and elicit information from students to complete the right-hand side.

Company	InStep
Offices in	Paris
Factory in	Beauchamp – small industrial town in N. France
Key issue	Following move of production there, whether to move offices to Beauchamp, too
Beauchamp's characteristics	Population 25,000. High proportion of young people. Jobs for local inhabitants if move goes ahead.

● Get students to discuss the two questions in pairs.

● Bring the students to order and discuss as a class.

For example:
● Staff may react badly
● They may have to move their families and find new homes in Beauchamp
● They may not like the new area

A 'getting to know you' meeting

● Go through the information and ensure that students understand *parent company* (a company that owns another) and *subsidiary* (a company owned by another).

● Divide the class into fours and allocate the roles: Students A, B, C and D.

● Get students to introduce themselves to each other, and use some of the social English from the previous section. (Obviously Students B and C, as managers of the Paris subsidiary, already know each other.)

● Go round the class and monitor correct use of the language. Bring the class to order, praise good points and point out language that still needs work, getting individual students to say the right thing.

A communication from the Vice-President

● Get one of the students to read the message aloud, then work on any difficulties.

● With the whole class, get students to discuss the issues but without pre-empting the role-play discussion that will come later.

C ◀)) CD1.30

● Students listen to the recording once or twice, noting key points.

Then, in pairs, get them to compare notes with their partner.

Task

● Tell students to read their role cards and prepare their roles. Go round the room and help where necessary. Tell the Student As that they will be chairing the meeting, a) noting the views of the different participants, b) giving their own views, c) asking participants to make a recommendation, and d) noting down what it is. They should ensure that everyone participates by inviting their contributions where necessary.

● When the students have absorbed their role information, bring the class to order and explain anything that has been causing general difficulties.

● When students are ready, get them to start the role play in parallel groups. Go round the room and monitor the language being used. Note down strong points and points that need correction or improvement. Make sure that the Student As are including everyone in the discussion.

● When you feel the discussion is reaching an end in most groups, ask them to make a recommendation, if necessary by voting, if they have not already done so.

Feedback

● Bring the class to order. Ask the chair of each group to report on what happened in their group and the recommendation that they made.

● Praise some of the good language points that you heard and work on half a dozen others that need improvement, getting individual students to say the correct thing.

● If there is time and interest, have a general class discussion about the merits of each solution. Encourage students to talk about their own experiences of life and work in bigger and smaller places, being tactful, as ever.

One-to-one

Work on the background to bring out the key points in the table.

Get the student to look at and express in their own words the information in the message from the Vice-President.

Then choose the role of the Vice-President and one other – your student should then take the role of the VP and you take the other for the initial social English session and then the main decision-making discussion.

Monitor the language that you both use. After the activity, underline some of the key discussion language that you chose to use and some that your student used correctly and work on five or six points from what they said that need improving.

If there is time and interest, do the role play again, with you as the VP and your student taking one of the other roles. Monitor and correct as above.

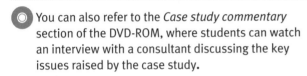 You can also refer to the *Case study commentary* section of the DVD-ROM, where students can watch an interview with a consultant discussing the key issues raised by the case study.

Writing

- Get your students to write an e-mail summarising the discussion and making a recommendation about the relocation. Students could do this for homework or in pairs in class.

⇒ Resource bank: Writing (page 207)

⇒ Writing file, page 127

CASE STUDY

UNIT 5 Advertising

	Classwork – Course Book	Further work
Lesson 1 *Each lesson (excluding case studies) is about 45 to 60 minutes. This does not include time spent going through homework.*	**Starting up** Students look at some advertisements, say which ones they like and why. **Vocabulary: Advertising media and methods** Students look at some advertising-related vocabulary and use it in context. **Reading: A new kind of campaign** Students read about an attention-grabbing advertising technique.	**Practice File** Vocabulary (page 20) **i-Glossary** (DVD-ROM) **Text bank** (pages 130–133)
Lesson 2	**Listening: How advertising works** An advertising executive talks about what is involved in preparing a campaign and gives an example of a memorable campaign.	**Resource bank: Listening** (page 192) **Course Book Listening** (DVD-ROM)
Lesson 3	**Language review: Articles** Students look at the places where articles are used and, just as important, where they are not. **Skills: Starting and structuring presentations** Students look at the language and techniques used for starting and structuring presentations and use them in context.	**Practice File** Language review (page 21) **ML Grammar and Usage** **Resource bank: Speaking** (page 180) **Practice File** Giving presentations (page 63)
Lesson 4 *Each case study is about 1½ to 2 hours.*	**Case study: Alpha Advertising** Students prepare and deliver presentations on different advertising campaigns.	**Resource bank: Writing** (page 208) **Practice File** Writing (pages 22–23) **Case study commentary** (DVD-ROM)

For a fast route through the unit focusing mainly on speaking skills, just use the underlined sections.

For one-to-one situations, most parts of the unit lend themselves, with minimal adaptation, to use with individual students. Where this is not the case, alternative procedures are given.

BUSINESS BRIEF

Whether or not you agree with communications guru Marshall McLuhan that advertising was the greatest art form of the twentieth century, it is a big part of modern culture. Shared references feed into it, and it in turn feeds into daily life: advertising catchphrases turn up in TV comedy sketches and everyday conversation. And we become 'ironic' about advertising, perhaps to show that we think are able to resist it. TV advertising is still glamorous, even if its heyday is over, what with the proliferation of channels and the saturation of the markets (at least in advanced economies) of the **consumer goods** it normally promotes. But the other **media** are not to be ignored – radio, cinema and the press – while **hoardings** (BrE) or **billboards** (AmE) are an integral part of the urban landscape. All these will be around for some time.

Internet advertising expenditure is on the increase. Some people find **banner** and **pop-up advertisements** have become a major source of irritation, but others find them a useful source of information. Debate about the relationship between Internet advertising and search engines such as Google is intensifying.

Advertising can be continued by other means, such as **sponsorship** of particular events or **product placement** in films. This is where the product's makers negotiate for their products to appear and be used by the film's characters. A related phenomenon is **product endorsement**, where a celebrity is used in advertising a particular product. This can be dangerous if, for whatever reason, the celebrity falls from favour.

Some very creative minds come up with seductive combinations of sound, image and words, but tests show that we often don't remember the brand being advertised. Quantifying the effect of advertising is very difficult, and there has been a backlash against it in favour of other, supposedly more **targeted**, forms of communication. This usually means **direct marketing**, otherwise known as **direct mail**, but, as those living in apartments who receive **mailshots** for gardening products know, the targeting can still be ludicrously imprecise.

Advertising agencies may offer to run direct-mail campaigns, but what they are best at is creating **advertising campaigns**. When a client becomes dissatisfied and the agency loses the **account**, this is major news in the advertising industry and means a big loss of revenue (and self-esteem) for the agency. Agencies develop a **creative brief** for clients, with proposals on the ideas to be used in the campaign. One key problem is reaching the right **target audience** (for example, young women between 28 and 30), so the selection of **media** (the right TV channels, magazines, etc.) or **new media** (such as the Internet) is very important. And the advertising must fit into the company's overall **marketing strategy** – its plans on how it will compete and succeed in particular markets.

All these activities, all this expenditure. But the ultimate in advertising is **word of mouth**: friends and colleagues are often our most reliable sources of information. This form of advertising is usually free. All the advertiser can do is hope that it is positive.

Advertising and your students

Pre-work and in-work students should have no trouble relating to advertising, as its willing or unwilling consumers! They will also be able to talk about the place of advertising in their industry or one they would like to work in.

Read on

Mario Pricken: *Creative Advertising: Ideas and Techniques from the World's Best Campaigns*, Thames and Hudson, revised edition, 2008

David Ogilvy: *Ogilvy on Advertising*, Prion, new edition, 2007

Rajeev Batra, John Myers, David Aaker: *Advertising Management*, Pearson Education, 5th edition, 1996

Kevin Lee and Catherine Seda: *Search Engine Advertising*, New Riders, 2nd edition, 2009

LESSON NOTES

Warmer

- Write the words in the box below on the board and get students to say them, with the correct stress, as you write them. Then underline the stressed syllables.

> ad <u>ad</u>vert ad<u>ver</u>tisement <u>ad</u>vertiser <u>ad</u>vertising
>
> com<u>mer</u>cial
>
> pub<u>lic</u>ity pub<u>lic</u>ise

- Get students to look in a good monolingual dictionary (e.g. *Longman Dictionary of Contemporary English*) or a bilingual one to find out about these words and then tell the class about them. (You could give each student or pair one or two words.) However, don't anticipate the Vocabulary section of the Course Book too much.

  For example, they should discover that *commercial* is a noun used to talk about ads on TV and radio and also that it is an adjective relating to commerce, etc.

  This will help them with the basic vocabulary of advertising and also help them distinguish words (e.g. *advertising* and *publicity*) that may be the same in their own language.

Overview

- Tell students they will be looking at advertising.
- Go through the overview panel at the beginning of the unit, pointing out the sections that students will be looking at.

Quotation

- Get students to look at the quotation. (Bernbach was behind the 'We try harder' campaign for Avis car rental and 'Think small' for VW – the latter of which students will see mentioned later in the unit (in Language review Exercise C) – among many others. Bernbach was active in the heyday of American advertising in the 1960s. You could ask students if they have seen *Mad Men*, a fictional TV series that recreates that era.)
- Ask students what they think of the quote. Be tactful to both those with an arts background and those with a scientific education!

Starting up

Students look at some advertisements, say which ones they like and why.

- Explain the task and get students to look at the ads in pairs.
- Go round the room and help where necessary.
- With the whole class, get individual students to talk about their neighbour's favourite ads as well as their own.

- Work on increasing students' vocabulary with words such as *striking*, *powerful*, *colourful*, etc. Don't let them just say that the advertisements are good or bad. This will also help them when they come to Exercise G in the next section.

Vocabulary: Advertising media and methods

Students look at some advertising-related vocabulary and use it in context.

A

- Point out that *media* is the plural of *medium*, as in *advertising medium*. Get students to call out other possibilities – e.g. Internet, TV, cinema, radio, magazines, hoardings/billboards, etc.

B

- Put students into pairs. Get them to go through the expressions in the list, assigning the labels, perhaps using a monolingual or bilingual dictionary. Tell them to leave any that they don't understand.
- If students are unfamiliar with *viral advertising*, you can explain it as being a campaign that uses the Internet to rapidly spread its message among computer users.
- Go through the answers with the whole class. Explain any difficulties and work on pronunciation and stress where necessary, e.g. *comMERcials*.

> 1 (Advertising media) cinema, exhibitions, Internet, outdoor advertising, point-of-sale, press, radio, television
> 2 (Methods of advertising) advertorials, banner ads, billboards/hoardings, commercials, free samples, leaflets/flyers, pop-ups, posters, product placement, sponsorship, viral advertising
> 3 (Verbs to do with advertising) communicate, endorse, place, run, sponsor, target

C

- Do as a quick-fire whole-class activity. Get students to call out the answers.

> Cinema: commercials, posters, product placement
> Exhibitions: free samples, leaflets/flyers
> Internet: pop-ups, banner ads, viral advertising
> Outdoor advertising: billboards/hoardings, leaflets/flyers, posters, sponsorship
> Point-of-sale: free samples, leaflets/flyers, posters
> Press: advertorials
> Radio: commercials
> Television: commercials, product placement, sponsorship

UNIT 5 ▸▸ ADVERTISING

D – F

- Put students into pairs. Go round the room and help where necessary.

- With the whole class, get students to call out the answers to Exercises D and E and examples they found for Exercise F – try to think of topical examples rather than old ones.

Exercise D

1	run a campaign	4	sponsor an event
2	endorse a product	5	target a consumer
3	place an advertisement	6	communicate a message

Exercise E

1	free samples	4	word of mouth
2	slogans	5	mailshots
3	endorsement		

- Work on any remaining difficulties of meaning or pronunciation.

- Do Exercise F as whole-class discussion, getting students to use advertising-related vocabulary correctly.

G

- Do as a quick-fire whole-class activity. Refer back to the words you encouraged students to use in the Starting up section. Work on stress, e.g. *inSPIRing*.

H – I

- Put students into pairs again. Allocate three or four discussion points to each pair. Go round the class and assist where necessary.

- Bring the class to order. Get members of each pair to report on their findings.

- Praise strong language points that you heard and work on any remaining difficulties.

➡ i-Glossary

Reading: A new kind of campaign

Students read about an attention-grabbing advertising technique.

A

- Put students into pairs. Get students to look through the three possible headlines.

- Get students to read the article fairly quickly. Go round and assist where necessary.

- With the whole class, get them to call out the answer: b. Work on the reasons for this.

B – C

- Get students to read through the whole article again.

- With the whole class, get them to call out the answers.

Exercise B

1 To tackle the problem of viewers tuning out of traditional television advertising.

2 Because it was a live event.

3 Because they enable viewers to skip adverts.

4 Nineteen stuntmen did a live skydiving jump and spelt out Honda's name.

5 LG ran adverts which appeared to trail a glamorous new television show but which really promoted its new screens.

6 They pushed the slogan on different media before the live advert went out.

7 Posters, TV ads, website, digital advertising, press coverage.

Exercise C

television/TV advertising, live advertisement, advertising agency, (to) run advertisements, teaser advertisement, digital advertising, advertising campaign, word-of-mouth advertising

- Work on any remaining difficulties of stress in *ADvertising* and *adVERTisement*, especially as they are used in the expressions here.

D – E

- Get students to do the exercises in pairs. Go round the room and help where necessary.

- With the whole class, elicit answers, again working on any problems of pronunciation, e.g. *design* and *features*.

Exercise D

1 e   2 d   3 b   4 c   5 a

Exercise E

1 publicity stunt

2 advertising campaign

3 teaser advertisements

4 poster campaign

5 design features

6 press coverage

7 slogans

8 live advertisement

9 word-of-mouth advertising

F

- Put students into groups of three or four and get each group to come up with an idea for one big publicity stunt.

- If there is time and interest, you could hand out overhead transparencies and pens and get students to outline their ideas on the transparencies (one or two transparencies for each group would probably be enough). Go round the class to monitor language and ideas.

- Then get students from two or three of the groups with the most interesting advertisements or stunts to come to the front of the class and present their ideas using the OHP.

- Praise strong language points and work on half a dozen that need more attention.

➡️ Text bank (pages 130–133)

Listening: How advertising works

An advertising executive talks about what makes a good campaign and how to plan one and gives an example of a recent successful campaign.

A 🔊 CD1.31

- Tell students that they are going to hear Marco Rimini, an advertising executive, talking about advertising campaigns.

- Get students to look at the text and anticipate what might go in the gaps, bearing in mind that there could be up to three words per gap, not just one (but without giving the answers away)!

- Play the recording a couple of times. Don't explain every unfamiliar word at this point – get students to focus on the answers to the key questions.

- Elicit the answers.

1	ask the question	4	wants to happen
2	trying to achieve	5	spending money
3	objectives		

B 🔊 CD1.31

- Tell students they are going to hear the first part of the interview again and get them to look at the question. (Obviously they will already have some ideas about the answers but, in any case, prepare them by telling them they will hear three main reasons, with three examples of the last reason.)

- Play the recording a couple of times, stopping at key points, explaining any difficulties and then, with the whole class, get students to identify the reasons and examples one by one.

1 To change the image of a company

2 To change people's views of an issue

3 To get people to change their behaviour:
   a) to drink less alcohol
   b) to do up their seat belts
   c) to change the way in which they use energy

C 🔊 CD1.32

- Get students to read the question and then play the recording once or twice.

- With the whole class, elicit the answers. Ensure that students correctly pronounce words like *brief* and *creative* when giving the answers.

1 Identify the brief from the client and agree the brief with the client.

2 Take the brief and articulate it for the people who have to make recommendations and have ideas about the campaign.

3 Present ideas to the client for discussion and agreement.

4 Execution phase (where creative material is produced and the space and places in the channels of distribution are bought).

D 🔊 CD1.33

- Get students to read the two questions. If they haven't noticed it already, point out the link between *viral* and *virus*, so that they understand better the idea of something that spreads spontaneously.

- Play the recording once or twice. Elicit the answers.

1 Viral campaigns are pieces of film or content which are picked up by individuals who see it, perhaps on YouTube, and passed on to their friends with comments.

2 Whether it was real or fake

E

- Whole-class discussion. First ask students if they know the Ronaldinho campaign and what they think of it. Then get them to talk about other campaigns. Alternatively, get them to find some (viral) campaigns on YouTube and report on them in the next lesson.

➡️ Resource bank: Listening (page 192)

🔘 Students can watch the interview with Marco Rimini on the DVD-ROM.

Language review: Articles

Students look at the places where articles are used and, just as important, where they are not.

- Get students to look through the commentary and the examples in the panel. Remind them about the Grammar reference section at the end of the book and get them to look at it for homework.

- Depending on the level of the class, you could give some of this extra information, but don't confuse students.

We do not use an article before the names of many places. However we do use *the*:

a) before some countries that have *Kingdom*, *States*, *Republic* in the name: **the** *United States*, **the** *Republic of South Africa* but not *-land* in the name: *New Zealand*. But we do use the article in names of countries and regions where there is *-lands* in the name: **the** *Netherlands*, **the** *Midlands*, **the** *Lowlands*, **the** *Highlands*...

b) before some institutions: **the** *United Nations*, **the** *BBC*

c) with superlative expressions: *Harley Davidson is* **the** *most popular motorbike.*

d) when two nouns are joined with *of*: **the** *advertiser of* **the** *year award*

e) before adjectives to specify a collective group of people or things: **the** *advertising industry*, **the** *rich*

A

- Do as a quick-fire whole-class activity.

Because they have not been referred to before.

B – C

- Explain the tasks and get students to work on them in pairs. Go round the room and help where necessary.

- With the whole class, go through the answers.

Exercise B

1 The problem of viewers tuning out of traditional television advertising. (para. 1)

2 Channel 4 (para. 1)

3 Honda (para. 1)

4 The Honda live advertisement ('the first', para. 2)

5 The Channel 4/Honda campaign (detailed in previous paragraphs)

Exercise C

1 Knowledge of <u>the</u> advertising code of practice is vital to those wishing to work in <u>the</u> advertising industry.

2 We want to film a TV commercial in Russia. ✓

3 The 'Think small' Volkswagen Beetle advert was one of <u>the</u> most successful advertising campaigns of <u>the</u> 20th century.

4 Four major brands – AOL, Yahoo!, Freeserve and BT – all achieve awareness of over 40% amongst <u>the</u> UK adult population.

5 Next year, I am going to work for an advertising agency in <u>the</u> USA.

D

- Now that students should be getting the hang of things, do this exercise as a quick-fire whole-class activity.

Almost as soon as the 'gorilla' television commercial for Dairy Milk chocolate was first shown on 31 August, people started posting it on YouTube. People also started asking questions, like did it feature <u>a</u> real gorilla playing (<u>the</u>) drums?

So what role did the extraordinary take-up of <u>the</u> gorilla ad on <u>the</u> Internet play in Dairy Milk's success?

And was <u>the</u> success of the advert a lucky break? For like Unilever and Diageo, Cadbury has benefited from the free 'viral' distribution of its advertising on <u>the</u> Internet as consumers e-mail, post and create spoof versions of <u>the</u> gorilla campaign.

<u>The</u> gorilla commercial is <u>the</u> most viewed advertisement so far this year on YouTube, the content-sharing website.

- Get students to go and look at the ad on YouTube in their own time if they are interested.

Skills: Starting and structuring presentations

Students look at the language and techniques used for starting and structuring presentations and use the techniques themselves in context.

A

- Do as a whole-class activity.

Students might mention the need for preparation, including thinking about the needs of the audience and the purpose of the presentation, right length and style, good visuals, body language, voice, among many others.

B – C 🔊 CD1.34

- Play the recording and get students to say which is more formal and which less, and ask for the one that they prefer. (You might get some interesting discussion about different cultural expectations of presentations. Be tactful as ever, of course.)

Exercise B

1 is more formal; 2 is more informal

- Play the recording again and get students to check the expressions against those in the Useful language box, deciding if they are formal or informal.

- With the whole class, go through the answers, explaining any difficulties.

Exercise C

Three sections

Formal

On behalf of Alpha Advertising, I'd like to welcome you. My name's Marc Hayward.

This morning, I'd like to outline the campaign concept we've developed for you.

I've divided my presentation into three parts. Firstly, I'll give you the background. Secondly, I'll discuss the media we plan to use. Finally, I'll talk you through the storyboard.

I'd be grateful if you could leave any questions to the end.

Informal

Hi, everyone, I'm Marc Hayward. Good to see you all.

I'm going to tell you about the ideas we've come up with for the ad campaign.

My talk is in three parts. I'll start with the background to the campaign, move on to the media we plan to use, and finish with the storyboard for the commercial.

If there's anything you're not clear about, feel free to stop me and ask any questions.

D

- Put students into pairs. Allocate one of the three presentation situations to each pair. (Don't let them choose, as this wastes time.) Remind them about the importance not just of greeting the audience, but of signalling structure as well.

- Get students to prepare their presentation openings, writing notes rather than a complete text. Go round the class and help where necessary. Get them to practise their presentation opening with each other.

- Bring the class to order. Get members of the pairs to give 'examples' of each type of opening for the whole class. Correct any key mistakes that are cropping up generally.

E – G 🔊 CD1.35

- Get students to look at the extract and to anticipate what might be in the gaps. Ask them to call out suggestions.

- Play the recording and get students to see if their predictions are confirmed.

Exercise E

1 if you look at; we can see from
2 that's all I have to say about; Let's now move on to
3 So, to sum up, then; the key points again

- Get them to say what the function of each of the missing expressions is.

Exercise F

1 c   2 b   3 a

- Then play the recording again and get them to give other examples of sequencers.

Exercise G

Then, Finally, Secondly

- Recap what students have seen in this section on presentations so far by going through the language in the Useful language box again if necessary.

H

- Get students to work on their presentations in pairs or individually. (If there are a lot of students in the class, you could get one member of each pair to work on the first half and the other the second half of each presentation, so that everyone has to give at least half of a presentation.)

- Go round the class and assist where necessary.

- Bring the class to order and work on any remaining difficulties, especially in relation to signalling language.

- Get one or two students to give their presentations and save the others for later classes, but don't forget to come back to them.

- Again, go over any problems and tell remaining students that they should be particularly aware of these when they give their presentations later.

➡ Resource bank: Speaking (page 180)

CASE STUDY

Alpha Advertising

Students prepare and deliver presentations on different advertising campaigns. The presentations are assessed in terms of the campaigns they describe and the presentation skills and language they use.

Introduction

- Get students to talk again briefly about the ads that they looked at on the opening page of the unit and what makes them effective.

- Write the headings on the left-hand side of the table and elicit information from students to complete the right-hand side.

Company	Alpha Advertising
Based in	Turin, Italy
Task	Develop ideas for three advertising campaigns

Preparation

- Explain to your students that they are going to work on one of the three campaigns. Go through the key questions that each team will have to look at when preparing their campaign and explain any difficulties. Explain that they will be presenting their campaigns to the managements of the companies concerned (the other students).

- Divide the class into fours and allocate the campaigns.

- Go round the room and help students understand the task where necessary. Tell students not to work on the text, script, etc. for specific advertisements yet.

- Once students have answered the key questions, tell them to start working on specific advertisements. If available, hand out overhead transparencies and pens so that students can prepare transparencies that they will use to explain their campaign to their clients. (You could get them to do this for homework. For students in an educational institution with appropriate facilities, you could even get them to do actual recordings for TV commercials and radio spots and bring them to the next lesson. Of course, this will depend on levels of interest, time available, etc.)

Optional extra activity: Songs in advertising

- If there is time, you could get students to do this optional extra activity. With the whole class, discuss the following:

Songs are often used in advertising to help reinforce the message and to fix the image of the product in the mind of the consumer. For example, Nike used the Beatles song *Revolution* in an advertisement. Match the following songs to the most appropriate type of company.

type of company	songs
1 An optician's	a) *Smooth Operator* (Sade)
2 A construction company	b) *Let's Get Physical* (Olivia Newton John)
3 A chain of health clubs	c) *Everybody's Talking* (Harry Nilsson)
4 A bank	d) *Another Brick in the Wall* (Pink Floyd)
5 A razor blade company	e) *Are you Lonesome Tonight?* (Elvis Presley)
6 A mobile phone company	f) *I Can See Clearly Now* (Chantal Jones)
7 A dating agency	g) *Money, Money, Money* (ABBA)

1 f **2** d **3** b **4** g **5** a **6** c **7** e

- This could be used to encourage students to think about the songs they will be using in their campaigns.

Presentations and assessment

- Tell the class that for each campaign, two members of each group of four are managers from the client company and the other two are members of the Alpha creative team. Get all the students to look through the points on the assessment sheet – the two managers should concentrate on the campaign concept points and the two members of the creative team should look at the presentation points.

- Groups present their campaigns. (It would be good if each member of the group can present a different part of the campaign.)

- While each group is giving its presentation, the other groups should pay attention, make notes and not talk among themselves. When the presenting group has finished its presentation, ask the other groups to confer among themselves and award points on the campaign concept and the presentation skills. (Deal with the latter especially tactfully. Try to balance any negative comments that students make by positive comments of your own or from others. Avoid students giving language feedback under the 'Accuracy' heading – that's your job.)

- After all the presentations have been given, praise some of the good language points that you heard, especially in the area of presentations language, and work on half a dozen others that need improvement, getting individual students to say the correct thing.

One-to-one

Discuss one of the campaigns with your student, using the Key questions.

Get your student to give the presentation, monitoring it from both the campaign concept and the presentation skills points of view.

After the presentation, discuss the skills and the language used, as above.

If there is time and interest, get your student to prepare and present another campaign, integrating the improvements in presentations language that you suggested.

◎ You can also refer to the *Case study commentary* section of the DVD-ROM, where students can watch an interview with a consultant discussing the key issues raised by the case study.

Writing

● Get your students to write a summary of 200–300 words of their campaigns. Point out that it's a discussion document, so it should be clearly structured with key points, like the presentations that they gave. Students could do this for homework or in pairs in class.

⇒ Writing file, page 131

⇒ Resource bank: Writing (page 208)

AT A GLANCE

	Classwork – Course Book	Further work
Lesson 1 *Each lesson (excluding case studies) is about 45 to 60 minutes. This does not include time spent going through homework.*	**<u>Starting up</u>** Students think about and discuss their own attitudes to money. **Vocabulary: Financial terms** Students look at and learn some key financial expressions and see how they are used in context.	**Practice File** Vocabulary (pages 24–25) **i-Glossary** (DVD-ROM)
Lesson 2	**Listening: Managing investments** Students listen to an investment manager talking about investment strategy. **Reading: An inspirational story** Students read about a particularly gifted financial trader at an investment bank.	**Resource bank: Listening** (page 193) **Course Book Listening** (DVD-ROM) **Text bank** (pages 134–137)
Lesson 3	**Language review: Describing trends** Students develop their knowledge of and ability to use the language to talk about trends and changes. **<u>Skills: Dealing with figures</u>** Students look at how to say numbers in different contexts.	**Practice File** Language review (pages 25–26) **ML Grammar and Usage** **Resource bank: Speaking** (page 181)
Lesson 4 *Each case study is about 1½ to 2 hours.*	**<u>Case study: Make your pitch</u>** Businesspeople appear on a business TV programme looking for entrepreneurs with attractive products in which to invest.	**Resource bank: Writing** (page 209) **Practice File** Writing (pages 26–27) **Case study commentary** (DVD-ROM)

For a fast route through the unit focusing mainly on speaking skills, just use the underlined sections.

For one-to-one situations, most parts of the unit lend themselves, with minimal adaptation, to use with individual students. Where this is not the case, alternative procedures are given.

BUSINESS BRIEF

One of the main features of globalisation is that capital can flow freely to and from almost everywhere. People are always looking to place money where it will be most profitable and earn the greatest **return on investment**. As an individual, you can put your money on **deposit** in a bank and you will get **interest**. Your money is lent out to people, businesses and governments who need it to finance their own projects, and the bank will make *its* money on the difference between what it pays out in interest on deposits and what it gets in interest from **loans**.

You could buy some **bonds** and, as long as the organisation or country you've invested in by lending it money doesn't **default**, you will get your interest payments, and later your bonds will eventually be repaid. Or you could buy some **shares** and share in the profitability of your chosen company. In good times, the **dividends** will be more than what you would get from bonds. In addition, the shares themselves will increase in value, giving you a **capital gain** if you sell them. But if the company runs into trouble and goes **bankrupt**, you will be among the last to be paid back and you may get only part of what you put in or you may lose all your money.

This is the **trade-off** between **risk** and **return**. The higher the risk of your investment not being repaid, the more you will want it to pay back in return on investment. **Investors** use the world's financial markets to channel money into profitable investment activities and projects. **Borrowers**, such as companies and governments, use them to find capital on the best terms.

Most investors are not private individuals but **institutions** like **banks**, **insurance companies**, **mutual funds** (**unit trusts** in Britain) and **pension funds**, who are, of course, investing the money of private individuals indirectly. The markets they invest in include the **money** and **currency markets**, **stock markets** for shares (also known as **equities**), **commodities markets** for anything from gold to pork bellies (used for making bacon), and **property** (buildings and land).

There are also markets for **futures** in currencies, equities, bonds and commodities: a future is a fixed-price contract to buy a certain amount of something for delivery at a fixed future date. There are markets for **options** in currencies, equities and bonds. Here, an investor buys the right to buy or sell a certain amount of these things at a certain price on a particular date in the future. This is a form of betting on how prices will move.

Options and futures are types of **derivatives**. It was with derivatives that the **credit crunch** of 2007–8 began. Loans to borrowers in the US housing market were resold or **securitised** by the banks who made the original loans: interest payments on the loans were used to pay investors who were buying the related derivatives. But **sub-prime** borrowers were unable to repay the original loans, and this led to the **collapse** of a large number of banks and other financial institutions, with governments having to **bail out** (rescue and assist) many of the remaining banks. Following their traumatic experience, many banks are very reluctant to start lending again, leading to dire consequences for economic activity.

Money and your students

Following the credit crunch and its aftermath of the last few years, your students may have strong views on the financial system and the social usefulness or otherwise of some of its activities, for example derivatives trading. As ever, discuss tactfully, especially if your students work in the financial sector.

Read on

Michael Brett: *How to Read the Financial Pages*, Random House, new edition, 2003

Longman Dictionary of Business English, Pearson Education, 2nd edition, 2007

Graham Bannock: *Penguin International Dictionary of Finance*, Penguin, new edition, 2003

Graham Turner: *The Credit Crunch: Housing Bubbles, Globalisation and the Worldwide Economic Crisis*, Pluto, 2008

LESSON NOTES

Warmer

- Write this question on the board: *Where do people put their money?* Give one or two answers, e.g. in their wallet or handbag, in a piggy bank (draw one on the board), on deposit (teach this expression) in a bank, etc. Get students to suggest different places and work towards the idea of investment, e.g. You can put your money in a company by buying its shares.

- Start building up a permanent list of financial expressions on one side of the board, to which you can add during the lesson.

Overview

- Tell students they will be looking at the subject of money.

- Go through the overview section at the beginning of the unit, pointing out the sections that students will be looking at.

Quotation

- Ask students if they agree with the quote. Ask why or why not.

Starting up

Students think about and discuss their own attitudes to money.

A

- Go quickly through the questions with the whole class. Explain any difficulties, e.g. *bank statements*, meaning and pronunciation of *receipts*, etc.

- Get students to discuss the questions in pairs. Go round the room and help where necessary.

- Bring the class to order and ask members of different pairs to talk about the answers that their neighbour gave, comparing them to their own answers. (Ensure that individual students don't just give their own answers.)

B

- With the whole class, ask two or three students what answers they gave. Don't be surprised by differing cultural attitudes, for example towards giving to charity and tax evasion (teach this expression). Be tactful as ever.

Vocabulary: Financial terms

Students look at and learn some key financial expressions, see how they are used in context and apply them themselves.

A – B

- Explain the tasks and get students to work on them in pairs.

- Go round the room and help where necessary. Correct any mispronunciation of *debt*.

- With the whole class, go through the answers.

Exercise A			
1	shares	4	stock market
2	recession	5	forecast
3	equity stake	6	debt

Exercise B					
1 b	2 c	3 e	4 a	5 f	6 d

C – D 🔊)) CD1.36

- With students still in pairs, explain the task. Go round the room and help students, where necessary, to complete the text. Don't play the recording yet.

Exercise C			
1	recession	6	debt
2	stock market	7	equity stake
3	forecast	8	pre-tax profits
4	investment	9	annual turnover
5	bankruptcy	10	dividend

- Then play the recording and, with the whole class, elicit answers. Explain that *turnover* is British English. Americans talk about *sales*.

E

- Do as a quick-fire whole-class activity, getting students to call out the answers.

> **Sample answers**
> Asia-Pacific region, share values, market confidence, luxury hotel group, interim results, strong performance, emerging markets

F

- Put students into threes. Get them to discuss the different points. Go round the class and assist where necessary. Monitor the financial terms that they use.

- Bring the class to order and ask a spokesperson for each group to say what its findings were. Compare the answers from different groups.

- Then praise strong language points that you heard and work on half a dozen finance-related points that still need improvement.

 i-Glossary

Listening: Managing investments

Students listen to Darrell Mercer, an investment manager, talk about the investment strategy that he follows.

A 🔊 CD1.37

- Explain to students that they are going to listen to an investment manager talking about what he does.

- Get them to look at the text and guess what might be in the gaps before they hear the recording. (They might talk about money and the return that his clients are looking for.)

- Play the recording once or twice. Explain any difficulties, without giving away the answers, of course.

- With the whole class, elicit the answers.

1	investment solutions
2	capital
3	level of return
4	design the strategy

- Explain any difficulties.

B 🔊 CD1.38

- Get students to look through the chart, but don't say too much about the expressions in the left column as they will be explained in the recording.

- Play the recording twice, stopping at convenient points for students to complete the chart. You may have to play the recording more than twice as there is a lot of information for them to absorb.

1	government	6	commercial
2	company	7	commodities
3	rate of inflation	8	agriculture
4	stock	9	hedge
5	share	10	absolute return

- Go through any difficulties and any pronunciation problems (e.g. *precious*).

C 🔊 CD1.39

- Get students to look at the four points.

- Play the recording once or twice (or more if necessary). Again, help with any difficult expressions without giving away the answers.

- Elicit the answers.

He does not mention 3 (hedge funds).

➡ Resource bank: Listening (page 193)

◉ Students can watch the interview with Darrell Mercer on the DVD-ROM.

Reading: An inspirational story

Students read about a particularly gifted financial trader at Goldman Sachs.

A

- Get students to look at the headline and find the two expressions. Elicit the answers.

1	wheeler dealer	2	whizz-kid

B – C

- Put students into pairs and tell them that they have to find the information to complete the profile. Go round the room and help where necessary.

- Bring the class to order and get them to give the answers to complete the profile.

Name	Kieran Prior
Age	29
Job	Financial Analyst
Duties	Running a group of European equities and derivatives
Company	Goldman Sachs
Work location	London
IQ	238
Personality/ Strengths	Determined, smart, perceptive, likes challenges
Current area of specialisation	Focusing on 20 companies

- Explain any remaining difficulties.

- Then get students to give their reactions to the article.

D

- Explain what students have to do: find the vocabulary matching the definitions. Do as a quick-fire whole-class activity.

- Get students to call out the answers.

1	bear market	6	equities
2	traders	7	research analysis
3	financial analyst	8	business sector
4	volatility	9	earnings
5	trading desk	10	derivatives

E

- Explain *volatile* – changing rapidly and in unpredictable ways. Point out that it is the adjective linked to *volatility* (see Exercise D).

- Put students into threes and get them to discuss the different industries in relation to recessions, making sure they understand that they will have to give their reasons. Go round and assist where necessary.

- With the whole class, get someone from each group to say what its findings were and discuss them and their reasons for them. For example, food might be less volatile than cars, as people always have to eat but they can put off buying a new car if necessary. With in-work groups, people working in different industries should have a lot to say about how their companies do in recessions!

- If there is interest, get students to do research for homework on how particular industries are faring at the moment and how they fared in the last recession. Point out that the *Financial Times* website (www.ft.com) is a very valuable resource for this type of search. Don't forget in the next lesson to ask students what they found if you ask them to do this task.

➡ Text bank (pages 134–137)

Language review: Describing trends

Students develop their knowledge of and ability to use the language to talk about trends and changes.

- With the whole class, go through the three categories of examples in the panel. Explain any difficulties. (Explain *soar* if necessary.) Remind them about the further information in the Grammar reference section, which they can look at for homework.

A

- Get students to do the exercise individually. Go round the room and help where necessary with difficult words, e.g. *plummet*.

- Then get students to compare their answers with those of their neighbour.

- Go through the exercise with the whole class.

1 decline, drop, fall, decrease
2 double
3 fluctuate
4 gain, increase, rise, improve (unless you're talking about something bad like unemployment)
5 halve
6 level off
7 peak
8 plummet
9 recover
10 rocket, jump
11 triple

- Remind students that the other parts of the verb *fall* are *fell* (past simple) and *fallen* (past participle), not to be confused with *feel*, *felt* and *felt*.

- Remind them also that *rise* is intransitive, i.e. it isn't followed by an object (e.g. *Unemployment rose.*) and *raise* is transitive (e.g. *The finance minister raised taxes.*).

B

- Whole-class activity. Get students to call out noun equivalents and write them up on the board.

a decline
a gain
a drop
an increase
(*rocket* does not have a noun form in this context)
a plummet (rare, but it does exist as a noun)
a doubling
a fall
a halving
a levelling off
a tripling
a recovery
a decrease
a fluctuation
an improvement
a peak
a rise
a jump

C

- Do these as a quick-fire whole-class activity.

1 from; to
2 by
3 of
4 at
5 of
6 of

D

- Tell students to work individually or in pairs to write their sentences, using nouns or verbs. Go round the room and help where necessary.

Sample answers
Graph 1

Sales rose from just under €5 million last year to €7 million this year. There has been an increase in sales of €2 million.

Graph 2

Sales reached a low point of €1 million in April. Sales reached a peak of €7 million in July.

- With the whole class, ask three or four students for their sentences and write some of them on the board.

Skills: Dealing with figures

Students look at how to say numbers in different contexts.

- With the whole class, point out that *figures* is another way of referring to numbers. Go through the examples in the Useful language box. (You could also point out that the year 2012 is *two thousand twelve* in American English. With decimals, the important thing to remember is to say the figures individually, i.e. *one point one eight five* not *one point one hundred and eighty-five*.)

- Also point out that it's rare to say exact figures in full. Teach *roughly*, *about* and *approximately*, *nearly* and *almost*. Give the example: *3,560 is roughly three and a half thousand*. Write this up on the board. Get individual students to talk about the other bigger numbers in the box in the same way.

> 598,347 – roughly 600,000
> 1,300,402 – about 1.3 million
> €478m – nearly €500 million

A

- Explain the task and get students to work in pairs. Make sure the Student As turn to the correct page and also ensure that everyone understands that Student A is looking at the correct version of the article and Student B is looking at a version with errors in some of the figures.

- Go round the room and help where necessary with any difficulties.

- Bring the class to order. Work on problems that were causing particular difficulty.

> The figures that are wrong in Student B's article are underlined:
>
> It was a bad day for the London market. Following disappointing results from FedEx in the US and fears of a credit crunch, the FTSE 100 fell <u>125</u> points or 1.8 per cent to 5,756.9, while the FTSE 250 fell 189.1 points or 1.9 per cent to <u>9,538</u>.
>
> Only eight blue-chip stocks managed to make gains. The best was Smith & Nephew. Shares in the medical devices group rose 2.9 per cent to <u>599p</u> after UBS upgraded the stock to a 'buy' recommendation. S&N was also supported by rumours of a bid approach from a Japanese company.
>
> On the other hand British Airways, down 5.2 per cent to 225$^1/_4$p, fell even further after Morgan Stanley cut its target to 149p. This was because of worries about increasing fuel prices.
>
> Tate and Lyle, the sugar and sweeteners group, lost <u>5.8</u> per cent to 402$^3/_4$p after CityGroup lowered its forecasts because of rising corn prices. Following recent floods in the US, the cost of corn has risen <u>2.5</u> per cent.

B 🔊 CD1.40

- Tell students that they are going to hear Student B's version of the article, so ensure that everyone is looking at page 57 of the Course Book.

- Play the recording, stopping at key points, and get students to repeat the numbers, concentrating on their pronunciation.

C

- Get students to work on the task individually. Go round the room and help where necessary.

- With the whole class, work on problems that have caused particular difficulty. (Don't write up all the answers on the board, as this would be very tedious.)

125 points	a hundred and twenty-five points
1.8 per cent	one point eight per cent
5,756.9	five thousand, seven hundred and fifty-six point nine
189.1 points	a hundred and eighty-nine point one points
1.9 per cent	one point nine per cent
9,538	nine thousand, five hundred and thirty-eight
2.9 per cent	two point nine per cent
599p	five hundred and ninety-nine pence
5.2 per cent	five point two per cent
225$^1/_4$p	two hundred and twenty-five and a quarter pence
149p	one hundred and forty-nine pence
5.8 per cent	five point eight per cent
402$^3/_4$p	four hundred and two and three-quarter pence
2.5 per cent	two point five per cent

➡ Resource bank: Speaking (page 181)

CASE STUDY

Make your pitch

Businesspeople appear on a business TV programme looking for entrepreneurs with attractive products in which to invest. As either investors or entrepreneurs, students look at various projects, present or analyse each one and decide how to allocate their investment money.

Background

● Get students to focus on the case study by asking them to talk about the picture on page 58 and explain the background briefly. Ask them if they have a similar TV programme in their own country.

● Write the headings on the left-hand side of the table and elicit information from students to complete the right-hand side.

TV channel and programme	BNT, *Make your pitch*
Based in	US
Concept	Entrepreneurs present new products or services and wealthy businesspeople choose which ones to invest in.
Money available in return for	An equity stake in the business

Rules of the competition

● With the whole class, quickly go through the rules and explain any difficulties.

🔊 CD1.41, 1.42

● Tell students that they will hear an entrepreneur ending a presentation of the product.

● Play track 41 and elicit the answers.

> The correct statements are: 1, 2, 3.

● Get students to look through the questions relating to track 42.

● Then play the recording and ask a few quick comprehension questions to see if students have followed it.

● The audio is designed to inspire discussion about the four questions. Get students to discuss them in groups of four and report back to the whole class.

Possible issues

1 Tycoons might want to ask about previous business experience of the entrepreneurs.

2 Encourage students to give their personal reasons as to whether they would invest or not.

3 Again, ask students to justify their reasoning, e.g. the fact that particular entrepreneurs would bring their expertise and expect to be rewarded for it.

4 Get students to say what experience and qualities would be important, e.g. skill in negotiating with retailers.

● Get students to look through the four products that are on tonight's programme, i.e. the ones for which they will be making pitches about in the task.

Task

● Divide the class into fours again. Allocate two products or services to each group. Explain that they will take turns in being tycoons and entrepreneurs. Two students will present one of the products to the other two, the tycoons. Then they reverse roles and the latter pair of students will present one of the other products to the former pair. Make sure everyone understands which pages to turn to. Underline the instruction that the pitches should be relatively short (one to two minutes) rather than full-length product presentations.

● Start the task. Go round the room and monitor the language being used, both examples of correct usage and points that need correcting.

● When most of the groups have done their presentations, bring the class to order.

● Praise some of the good language points that you heard and work on half a dozen others that need improvement, getting individual students to say the correct thing.

● With the whole class, talk about all four products and rank them in terms of their investment potential. Get students to vote for each one.

One-to-one

Work on the background to bring out the key points about possible issues when a tycoon invests in an entrepreneur's product or service.

Run the task. Present one of the products to your student (the tycoon). Monitor the language that you both use. Then reverse roles, with your student presenting another of the products to you.

After the activity, underline some of the language that you chose to use and some that your student used correctly and work on five or six points from what they said that need improving.

◎ You can also refer to the *Case study commentary* section of the DVD-ROM, where students can watch an interview with a consultant discussing the key issues raised by the case study.

Writing

● Get your students to write en e-mail of 120–150 words, outlining their recommendations. Students could do this for homework or in pairs in class.

➡ Resource bank: Writing (page 209)

➡ Writing file, page 127

WORKING ACROSS CULTURES 2 — International meetings

Introduction

This Working across cultures unit focuses on the language of meetings and how people from different cultures have different ideas about how meetings should be run and what they should achieve.

A

- Do as a quick-fire whole-class activity and write up what students tell you on the board in note form. For question 4, discuss how students would define 'success' for each type of meeting.

B

- Put students into pairs and get them to do the quiz. Go round and assist where necessary.

- Bring the class to order. Get students to give their answers and write up correct answers on one side of the board.

1 b	**2** c	**3** a	**4** b	**5** c	**6** b	**7** a	**8** a

C

- Get students to discuss with a partner. Then bring the class to order and get students to talk about the importance of the different things in relation to different types of meeting they go to. (There will, for example, be very different answers depending on whether meetings are internal to an organisation or with outsiders such as clients or suppliers.)

D

- Get students to look through the four questions.

- Then get them to look at the five different experiences in pairs. Go round the class and assist where necessary with the vocabulary in the texts that they might find challenging.

- Bring the class to order and get students to discuss their 'findings' with the whole class. Students may identify particular situations with particular countries, but be tactful when dealing with this.

E 🔊 CD1.43

- Get students to look at the questions and then listen to the recording.

- With the whole class, elicit the answers.

> 1 Time, hierarchy, objective
> 2 Clarifying is key, constant checking and feedback are crucial; summarise main areas of agreement and disagreement; plan and organise meetings; predict potential cultural problems

- Work on any remaining difficulties.

F 🔊 CD1.43

- Get students to look at the questions. Explain any difficulties, such as the meaning and pronunciation of *hierarchical*, and then play the recording once or twice.

- With the whole class, elicit the answers.

1 False	**2** False	**3** False	**4** False	**5** True

G 🔊 CD1.43

- Get students to look through the expressions and see if they can remember what goes in the gaps.

- If necessary, play the recording again, stopping at convenient points so that students can write the missing words.

- With the whole class, elicit the answers.

1	money	3	face	5	talk
2	agenda	4	business	6	building

- Discuss the importance of these issues with the whole class. The answer may often be *It depends ...* on the type of meeting, etc.; however, cultural differences will probably emerge in multinational classes.

Task

- Go through the task with the whole class and make sure they understand it.

- Put students into groups of four and appoint one member of each group as its chair. Get them to work on the task and produce their list of tips.

- Go round the class to assist if necessary. Monitor the language being used, but monitor also the cultural attitudes to the subjects that students are talking about.

- Bring the class to order. Ask a spokesperson for each group to move to the next group and to say what they put in their list.

- Bring the class to order again and praise five or six good language points that you heard. Then work on some language points that need correction or improvement. However, pay as much attention to cultural issues, pointing out some of the cultural differences that have emerged if the class is multinational or asking them what they think some of the differences might be between people from different cultures if the class is monocultural. Treat tactfully, as ever.

UNIT B Revision

This unit revises and reinforces some of the key language points from Units 4–6 and from Working across cultures 2. Links with those units are clearly shown. You can point out these links to your students.

4 Organisation
Vocabulary

- Students work on the vocabulary used to describe organisations and further develop their knowledge of typical collocations in this area.

Exercise 1

1 b 2 d 3 e 4 f 5 c 6 a

Exercise 2

1 Carry out research
2 Issue press releases
3 Draw up contracts
4 Install and maintain systems
5 Train staff
6 Keep records

Noun combinations

- Students work further on typical collocations in the area of organisations.

1 management style
2 product range
3 consumer awareness
4 sales revenue
5 company headquarters

Writing

- This exercise provides practice in arranging the contents of a follow-up e-mail in the correct order.

g b d c e a f

5 Advertising
Vocabulary

- Students think about appropriate use of advertising expressions.

1 advertorial
2 commercials
3 endorsed
4 pop-ups
5 hoardings
6 point-of-sale
7 free samples

Articles

- Students get more practice in the use or articles.

Sweden has a long history of rules and regulations aimed at guiding citizens on the right path. A majority of Swedes seem content with the prohibitions they believe help keep their country one of the safest on Earth. As Sweden is an extremely child-focused society, much of the paternalistic protection is directed towards children. For example, all television advertising aimed at children under the age of 12 – from junk food to toys to video games – has been banned on terrestrial channels before 9 p.m. since 1991. Although it has many admirers, the ban is not entirely successful because the satellite television stations that broadcast from outside Sweden are free to target children as much as they like. Despite this, health professionals say the relatively low incidence of children's advertising has been a big factor in the exceptionally low levels of overweight children in Sweden.

Skills

- This exercise provides further practice in the language of presentations.

1 behalf
2 welcome
3 talk
4 divided
5 parts
6 Firstly
7 like
8 Secondly
9 finally
10 interrupt
11 question

6 Money
Vocabulary

- Students practise words and expressions related to money.

1 bankruptcy
2 gains
3 Turnover
4 recession
5 Pre-tax profits
6 Shareholders
7 dividend
8 share
9 Forecasts
10 investment

61

Describing trends

● Students develop their knowledge of the language used to describe trends.

Exercise 1

1	plummet	**5**	increase
2	drop	**6**	rise
3	fall	**7**	rocket
4	decline	**8**	jump

Exercise 2

1	decreased	**6**	fall	**11**	peaked
2	decreased	**7**	dropped	**12**	peak
3	decrease	**8**	dropped	**13**	rose
4	fell	**9**	drop	**14**	risen
5	fallen	**10**	peaked	**15**	rise

Exercise 3

1	in	**4**	at
2	from; to	**5**	of; in
3	by		

Skills

● Students are provided with more practice in dealing with numbers.

---

1 fourteen

2 forty

3 eight pounds fifty

4 five hundred and fifteen euros

5 twelve point five

6 thirteen point three six per cent

7 zero (*or* oh *or* nought) point one two five

8 a (*or* one) third

9 three quarters

10 five thousand, six hundred and seventy-eight

Cultures: International meetings

● Students look again at some of the vocabulary relating to cross-cultural issues.

1	body	**5**	key
2	face	**6**	building
3	action	**7**	small, business
4	times	**8**	agenda

UNIT 7 Cultures

AT A GLANCE

	Classwork – Course Book	Further work
Lesson 1 *Each lesson (excluding case studies) is about 45 to 60 minutes. This does not include time spent going through homework.*	**Starting up** Students are encouraged to think about cultural issues and their relevance to business. **Listening: Cultural differences** Students listen to the Marketing Director at an international cultural training centre in the UK.	**Resource bank: Listening** (page 194) **Course Book Listening** (DVD-ROM)
Lesson 2	**Vocabulary: Idioms** Students look at some common idioms and use them in context. **Reading: Culture shock** Students read about how an international bank works to ease cultural misunderstandings between its staff from different countries.	**Practice File** Vocabulary (page 28) **i-Glossary** (DVD-ROM) **Text bank** (pages 138–141)
Lesson 3	**Language review: Advice, obligation and necessity** Students look at some modal and other verbs and use them in the context of intercultural advice. **Skills: Social English** Students look at, listen to and practise the language of social interaction.	**Practice File** Language review (pages 29–30) **ML Grammar and Usage** **Resource bank: Speaking** (page 182) **Practice File** Using English in social situations (page 67)
Lesson 4 *Each case study is about 1½ to 2 hours.*	**Case study: Business culture briefing** A group of managers is attending an informal briefing about the business culture of a country where they will soon be doing business. Students give advice on the cultural issues that may arise.	**Resource bank: Writing** (page 210) **Practice File** Writing (pages 30–31) **Case study commentary** (DVD-ROM)

For a fast route through the unit focusing mainly on speaking skills, just use the underlined sections.

For one-to-one situations, most parts of the unit lend themselves, with minimal adaptation, to use with individual students. Where this is not the case, alternative procedures are given.

BUSINESS BRIEF

As the world gets smaller, we need to learn more about each others' values, beliefs, habits and expectations. Culture is, in the famous phrase, the way we do things around here. The 'here' in question may be a country, a region, a social class, a company, a university. Clearly, we each live in a set of cultures and **subcultures** that interlock in complex ways and, to make a generalisation, one of the most dangerous things is to generalise about them. **Stereotypes** are, of course, to be handled with caution. The stereotype may represent the middle of a range of differing behaviours, it may be at one extreme or it may just not be true. And there may be more variety in behaviour within a culture than between one culture and another.

Neighbouring countries or regions or two companies in the same industry often see themselves as very different from each other, but that difference may be hard for the outsider to grasp at first glance. A few years' working in one of the two places will make it seem more apparent, as one gets 'involved' in one of the cultures.

Here are some **intercultural issues** (*intercultural* is nowadays often preferred to *cross-cultural*), areas where there are variations in behaviour across different cultures.

- Religion: Is it expected of people or a matter of individual choice? Does it play a role in business life?
- Roles of men and women: Are women often found at the highest levels of business and society?
- Hierarchy: What is the distance between managers and the people who work for them?
- Levels of formality in language and behaviour: Is there an elaborate system of levels of deference in addressing different people?
- Conversation, discussion: Settings (formal and informal meetings, social situations, etc.), turn-taking, proximity, body language, contact, etc.
- Dress for different settings and occasions: Is the business suit *de rigueur*?
- The relation of work to private life: Are spouses expected to attend certain types of company event? Do businesspeople invite colleagues and contacts to their homes, or is everything done in the office and restaurants?
- Time: Timescale of the activity/organisation, planning, punctuality, the working day/week/ year, meals, recreation, holidays, etc. Do meetings start on time? Is the summer break sacrosanct?

Cultures and your students

Language trainers and teachers, like their students, are often fascinated by intercultural issues. Obviously, culture has to be discussed tactfully, bearing in mind that we are not judging whether other ways of doing things are right or wrong, but we should be aware of the differences and not see our own culture as the 'normal' one.

However, language issues are equally important: for example, getting students to greet people in an appropriate way, with the correct intonation. Situations such as this require very formulaic language, and one thing wrong or out of place can destroy the whole effect and may lead to 'cultural' misunderstandings (e.g. the use, intonation and place in the sentence of *please*). One of our jobs is to teach and practise the formulae, the language blocks, for these situations. Of course, this can be done in simulation activities where awareness of cultural issues also has its place.

Read on

Fons Trompenaars: *Riding the Whirlwind: Connecting People and Organisations in a Culture of Innovation*, Capstone, 2003

Fons Trompenaars: *Managing People across Cultures*, Infinite Ideas, 2007

Geert Hofstede: *Cultures and Organizations: Software of the Mind*, McGraw Hill, 2nd edition, 2004

Susan Schneider and Jean-Louis Barsoux: *Managing across Cultures*, Prentice Hall, new edition, 2007

Craig Storti: *The Art of Crossing Cultures*, Nicholas Brealey, new edition, 2008

LESSON NOTES

Warmer

- Get students to look in a good dictionary, e.g. *Longman Dictionary of Contemporary English*, at the word *culture*. What does it say about the word, as a countable noun and an uncountable noun? How would students translate each sense of 'culture' into their own language?

Overview

- Tell students they will be looking at the subject of cultures (and culture). Point out the difference in meaning between the uncountable noun (culture in general) and the countable one (used to talk about particular cultures).

- Go through the overview panel at the beginning of the unit, pointing out the sections that students will be looking at.

Quotation

- Get students to look at the quotation and ask them if they agree with it. (Borgen has an interesting background in international development: students can look at http//borgenproject.org/Clint_Borgen.html if they are interested.)

Starting up

Students are encouraged to think about cultural issues and their relevance to business.

Throughout the unit, be very tactful about how you treat cultural issues. It's probably a good idea not to praise or criticise any particular country's way of doing things.

A

- Discuss with the whole class. You could give examples of what you miss about your culture when you go abroad.

B

- With the whole class, get students to give examples, if possible, of business incidents where culture has been a problem, e.g. unintended rudeness, breakdowns of communication.

C – D

- Get students to discuss the points in pairs and choose the four points from Exercise C that they think are the most important. Go round the room and help where necessary.

- Discuss with the whole class, getting pairs to give the ideas they came up with.

- Then follow the same procedure for Exercise D, getting students to say why they hold the opinions that they do. (It'll be interesting if you can find someone who doesn't agree that cultures are becoming more alike – don't ignore it as a possible point of view.) ASEAN is a trading bloc of countries in south-east Asia.

- You could give your students the most famous definition of culture – 'The way we do things round here' – and discuss the possible 'heres' – a club, a company, an institution, a whole country, ...

E

- Get students to discuss in pairs and then with the whole class.

- **Exchanging business cards:** The etiquette is very important in some places. In Asia, hand over with both hands and do not write anything on cards you give or receive.

- **Shaking hands:** Every day? Only on seeing someone for the first time or after a long time?

- **Bowing:** How far should Westerners be expected to follow the rules in cultures such as Japan?

- **Kissing:** Get students to say when and how often (e.g. on every meeting?) you should shake hands or kiss, if at all, in their country.

- **Being formal or informal:** In dress, language and behaviour, do you err on the safe side (teach this expression), or is there a risk of appearing stuffy in some places?

- **Punctuality:** How late do you have to be before it is considered unacceptable?

- **Humour:** Is this best avoided altogether?

- **Eye contact:** Is keeping eye contact for about half the time a good guide? Or might this be too much, or not enough, in some cultures?

- **Socialising with contacts:** Do people invite business guests to their homes, or is everything done in restaurants? If so, is lunch or dinner the key meal?

- **Small talk before meetings:** How much is expected, if any? Or is it considered to be time-wasting?

- **Accepting interruption:** When someone is speaking, are interruptions rude? In some places, there can be quite long pauses before the next speaker begins. Does/Would this make your students uncomfortable?

- **Giving presents:** When and what should you give? When should you open presents?

- **Being direct (saying exactly what you think):** People in some countries may pride themselves on this, but is it always appropriate, or even possible, with 'normal' social relations?

- **Using first names:** In general, is this something to avoid unless invited to use them?

Listening: Cultural differences

Jeff Toms, Marketing Director at an international cultural training centre in the UK, talks about some cultural issues and their impact on doing business internationally.

A 🔊 CD1.44

- Explain who Jeff Toms is and get students to look at the two questions.

- Then play the recording once or twice, explaining any difficulties, and elicit the answers.

- Have a class discussion about the issues. As ever, be tactful.

> 1 The perception of time-keeping is different because of prayer times and awareness of the movements of the sun and moon.
> 2 Americans want to get down to business immediately but, in other cultures, relationship building is very important.

B 🔊 CD1.45

- Get students to read the rubric and play the recording, again explaining any difficulties.

- Then elicit the answer.

> It's not enough for staff to be brilliant in their area. They have to be adaptable and flexible – prepared to change when necessary.

C 🔊 CD1.46

- Play the recording two or three times. Explain any remaining difficulties, but don't give the answers away.

- Elicit the answers.

> 1 international businessperson
> 2 judgemental
> 3 hierarchy
> 4 decision-making process
> 5 influence

- Work on any difficulties, e.g. pronunciation of *hierarchy*.

- Ask students with international experience if they have had problems in these areas themselves.

D

- Put students into pairs. Get each member of the pair to explain their choice, and reasons for it, to their partner. Go round the class and assist where necessary.

- Bring the class to order. Get students to talk about their partners' choices, rather than their own.

- Praise good language points you heard and work on half a dozen, preferably related to culture, that have been causing difficulties.

➡ Resource bank: Listening (page 194)

◎ Students can watch the interview with Jeff Toms on the DVD-ROM.

Vocabulary: Idioms

Students look at some common idioms and use them in context.

A

- Point out that idioms can mystify non-native speakers. Get students to tell you some idioms from their own language(s).

- Do the exercise as a quick-fire whole-class activity. Explain any difficulties.

1	ice	5	foot
2	end	6	fire
3	eye	7	water
4	water	8	eye

- You could ask students if they have similar idioms in their own language(s) or what the equivalents would be. This can be amusing, but don't spend too much time on it.

B – D 🔊 CD1.47

- Ensure that students understand the task, which is to identify the idiom being used in each extract. Then play the recording once or twice and elicit the answers.

> 1 break the ice – g (positive)
> 2 thrown in at the deep end – a (negative)
> 3 we don't see eye to eye – e (negative)
> 4 got into hot water – h (negative)
> 5 put my foot in it – d (negative)
> 6 get on like a house on fire – b (positive)
> 7 fish out of water – c (negative)
> 8 a real eye-opener – f (positive)

- As a quick-fire whole-class activity, get students to match the meanings in Exercise D and say which are positive and which negative.

E

- Get students to discuss in pairs or threes. Go round the room and help where necessary.

- With the whole class, get students to talk about particular situations, either ones they were in themselves or ones they heard about from other members of their pairs/threes.

◎ i-Glossary

Reading: Culture shock

Students read about how an international bank works to ease cultural misunderstandings between its staff from different countries.

A

- Get students to read the article quickly and, in pairs, find the positive and negative items.

- Go round the room and help where necessary.

- With the whole class, elicit the answers.

> 1 a   2 b   3 c   4 a   5 c

B

- Get students, in their pairs, to look at the questions and read the article a second time. Go round and assist where necessary.

- With the whole class, elicit the answers. You could get students to find the parts of the article that relate to each question, then get them to rephrase the answers in their own words and then discuss them.

> 1 a) '[They] might share similar professional knowledge and skills ... ' (lines 15–16)
>
> 1 b) ' ... their ways of working, social skills, body language and ways of doing business are likely to be completely different. They may have different patterns of behaviour ... ' (lines 17–22)
>
> 2 'It is about understanding how and why cultures work differently.' (lines 46–47)

C

- Get students to discuss the question, still in pairs. Go round and assist where necessary. If students are stuck for ideas, they could go back to the issues in *Starting up* and decide which should be included in their course. Monitor the language that they are using, especially the language that relates to cultural issues.

- Bring the class to order and elicit some of the students' ideas, comparing and contrasting those of different pairs.

D

- Get students to write their paragraph individually in class, or for homework. Don't forget to check what they have written at some point.

➡ Text bank (pages 138–141)

Language review: Advice, obligation and necessity

Students look at some modal and other verbs and use them in the context of intercultural advice.

- Talk students through the commentary and examples in the panel. Also bring their attention to the extra information in the Grammar reference on page 149 and tell them to look at it for homework.

A

- Go through the exercise with the whole class. The important thing is to discuss why the answer is appropriate in each case.

> 1   should
> 2   mustn't
> 3   both (this may be advisory or compulsory)
> 4   mustn't
> 5   both (may be advisory or compulsory)
> 6   both (two senses: she needn't work so hard; it's not good for her to do so)
> 7   both (depends on the strength of the advice)
> 8   don't have to

B

- Get individual students to read aloud the advice on Chinese business protocol. Practise difficult words like *honour*.

- Either as pairwork or a whole-class activity, get students to talk about differences and similarities with their own countries.

- If you have done the last step as pairwork, do a whole-class round-up of the pairs' findings.

Skills: Social English

Students look at, listen to and practise the language of social interaction.

A 🔊 CD1.48

- Tell students that they will be doing 'social English'. (You should have no trouble 'selling' this – it's something that students often request and see as a key area.)

- Get students to listen to the dialogue once right through, then again, stopping after each exchange and getting students to suggest improvements.

> **Sample answer**
> **A** So where did you go on holiday, then?
> **B** We went to Italy this year.
> **A** Did you have a good time? [enthusiastically]
> **B** Yes, it was great!
> **A** And which part of Italy did you go to?
> **B** We rented a villa in Sicily.
> **A** I've been to Sicily – Taormina. I really enjoyed it. What did you think of it?
> **B** Yes, I thought it was wonderful – the scenery is so beautiful.
> **A** Yes, it's a marvellous place. We want to go back next to Italy next year. So ... how's it going at work?
> **B** We're really busy.
> **A** That's really good, isn't it?
> **B** Yes, it's better that way!

- Get one or two pairs to perform the improved version, with feeling!

B

- Go through the expressions and explain any difficulties.

- Put students into pairs. Get them to suggest situations in which the expressions are used. Go round the room and help where necessary. (Students in the UK may point out that *Cheers* is used also to mean 'Goodbye' and 'Thank you' as well as when raising one's glass. Point out also that *I'm afraid* is often used when giving bad news, particularly in British English.)

C

- With the whole class, get individual pairs to have mini-conversations where they use the expressions, for example, **A**: *I've just been promoted.* **B**: *Congratulations.*

Sample answers

1 Sorry, I didn't catch that.

2 I'm afraid I won't be able to make it. I have to be at the airport by six.

3 No, thanks. I don't like black pudding very much, I'm afraid.

4 It was nice talking to you, but I have to get to my next meeting.

5 Hello. It's very nice to see you. Welcome to Prague. Have you been here before?

6 Jack, I'd like to introduce you to Ivan – Jack Smith, Ivan Brodsky.

7 I'll get this – it's on me.

8 I'd like to propose a toast. Here's to the success of our joint venture!

9 I'm very sorry to hear that.

10 I'm so sorry I'm late. The traffic's awful!

D 🔊 CD2.1

- Play the recording, stopping after each item. Get students to write down exactly what they hear.

1 I'm sorry. I didn't quite catch your name.

2 I'm really sorry – I'd love to, but I'm afraid I'm going to the theatre on Wednesday night.

3 Not for me, thanks. I'm not keen on seafood.

4 I'm sorry, but I really do have to be going. It was really nice talking to you.

5 Welcome to our headquarters. It's a pleasure to meet you. I'm James Clayton.

6 Katrina, can I introduce you to Greg? Greg's over from the States. Greg, this is Katrina Siedler, my boss.

7 Please, let me get this.

8 Here's to our future success.

9 I'm very sorry to hear about what happened.

10 I'm sorry I'm late, the traffic from the airport was terrible.

- As in Exercise C above, get individual pairs to perform exchanges with these expressions, either the ones they suggested themselves or the ones they heard in the recording, for example, **A**: *My name's Smolensky.* **B**: *I'm sorry. I didn't quite catch your name.*

E 🔊 CD2.2

- Ask students if they think it's true that we form our ideas about someone within the first few minutes of meeting them. Is it always easy to know what to say during this critical time?

- Explain the task and get students to work on it in pairs. Go round and assist where necessary.

- Bring the class to order and elicit the answers.

1 c	2 d	3 b	4 g	5 e	6 h	7 f	8 a
9 j	10 i				

- Play the recording and get students to check their answers.

- Get students to practise reading the conversation in pairs. Go round the room and help where necessary, especially with intonation.

- Get one or two pairs to 'perform' the conversation for the whole class.

F – **G**

- With the whole class, discuss the issues relatively quickly. Students might, rightly, suggest that the weather, food, hotels, length of time in a place are safe, but that religion and politics are best avoided.

- Decide which of the items of advice for a successful conversation are helpful and which are not as a quick-fire whole-class activity.

Exercise G

Useful: 1, 4, 5, 7, 8

But remind students not to overdo it. For example, ask questions but not too many and not very personal ones; keep eye-contact most of the time, but don't stare at the other person.

Not useful: 2, 3, 6

➡ Resource bank: Speaking (page 182)

CASE STUDY

Business culture briefing

A group of managers is attending an informal briefing about the business culture of a country where they will soon be doing business. Students give advice on the cultural issues that may arise.

Background

- Get students to focus on the case study by getting them to list all the things that could go wrong in a visit by overseas visitors from the cultural point of view. Get them to call out possible answers.

- Write the headings on the left-hand side of the table and elicit information from students to complete the right-hand side.

Company	Better Business Communications (BBC)
Activity	Prepares business people who are visiting a country for the first time
Situation	Group of top managers who are looking to set up a subsidiary in the country. BBC will prepare them culturally (for meetings, invitations to homes/restaurants, social visits and excursions)

Discussion of topics 🔊 CD2.3

- Put students into pairs. Get them to draw up a list of topics that they would think important for visitors. (If the class is multinational, put students from different countries together so that they can compare and contrast their findings.)

- Get one or two of the pairs to call out their answers.

- Then play the recording and ask students to see if the issues on their lists are mentioned.

1 Level of English
2 Formality
3 Greetings
4 Topics of conversation (There may be disagreement here: students might see it as tactless to ask any nationality, not just Russians, about the current state of their economy.)
5 Gifts

Task

- Talk students through the three steps of the task.

- Divide students into (national) groups of, say, three, or get them to work individually.

- Get them to work on step 1 of the task. Go round and assist where necessary.

- Bring the class to order. Get a representative of each group to come to the front of the class and give their presentation to the whole class. Encourage questions from the class, reminding students that they are top managers at BBC's cultural briefing session.

- Note down strong language points and ones that need correction or improvement. After each presentation, praise the strong points and work on half a dozen that need improvement, getting students to say the correct thing.

- Do step 3 as a whole class. When deciding on the most interesting talk, focus on the positive aspects of that talk and not the negative aspects of the other talks.

> **One-to-one**
>
> Work on the background and the recording to bring out the key points.
>
> Then get the student to work through the different steps of the task. Get them to give their presentation. Note down strong language points and ones that need correction or improvement as above.

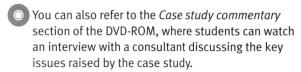 You can also refer to the *Case study commentary* section of the DVD-ROM, where students can watch an interview with a consultant discussing the key issues raised by the case study.

Writing

- Get your students to write a short report (130–150 words) about the most interesting information they have learned.

- Students could do this for homework or in pairs in class.

⇒ Resource bank: Writing (page 210)

⇒ Writing file, page 130

Human resources

AT A GLANCE

	Classwork – Course Book	Further work
Lesson 1 *Each lesson (excluding case studies) is about 45 to 60 minutes. This does not include time spent going through homework.*	**Starting up** Students look at the factors that are important in getting a job and their relative importance. **Vocabulary: Employing the right people** Students look at words used to talk about recruitment and words used to describe candidates and workers.	**Practice File** Vocabulary (page 32) **i-Glossary** (DVD-ROM)
Lesson 2	**Reading: Women at work** Students read about the situation for women at work in Vietnam and Japan. **Listening: Finding a job** Students listen to a professional recruiter's advice about finding a job and the latest trends in the job market.	**Text bank** (pages 142–145) **Resource bank: Listening** (page 195) **Course Book Listening** (DVD-ROM)
Lesson 3	**Language review: -*ing* forms and infinitives** Students look at and work on those verbs that are followed by -*ing* forms and those that are followed by infinitives. **Skills: Getting information on the telephone** Students look at language for obtaining information on the phone and practise using it in a role play.	**Practice File** Language review (page 33) **ML Grammar and Usage** **Resource bank: Speaking** (page 183)
Lesson 4 *Each case study is about 1½ to 2 hours.*	**Case study: Fast Fitness** People apply for the job of turning round a chain of gym clubs. Students discuss the candidates, listen to their job interviews and appoint the best one.	**Resource bank: Writing** (page 211) **Practice File** Writing (pages 34–35) **Case study commentary** (DVD-ROM)

For a fast route through the unit focusing mainly on speaking skills, just use the underlined sections.

For one-to-one situations, most parts of the unit lend themselves, with minimal adaptation, to use with individual students. Where this is not the case, alternative procedures are given.

BUSINESS BRIEF

Human resources (HR), formerly known as Personnel, is the Cinderella of company departments. Production managers manage production, sales directors head up their sales teams, but HR directors do not, strictly speaking, direct employees. They act more as facilitators for other departments: they deal with **recruitment** in conjunction with departmental managers, they administer **payment systems** in tandem with accounts, they are perhaps present at **performance appraisal reviews** when employees discuss with their managers how they are doing, they may be responsible for providing **training**; in **industrial relations**, they are involved in **complaints and disputes procedures**, and they often have to break the news when people are **dismissed**.

Human resources management specialists may be involved in:

- introducing more 'scientific' **selection procedures**: for example, the use of **psychometric tests** to see what people are really like and what they are good at, rather than how they come across in interviews.

- implementing policies of **empowerment**, where employees and managers are given authority to make decisions previously made at higher levels.

- employee **training** and, more recently, **coaching** (individual advice to employees on improving their career prospects) and **mentoring**: when senior managers help and advise more junior ones in their organisation.

- **diversity**: actions to eliminate **racial** and **sexual discrimination** in **hiring** and **promotion** and to fight **harassment** in the workplace (such as bullying and sexual harassment) and to encourage the idea that an organisation benefits when it has employees from different backgrounds and cultures.

- **incentive schemes** to increase **motivation** through **remuneration systems** designed to reward performance.

But their services may also be required when organisations **downsize** and **delayer**, eliminating levels of management to produce a **leaner** or **flatter** organisation, trying to maintain the **morale** of those that stay and arranging **severance packages** for employees who are **made redundant**, sometimes offering **outplacement** services, for example putting them in touch with potential employers and advising them on training possibilities.

Professional people who are made redundant may be able to make a living as **freelancers** or, in modern parlance, **portfolio workers**, working for a number of clients. They hope to be on the receiving end when companies **outsource** activities, perhaps ones that were previously done **in-house**.

This is all part of **flexibility**, the idea that people should be ready to change jobs more often, be prepared to work part time and so on. The message is that the era of **lifetime employment** is over and that people should acquire and develop skills to maintain their **employability**.

Human resources and your students

In-work students will, of course, know at first hand employment issues such as job interviews and payment systems. They may be unfortunate enough to have experience of complaints procedures and dismissal or redundancy. Discussing these things will obviously require sensitivity and tact.

Pre-work students will be less familiar with these areas, but may be about to enter the world of work. Allow for their lack of direct experience of employment issues.

Read on

Wayne Cascio: *Managing Human Resources,* McGraw Hill, 7th edition, 2005

Michael Armstrong: *A Handbook of Human Resource Management Practice*, Kogan Page, 10th edition, 2006

Derek Torrington, Stephen Taylor, Laura Hall: *Human Resource Management,* FT Prentice Hall, 7th edition, 2007

LESSON NOTES

Warmer
- As a quick-fire whole-class activity, get students to brainstorm all the ways of getting a job that they can think of, e.g. looking at job advertisements, asking friends, writing to companies, being headhunted, starting your own company. Write the suggestions on the board.

Overview
- Tell students they will be looking at the subject of jobs and employment.
- Go through the overview panel at the beginning of the unit, pointing out the sections that students will be looking at.

Quotation
- Ask your students if they agree with the quote. (Students may come up with counter-examples, such as chess-playing computers that beat world champions. If interested, they can find out more about Hubbard on Wikipedia.)

Starting up
Students look at the factors that are important in getting a job and their relative importance.

A
- With the whole class, get students to look through the list and explain any difficulties. (Don't be surprised by some of the factors. Blood group is very important in Japan, for example, and handwriting analysis is a priority in France. Ask your students particularly about these.)
- Get students to suggest other factors. These could include behaviour or manners and accent or way of talking. If they don't mention these, ask students about them.

B – C
- Put students in pairs and get them to ask each other about their best and worst jobs, boss, etc., and to discuss the statements in Exercise C. Go round the room and help where necessary.
- With the whole class, get students to talk about their neighbour's experiences and opinions, rather than their own. Of course, be tactful – especially, for example, if an in-work student says that their current boss is the worst they have ever had!

Vocabulary: Employing the right people
Students look at vocabulary used to talk about recruitment and words used to describe candidates and workers.

A – C 🔊 CD2.4
- Do Exercise A as quick-fire whole-class activities. Explain any difficulties.

> **Exercise A**
> 1 curriculum vitae (CV)/résumé
> 2 application form
> 3 covering letter
> 4 interview
> 5 psychometric test
> 6 probationary period

- Get students to match the verbs with the nouns in Exercise B and decide on a possible order.
- Play the recording and get students to listen out for the word partnerships in Exercise A (you could get them to raise their hands each time they hear one) and check their answers to Exercise B.

> **Exercise B**
> 1 e 2 c 3 a 4 b 5 f 6 d
> Point out that other partnerships are possible (e.g. *assemble the candidates*), but that the ones above are the most likely.
> Possible order: 3, 2, 4, 6, 5, 1
>
> **Exercise C**
> Well, what usually happens is that an employer will <u>advertise a vacancy</u> or new <u>post</u> – sometimes both inside and outside the company. Then, after they have received all the applications, they will screen them – go through and <u>shortlist the candidates</u> for interview – choosing those who appear to meet the criteria for the job. Next, they will <u>assemble an interview panel</u>, which is perhaps as many as four or five people in some cases, and then call the candidates to interview. Some employers choose to <u>check references</u> at this stage to avoid delays later, while others wait until after the interview when they have chosen one of the candidates. Provided the panel is happy, the employer will <u>make a job offer</u>, and the successful candidate starts work. Often he or she will attend induction sessions or be given a mentor who helps to <u>train new staff</u>.

D
- Give students the example of employers looking for people who are honest, loyal, etc.
- Get students to work in pairs to come up with other qualities. You could get them to use good bilingual dictionaries or good monolingual ones, like *Longman Dictionary of Contemporary English* if they get stuck.
- Go round the room and help where necessary. Get students to start thinking about using the words in context.
- With the whole class, elicit some ideas.

E

- Get students, again in pairs, to rank the qualities.

- Then, with the whole class, get pairs to give their rankings and compare them with those of other pairs.

- With the whole class, get students to match the meanings as a quick-fire activity.

> **1** g   **2** i   **3** f   **4** j   **5** e   **6** a   **7** c   **8** h
> **9** b   **10** d

- Work on any difficulties, e.g. the pronunciation of *creative*, but don't pre-empt the next activity too much.

F 🔊 CD2.5

- Get students to mark the stress on the words. Then play the recording or read the words out yourself and get students to check their answers.

> | | | | |
> |---|---|---|---|
> | **1** | cre<u>a</u>tive | **6** | enthusi<u>a</u>stic |
> | **2** | au<u>tho</u>ritative | **7** | me<u>tho</u>dical |
> | **3** | ob<u>jec</u>tive | **8** | ana<u>ly</u>tical |
> | **4** | <u>prac</u>tical | **9** | a<u>dap</u>table |
> | **5** | am<u>bi</u>tious | **10** | re<u>li</u>able |

- Get students to discuss the questions in pairs or threes.

- Discuss the findings of the different groups with the whole class.

- If there is time and interest, you could get students to do this task. Working in pairs or threes, students think about selecting three people for a team to work on a new project. They should decide what type of project it is and agree on the qualities the team should have. They can use the ideas on page 75 of the Course Book and their own ideas.

- Go round and assist where necessary, making sure that each group has identified the type of project for which they are recruiting people.

- Monitor the language being used. Note down some good points and half a dozen that need improvement, especially in language used in relation to human resources.

- Get individuals from each group to present their findings to the whole class or, if you have a big enough classroom, you could get groups to present to each other in parallel.

- Bring the class to order. Praise the good points that you heard in the group discussions and the presentations and work on those that need further attention.

 i-Glossary

Reading: Women at work

Students read about women at work in two different countries and compare them.

A

- Put students into pairs and allocate article A or B to each member of the pairs. Get them to read the article quickly and to think up a heading for each.

> **Possible headings** (some snappier than others!)
> **Article A**
> - The advancement of women in Vietnam
> - The increasing importance of women in Vietnamese business
> - Major progress for women in the Vietnamese workplace
>
> **Article B**
> - Women in the driver's seat in Japan
> - Changing the Japanese way of selling cars
> - Women lead change in Japanese car-selling methods

B

- Get students to work individually to find if the statements about 'their' article are true or false.

- Then they explain their answers to their partner, correcting the false statements, paraphrasing or quoting from the articles.

> **Article A**
> 1   True
> 2   False: Women account for nearly 52 per cent of the workforce in the service sector, 50 per cent in the agricultural and fisheries sector and 37 per cent in industry and construction.
> 3   True
> 4   False: More than a third (40.2 per cent) of university graduates are women but slightly under a third (30.5 per cent) of holders of Master's degrees are women.
> 5   False: She says that they jointly decide important issues in their life, such as work or education for their children. Her husband always respects her opinions.
> 6   True
>
> **Article B**
> 7   True
> 8   True
> 9   True
> 10 False: The number of women managers at Nissan … has risen from 2 per cent to 5 per cent.
> 11 False: The percentage of women managers in the Japanese car industry as a whole is 0.6 per cent.
> 12 False: Men are attracted by big pictures of cars and specifications about performance; most mothers were attracted by pictures of a family having a great time with the car.

C

- Students remain in their pairs and exchange information in order to make comparisons, for example, *Women in Vietnam make up more than half the workforce, but the number of women in parts of Japanese business, for example engineering, is very small.*

- With the whole class, get pairs to read out their comparisons.

D

- With the whole class, discuss the issue tactfully. (Don't be surprised if students are not convinced by this statement when talking about the business cultures from which they come.)

E

- Again in pairs, get students to identify the words under each heading. Go round and assist where necessary.

- With the whole class, get students to call out the answers.

> **a)** child(ren), mother, housewife, residents, community, husband, family, women, society, government, (university) graduates, PhDs, recipients
> sales executives, customers, salespeople, boy, women, men, family, graduates, managers, employees, engineers, mothers
>
> **b)** construction, real estate, service (sector), agricultural, fisheries, industry, education
> engineering, marketing, sales

- Then, with the whole class, give examples of one or two of these words in sentences. Get students to think specifically about their country and industry (or one they would like to work in).

- Get students to write six sentences in pairs and then, with the whole class, get students from some of the pairs to read them out.

- Work on any difficulties.

⟹ Text bank (pages 142–145)

Listening: Finding a job

Students listen to a professional recruiter's advice about finding a job and the latest trends in the job market.

A ◀)) CD2.6

- Focus students' attention on the speaker – Carys Owen, a recruitment specialist – and what they are going to hear – a professional recruiter talking about her organisation's services.

- Get students to look at the question. Then play the recording once or twice.

- Elicit the answer.

> Via a network of global offices; candidates work with a Hays consultant who helps them gain an understanding of the type of role they're looking for, what type of organisation they would like to work for, etc. They also work how to present their CV.
>
> Also via the website; candidates can apply for jobs and get advice on applications.

- Work on any language difficulties.

B ◀)) CD2.7

- Get students to look at the question. Then play the recording once or twice.

- Elicit the answers, preferably with students paraphrasing what they heard.

> 1 Look your best.
> 2 Research your employer.
> 3 Look at the duties of the vacancy and match them to your experience.

C ◀)) CD2.7

- Play the recording again and elicit the answers.

> 1 recommend   3 previous experience
> 2 duties   4 demonstrate

D ◀)) CD2.8

- Get students to look at the questions. Then play the recording once or twice, stopping if necessary to signal the two changes.

- Elicit the answers.

> 1 Intervention of online recruitment and websites; need for interim and temporary employees
> 2 Online recruitment means candidates have access to jobs all over the world.

E

- Do as a quick-fire whole-class activity. You might get into the increasing importance of the Internet for recruitment advertising, but encourage students to think about all the other possibilities: networking, unsolicited job applications (teach this expression – writing to companies 'on spec' to see if they need people), meeting employers at trade shows, etc.

⟹ Resource bank: Listening (page 195)

◉ Students can watch the interview with Carys Owen on the DVD-ROM.

Language review: *-ing* forms and infinitives

Students look at and work on those verbs that are followed by *-ing* forms and those that are followed by infinitives.

- Go through the panel with the whole class. Show the different structures by writing up some of (not all) the examples on the board.

A – **B**

- Explain the tasks and get students to work on them in pairs. Go round the room and help where necessary.

Exercise A
1 b   2 a   3 b   4 c   5 a

Exercise B
1 f   2 a   3 d   4 b   5 c   6 e

- With the whole class, elicit the answers from individual students and discuss any problems.

C

- Do as a quick-fire whole-class activity.

1	working	4	offering
2	to answer	5	to tell
3	to call	6	making

D

- Ask students individually to write down three or four sentences using the verbs in bold in Exercise B. Go round the class and assist where necessary.
- Get some of the students to read out their sentences and work on any remaining difficulties.

Skills: Getting information on the telephone

Students look at language for obtaining information on the phone and practise using it in a role play.

A 🔊 CD2.9

- Tell students they will be looking at the language for obtaining information on the phone.
- Get individual students to read sentences aloud from the Useful language box.
- Explain the situation and task to students and go through the list of points. Play the recording once or twice and elicit the answers.

a, d, f

B 🔊 CD2.9

- Get students to look through the conversation and to anticipate what might be in the gaps. Then play the recording again and get students to complete the conversation.
- With the whole class, elicit the answers.

1	I was wondering
2	still in time to apply
3	I'd also like to know
4	notice would you need to give
5	just to get this clear
6	Exactly
7	what the salary is
8	Are you saying
9	negotiable

- Play the recording again to clarify any remaining difficulties.

C

- Ensure students understand the situation. Put them into pairs, allocate roles and get them to turn to the correct page. Go round the class and assist where necessary.
- When students have absorbed their information, get them to turn back to back and start their phone calls or, better still, get them to use real telephone extensions.
- Go round the class and monitor the language being used. Note down some good points and half a dozen that need further work, especially in relation to the language used when getting information on the telephone.
- Bring the class to order. Praise good points you heard and work on those that need further practice, getting individual students to say the correct thing.
- Get one or two pairs to repeat their role play for the whole class.

➡ Resource bank: Speaking (page 183)

Fast Fitness

People apply for the job of turning round a chain of health clubs in Brazil. Students discuss the candidates, listen to their job interviews and appoint the best one.

Background

- Get students to focus on the case study by asking them about gyms and health clubs in their town or city – if they belong to one, how much it costs to join, etc.

- Write the headings on the left-hand side of the table and elicit information from students to complete the right-hand side.

Company	Fast Fitness
Industry	Health and leisure clubs
Based in	US
Number of clubs in São Paulo	6
Clientele	People aged 20–40
Facilities	Gymnasium, an aerobics studio, a swimming pool, sun decks, a café, bar and clubroom
Locations	Japanese, Spanish, Chinese, Italian areas
Problems	Disappointing performance, targets not reached
	Members don't renew memberships
	Not enough new members attracted
Action	Advertised for a General Manager
Job	Boost sales and increase profits

Job advertisement

- Get students to look at the job advertisement in pairs. Tell them to talk about the job and the requirements in their own words and in complete sentences, e.g. *Fast Fitness wants to increase sales and profits. To do that, it needs to recruit someone who is dynamic, flexible, … .*

- Go round the room and help where necessary with the meaning, pronunciation and stress of difficult words, e.g. *liAIsing*, *opporTUNities*, etc.

- With the whole class, get individual students to talk about the advertisement in the way described above.

Appraising the applicants

- Explain the task. Divide the class into groups of four – all the groups work in parallel. Get each member to look in detail at one of the candidate file cards. Go round the room and help where necessary.

- When the groups are ready, get each member of each group to paraphrase the information that they read about 'their' candidate for other members of the group, again in parallel.

Job interviews 🔊 CD2.10, 2.11, 2.12, 2.13

Play each recording once or twice and get students to note down their general impressions of each candidate. Help with any difficulties, but it's the overall impression that counts. It's not necessary for students to understand every single word.

Selection

- Each group discusses the candidates and makes its selection. Appoint one member of each group as chairperson.

- Go round the room and monitor the language being used, especially the language related to recruitment. Note down strong points and points that need correction or improvement.

- When groups have made their selection, bring the class to order and praise some of the good language points that you heard and work on half a dozen others that need improvement, getting individual students to say the correct thing.

- Then ask a representative of each group to explain their choice. Encourage a whole-class discussion about the merits of each candidate.

One-to-one

Work on the background to bring out the key points about Fast Fitness.

You could summarise the information about one of the applicants and then get your student to summarise the other three file cards.

Play the recordings and discuss the four candidates with your student. Then work on the candidate selection.

Monitor the language that you both use. Afterwards, underline some of the language that you chose to use and some that your student used correctly. Then work on five or six points from what they said that need improving.

- ◉ You can also refer to the *Case study commentary* section of the DVD-ROM, where students can watch an interview with a consultant discussing the key issues raised by the case study.

Writing

- Get your students to write a letter of about 100–120 words, offering the job to the successful candidate. (Make it clear whether everyone should write to the candidate that was selected by their group or whether each student can write to the candidate that they themselves think should get the job.) Students could do this for homework or in pairs in class.

⇨ Resource bank: Writing (page 211)

⇨ Writing file, page 126

International markets

AT A GLANCE

	Classwork – Course Book	Further work
Lesson 1 *Each lesson (excluding case studies) is about 45 to 60 minutes. This does not include time spent going through homework.*	**Starting up** Students work on some economic language relating to international markets. **Vocabulary: Free trade** A trade expert talks about free trade and its benefits; students then practise some of the vocabulary that he uses.	**Practice File** Vocabulary (page 36) **i-Glossary** (DVD-ROM)
Lesson 2	**Reading: Trade between China and the US** Students read articles about trade between the two countries and the economic issues arising from it. **Language review: Conditions** The first and second conditionals are compared and contrasted. Students then listen to a negotiation where they are used.	**Text bank** (pages 146–149) **Practice File** Language review (pages 37–38)
Lesson 3	**Listening: Training for negotiating** An expert gives advice on successful negotiating. **Skills: Negotiating** Students examine the stages of a negotiation and listen to one that illustrates them. They then role-play a negotiation.	**Resource bank: Listening** (page 196) **Course Book Listening** (DVD-ROM) **ML Grammar and Usage** **Resource bank: Speaking** (page 184)
Lesson 4 *Each case study is about 1½ to 2 hours.*	**Case study: Pampas Leather Company** An Argentinian manufacturer of leather and fur items and a US distributor negotiate a deal.	**Resource bank: Writing** (page 212) **Practice File** Writing (pages 38–39) **Case study commentary** (DVD-ROM)

For a fast route through the unit focusing mainly on speaking skills, just use the underlined sections.

For one-to-one situations, most parts of the unit lend themselves, with minimal adaptation, to use with individual students. Where this is not the case, alternative procedures are given.

BUSINESS BRIEF

An expanding business will eventually want to sell its products or services abroad, outside its **home market**. International trade takes place within the framework of agreements worked out by countries in the **World Trade Organisation (WTO)**, formerly known as the **General Agreement on Tariffs and Trade (GATT)**. Over the last 50 years, **trade barriers** have been coming down and **free trade**, **open borders** and **deregulation** now form the ideal for almost all nations, even if the situation is far from one of complete **laissez-faire**, with no government **intervention**. **Protectionism** is no longer the order of the day in most places; even if some developing countries argue that protectionist measures are the way to develop their economies, they avoid using the term.

Trade negotiations are well known for their epic eleventh-hour negotiating sessions, where individual nations argue for what they see as their specific interests. Countries argue for **protection** of their **strategic industries**, ones they consider vital to future prosperity, such as the electronics industry in the developed world. A less-developed country beginning car assembly might want to protect it as an **infant industry** with **quotas**, for example restrictions on the number of imported cars. European farmers argue for their **subsidies**, when governments guarantee farmers a higher price than they would normally get, making it hard for developing nations to compete in agricultural products.

Countries sometimes accuse each other of **dumping**, when exported goods are sold at a lower price than in the home market or for less than they cost to produce, usually in order to gain **market share** in the export market. The offending country may reply that it has a **comparative advantage** in producing these goods, the ability to produce them cheaper than anyone else, and that they are not selling at below cost.

Of course, there are **trading blocs** with no **trade barriers** at all, such as the **single market** of the **European Union**. The **North American Free Trade Agreement**, or **NAFTA** (the US, Canada and Mexico) is also eliminating its **tariff walls** and **customs duties**. Their equivalents in Asia and Latin America are **ASEAN** and **Mercosur**. All this is part of the wider picture of **globalisation**, the tendency of the world economy to function as one unit.

One major concern in international trade between smaller companies is payment. The exporter wants to be sure about getting paid, and the importer wants to be sure of getting the goods. A common solution is the **letter of credit**: a bank guarantees payment to the exporter's bank once it receives the related **shipping documents**, including the **clean bills of lading**, showing the goods have been shipped without damage or other problems. **Shipping terms** like **CIF** (**carriage insurance freight**), when the exporter pays for insurance of the goods while they are being transported, are part of the standard **Incoterms** defined by the **International Chamber of Commerce**. These terms are used in **standard contracts** that form the basis, with adaptations, for most international trade contracts.

International markets and your students

Your in-work students may work for organisations that export their goods and services, and you will be able to talk about how they do this. Pre-work and in-work students will be able to discuss issues of globalisation. Do they think that some industries, like agriculture, should be protected from international competition?

Read on

Kenneth Weiss: *Building an Import/Export Business*, Wiley, 3rd edition, 2002

Jim Sherlock, Jonatan Reuvid (eds): *Handbook of International Trade: A Guide to the Principles and Practice of Export*, Global Market Briefings, 2007

Eric Bishop: *Finance of International Trade*, Butterworth Heinemann, 2003

Martin Wolf: *Why Globalization Works*, Yale University Press, 2004

Joseph Stiglitz: *Making Globalization Work*, Penguin, 2007

LESSON NOTES

Warmer

- Get students to look at all the meanings of *market* as both noun and verb in a good dictionary like *Longman Dictionary of Contemporary English* or the *Longman Business English Dictionary*. Ask them to prepare statements about what they find, e.g. 'In the *Longman Business English Dictionary*, *market* has 13 senses as a noun and two senses as a verb. It also occurs as a noun in a number of compounds – *bear market*, *black market*, *bond market*, etc.' Go round the room and help where necessary.

- With the whole class, get individual pairs to give examples of what they found.

- Work towards the idea of international markets.

Overview

- Tell students they will be looking at the subject of buying and selling things internationally.

- Go through the overview panel at the beginning of the unit, pointing out the sections that students will be looking at.

Quotation

- Ask your students if they know Robert Louis Stevenson as the author of *Treasure Island*.

- Ask what they understand by the quote. (You could teach the expression *make a living* in this context.)

Starting up

Students work on some economic language relating to international markets.

A

- With the whole class, get students to look through the words in the box. Explain any difficulties and work on stress, e.g. *unemPLOYment*, *POVerty*, etc.

- Get students to do the exercise in pairs. Go round the class and assist where necessary.

- Bring the class to order and elicit the answers.

1	opportunities	6	gap
2	competition	7	prices
3	unemployment	8	companies
4	poverty	9	environment
5	workers	10	standards

B – D

- Get students to discuss the points from the three exercises in pairs. Go round the class and assist where necessary.

- Bring the class to order and have a discussion about some of the points, for example those which seem to be most controversial. (Refer to the Business brief for this unit for background to some of these issues.) In relation to Exercise D, you could ask which areas of the world students think will become more or less important in the future.

Vocabulary

Students listen to a trade expert talk about free trade and its benefits and recycle some of the vocabulary that he uses.

A – B 🔊 CD2.14

- With the whole class, elicit some definitions. Then play the recording once or twice, depending on the level of the class, and get students to listen out for missing words.

- With the whole class, ask them what they are.

1	controls	4	barriers
2	taxes	5	borders
3	liberalise	6	customs

C 🔊 CD2.15

- Play the recording once or twice, depending on the level of the class, and get students to listen out for the five things that stop people trading freely.

- With the whole class, ask them what they are. Explain any difficulties.

1	Tariffs – these are taxes on imported goods (they raise the price of goods and make them more expensive)
2	Subsidies to domestic producers – money given to them by the government
3	Quotas – limits on the number of goods that can be imported
4	Expensive import licences – special permission to import goods
5	Complicated regulations for documents – make trade slower and less attractive

- Then get individual students to recap and explain for the rest of the class the particular problems associated with each of these barriers to trade.

D 🔊 CD2.16

- Get students to look through the questions in this section. Then play the recording once right through and then once again, stopping after the answer to each question. Explain any difficulties, but don't give away the answers.

1 a

2 a, b, d

3 **a)** unfair

    b) strategic

    c) imports

4 **a)** The trend towards liberalising trade and removing trade barriers

    b) Because the most successful economies tend to have open markets and most of their industries have been deregulated.

E

- Do as a quick-fire whole-class activity.

open markets	protected markets
open borders, free port, laissez-faire, liberalise, deregulation	barriers, developing industries, dumping, tariffs, strategic industries, restrictions, quotas, customs, subsidise, regulations

F – G

- Get students to work on matching the sentence halves in pairs. Go round the room and help where necessary.

- Then get students to match the verbs and nouns to make partnerships and say who is normally the subject of sentences using these expressions.

Exercise F

1 e   **2** d   **3** f   **4** b   **5** g   **6** c   **7** a

Exercise G

1 to break into a market

2 to carry out a survey

3 to place an order

4 to meet a delivery date

5 to quote a price

6 to arrange insurance cover

7 to comply with regulations

a) 1, 4, 5

b) 2, 3

c) 6, 7

- Bring the class to order and check pairs' answers. Explain any remaining difficulties.

H

- Get students to discuss these questions in pairs and then with the whole class.

These are tricky questions. Here are some pointers.

1 Advanced industrial countries have quite open markets for consumer and industrial goods, but not food. Producers in developing countries complain that they are not given access to the markets for farm products in Europe and North America, where farmers are heavily subsidised. Without this government and European Union support, a lot of grain production, for example, would end, replaced by cheap imports from places where it is cheaper to grow grain. So you could ask students about their view of this example of 'unfree' trade.

2 Students might mention infant industries in their own countries that need to be protected. (A classic example is the South Korean car industry, which was protected while it developed in the 1980s and 1990s by very strict quotas on the number of imported cars.)

3 Here you could mention the outsourcing of services. India has provided software and call-centre services for some time, but is now moving on to other professional services such as accountancy and law. Professionals in these areas in the UK and the US are just starting to feel squeezed. The process is still at the very beginning, and the traditional advice from free-trade supporters is for the UK and US professionals to retrain in more advanced and specialised areas, areas where India cannot compete. But many professionals, naturally, are unwilling to do this because of the upheaval that it entails. Free trade usually brings down the cost of goods, but the personal 'costs' of this can be very high.

 i-Glossary

Reading: Trade between China and the US

Students read two articles about trade between the two countries and the economic issues arising from it.

A

- In pairs, get students to read the possible titles (headlines) and the two articles. Go round the class and assist where necessary.

Article 1: c

Article 2: a

- With the whole class, work on any difficulties that have been causing general problems.

B

- Get students to read the articles again. (If time is short, one member of each pair could read one of the articles.)

- With the whole class, elicit the answers.

1 True
2 False: 'The US should focus on improving its overall economic competitiveness instead of seeking protectionism to combat its economic slowdown, ...'
3 False: '... it should not argue for a stronger currency to reduce its trade deficit with China, since the value of the yuan is not the fundamental cause of the deficit ...'
4 True
5 True
6 True
7 False: 'China has also said the fact that Americans save much less of their incomes than the Chinese do has increased the trade deficit.'
8 True

C – D

● Do as a class activity, discussing the answers as you go.

Exercise C

1	protectionism	4	co-operation
2	slowdown	5	risen
3	deficit	6	save

Exercise D

1	protectionism	3	slowdown
2	co-operation	4	deficit

E

● Discuss the question with the whole class. You could get students to vote with a show of hands as to who thinks the deficit will go on increasing and how many think that the trend will be reversed. (You could quote the economist Herbert Stein, who said; 'If something can't go on forever, it will stop.' The problem is knowing when it will stop.)

➡ Text bank (pages 146–148)

Language review: Conditions

The first and second conditionals are compared and contrasted. Students then listen to a negotiation where conditionals are used.

● Talk students through the commentary and examples in the panel. Write some of the examples on the board to explain key tenses. Point out that *will* never occurs in the same part of the sentence as *would*.

A

● Get students to work on the exercise in pairs. Go round the room and help where necessary.
● Bring the class to order and elicit answers from individual students. Explain any remaining difficulties.

1	give us; 'll place	4	Would; sent
2	Will you deliver; pay	5	don't improve; 'll have
3	lower; 'll buy	6	joined; would get

B – C 🔊 CD2.17

● Explain the situation to students and play the recording once right through.
● Then play it again, stopping after each item and elicit the answers from students.
● Then discuss with students which events are very likely and which are less certain or imaginary.

Exercise B

1	order	5	was
2	we'll	6	were
3	would you be able	7	we would offer
4	order	8	I would love

Exercise C

a) If I **order** 30,000 silk scarves, what discount will you offer us? If you buy 50,000 scarves, then **we'll** offer you 10%. If you **order** at a peak time, like just before Chinese New Year, it will be impossible to deliver that quickly.

b) If we placed a very large order, **would you be able** to despatch immediately? If the order **was** really large, that would be negotiable. If you **were** a regular customer, **we would offer** you 30 days' credit. If I had more time, **I would love** to have dinner with you.

Listening: Training for negotiating

An expert, Andy Simmons, gives advice on successful negotiating.

A 🔊 CD2.18

● With the whole class, ask students if any of them have experience of negotiating. (This will apply more to in-work students that pre-work ones.) Get them to talk about their experiences.
● Get students to look at the questions.
● Play the recording once or twice. Explain any difficulties without giving away the answers.
● Elicit the answers.

Create an environment where people can do; keep the learning fresh; look at the feedback from negotiations

B 🔊 CD2.19

● Get students to look at the text. Play the recording once or twice and get students to fill in the gaps.

1	appropriateness	5	co-operative
2	different	6	win–win
3	competitive	7	wrong
4	conflict	8	circumstances

Work on the meaning and pronunciation of difficult words, e.g. *apPROpriateness*.

C ◀)) CD2.20

- Go back to the students who talked about their negotiating experiences in Exercise A and ask them to give advice on these two points before you play the recording.

- Play the recording once or twice and elicit the answers.

---

1 Be versatile, be adaptable, be able to change behaviour according to circumstances, be able to manage conflict and the pressure of face-to-face negotiation, be able to plan effectively, be analytical, be open-minded and creative, have self-discipline

2 Listen for certain language cues – soft exposing give-aways.

- Work on any difficulties.

- Discuss with students if any of the advice they gave earlier came up in the extract.

D

- Put students into pairs. Point out that the first question relates to really good negotiators, not just good ones. Get them to discuss the points. Go round the class and assist where necessary. Monitor the language being used. Note down good points and those that need further work.

- Bring the class to order. Praise the correct language that you heard and practise points that need further work.

- Get members of one or two pairs to present their findings and discuss them with the whole class.

➡ Resource bank: Listening (page 197)

◎ Students can watch the interview with Andy Simmons on the DVD-ROM.

Skills: Negotiating

Students look at the different steps in a negotiation, listen to a negotiation that illustrates these steps, and then put negotiating language to work in two role plays.

A

- Tell students they will be looking at the language of negotiation. If you think they will have difficulty with the first task, get one outgoing pair of students to role-play the situation for the whole class.

- Then get students in parallel pairs to do the task. Go round the room and help where necessary.

B

- Bring the class to order and ask students if they were pleased with the outcome. In what way(s)?

- Then ask about the strategy, tactics and language that they used. Write up some of their negotiating expressions on the board.

C

- Get students to work on the stages in pairs. Go round the room and help where necessary.

- With the whole class, elicit the answers.

---

1 Ready yourself

2 Explore each other's needs

3 Signal for movement

4 Probe with proposals

5 Exchange concessions

6 Close the deal

7 Tie up loose ends

RESPECT

- Discuss the points with students. Do they agree with them? In particular, are the divisions between the steps as clear-cut as the model implies? For example, is it always possible to move clearly from the signalling stage to the probing stage?

D ◀)) CD2.21

- Point out to the students that the stages a–g are the same as the ones in Exercise C. Tell them they will hear extracts that correspond to each stage.

- Play the recording once right through and then once stopping after each extract to ask students which stage is being illustrated.

---

1 c   **2** e   **3** g   **4** b   **5** f   **6** d   **7** a

---

E

- Get students to study the Useful language box in pairs. Go round the room and help where necessary.

- With the whole class, go over points that have caused difficulty: don't get students to repeat all the expressions, just one or two or each type.

- Put students into pairs. Get them to look at the information for the role play. Make sure they look at the correct page.

- When ready, get pairs to do the role play. Go round the room and help where necessary. Monitor the language being used for good points and points that will need correction.

- Bring the class to order. Praise strong points that you heard and work on points that need correction or improvement, getting students to say the correct thing.

- Ask different pairs to say what happened in their negotiations.

➡ Resource bank: Speaking (page 184)

CASE STUDY

Pampas Leather Company

An Argentinian manufacturer of leather and fur items and a US distributor negotiate a deal.

Background

- Get students to focus on the case study by studying the Background information.

- Write the headings on the left-hand side of the table and elicit information from students to complete the right-hand side.

Company 1	Pampas Leather Company (PLC)
Based in	Buenos Aires, Argentina
Represented by	Roberto González
Activity	Manufacturer of leather and fur jackets, as well as accessories such as handbags, belts and wallets
Reputation	Best quality leather, creative designs, excellent quality control, reliable delivery
Company 2	West Coast Apparel (WCA)
Based in	Seattle, US
President	Brad Schulz
Activity	Clothing distributor (i.e. retailer)
Outlets	Chain of stores in large cities on the West Coast of the US
Interested in	Three models of jacket
Current situation	Now May – PLC have agreed to make jackets and ship by early Nov.
Constraints	PLC has to make and deliver other large orders before WCA's
Contract conditions	Some points remain to be negotiated
Present at meeting	González, Schulz, plus the Marketing Directors of each company
Objectives of meeting	Reach an acceptable deal for both sides which could be the basis for a long-term relationship

Preparation

- Tell students they will be negotiating an agreement between the two companies. Divide the class into fours and make it clear who is Roberto González, who is his Marketing Director, who is Brad Schulz and who is his Marketing Director in each four. Get students to turn to the page with their respective information. Make sure they turn to the right one.

- Go round the room and help where necessary.

- When students have absorbed their information, bring the class to order and ask the representatives of each company to identify their priorities and to prepare their negotiating strategy and tactics. You could ask them to use the RESPECT model from the Skills section above if you think that would be useful.

- Go round the room and help where necessary with this part of the preparation.

The negotiation

- Get the groups to start their negotiations in parallel.

- Go round the room and monitor the language being used for good points and points that will need correction, especially in relation to negotiating language.

- As groups finish, make sure they are clear what has been decided – the tying-up of the RESPECT model. Make sure someone in each group writes this down.

Feedback

- Bring the class to order. Praise strong points that you heard and work on points that need correction or improvement, getting students to say the correct thing.

- Ask different pairs to say what happened in their negotiations.

> **One-to-one**
>
> Work on the background to bring out the key points about the companies and the situation.
>
> Take the role of González or Schulz (ignore the Marketing Directors). You should both prepare your respective negotiating approaches.
>
> Run the task. Monitor the language that you both use. After the activity, underline some of the language that you chose to use and some that your student used correctly and work on five or six points from what they said that need improving, especially in the area of negotiating language.
>
> Ask your student how they felt about the negotiation and what they learned from it.

◎ You can also refer to the *Case study commentary* section of the DVD-ROM, where students can watch an interview with a consultant discussing the key issues raised by the case study.

Writing

- Get your students to write an e-mail of 200–250 words, summarising the points agreed during the negotiation and not forgetting to indicate any terms of the contract requiring discussion or clarification. Students could do this for homework or in pairs in class. If doing for homework, make sure that students have noted down all the details from the negotiation that they will need to include in the e-mail.

→ Resource bank: Writing (page 212)

→ Writing file, page 127

Doing business internationally

Introduction

This Working across cultures unit focuses on cultural difficulties when doing business in an international context.

A

● Tell students about the text they are going to read and the task that follows. Then put them into pairs. Go round the class and assist with any difficulties where necessary.

● With the whole class, elicit their answers. Then ask students to check their answers on Course Book page 138.

3
Students can use the points given in the Course Book answers to give advice, for example:

If going to Saudi Arabia, bear in mind that you should …

1 be ready to say something positive about the city you are visiting.

2 know that delays before meetings are not unusual.

B

● Put students into pairs and get them to read the text together. Go round and assist where necessary.

● Bring the class to order. Get students to give their answers.

1 **a)** There were other people there in addition to Matsumoto.

   b) He did not realise Matsumoto could not take a final decision himself and that discussion with other colleagues meant the decision would be delayed.

2 **a)** He did not spend any time studying Matsumoto's business card.

   b) He asked a direct question that put Matsumoto in an embarrassing position.

   c) He gave white flowers, which remind the Japanese of death.

Task 🔊 CD2.22

● Prepare students for what they are going to hear by asking them what they already know about Japanese ways of doing business. (If there are Japanese students in the class, get them to talk as experts on the subject, of course.)

● Play the recording once or twice and get students to take notes.

● Then discuss the notes with the whole class. Are there any points that they had not anticipated (teach them this word)?

● Work on any difficulties.

C

● Ask students to anticipate what the problems might be when Scandinavians deal with Brazilians (use of time, attitudes to hierarchy, etc.).

1 🔊 CD2.23

● Play the recording and elicit the answers.

a) During the meeting, they talked about football, the thunderstorm, his family and life in Denmark.
   At the restaurant, they talked about the crime rate, Amazon rainforests, the government and food.

b) They played snooker (a kind of pool).

2 🔊 CD2.23

● Play the recording again and elicit the answers.

a) He refused the cup of coffee.
   He tried to talk about sensitive issues such as politics.

b) Food in different countries

3 🔊 CD2.24

● Play the second part of the dialogue and get students to answer the question.

He wasn't very sure about it, as he thought their ways of doing business were too different.

4 🔊 CD2.24

● Play the second part of the dialogue again and get students to answer the question.

a) Delays in giving his presentation

b) The agenda not being followed

d) Too many questions during his presentation

g) No progress at the meeting

Task

● Get students to discuss the first part of the task in pairs.

● Bring the class to order. Elicit some of the pairs' opinions.

- Students could do the second part for homework. Suggest that the report should be about 100–120 words. Don't forget to give feedback on the task next time.

Sample answer

From: Pedro Oliveira

To: All directors

Subject: Meeting with Sven Selig re joint venture

As some of you may know, I recently met with Sven Selig, the Chief Executive of a Danish retail store group, to discuss a possible joint venture between our organisations.

He's a very nice guy, but there were times during our discussions where there were tensions; for example, he tried to discuss difficult political issues, which he should have avoided.

There were other difficulties: for instance, he was not flexible enough when we did not follow the items on the agenda and seemed irritated by questions during the presentation when he should have welcomed them.

These are just some of the difficulties that occurred and there would certainly be others if we went ahead and worked with Selig. For this reason, I recommend that we do not proceed with a joint venture with his company.

UNIT C Revision

This unit revises and reinforces some of the key language points from Units 7–9 and from Working across cultures 3. Links with those units are clearly shown. You can point out these links to your students.

7 Cultures

Vocabulary

● Students practise some idioms.

Exercise 1	Exercise 2
1 to get on like a house on fire	1 put my foot in it
	2 break the ice
2 to put one's foot in it	3 get on like a house on fire
3 to break the ice	

Advice, obligation and necessity

● Students get further practice in this tricky area.

1 shouldn't	3 should	5 should
2 shouldn't	4 don't have to	6 must / have to

Writing

● The first exercise gives students practice in the language of accepting invitations.

● The second exercise gives further writing practice.

Exercise 1

1 would like to	5 very much hope
2 would be delighted	6 seeing you
3 are willing	7 sincerely
4 invited	

Exercise 2 Sample answer

To: Erman Bayar **From:** J. Ferreira
Subject: Forthcoming IRTA Sales Conference

Dear Mr Bayar,

Thank you very much for your kind invitation to speak at your sales conference, which I am delighted to accept.

The subject of my presentation will be 'Barriers to International Trade'. Please find the abstract attached. My fee will be €1,500. I hope this is acceptable to you.

Thanks also for your invitation to the dinner on the second day of the conference. Unfortunately, I won't be able to attend, as I am giving another presentation elsewhere that evening.

Yours sincerely,
J. Ferreira

8 Human resources

Vocabulary

● Students get practice with HR-related vocabulary.

Exercise 1

1 g	2 e	3 f	4 b	5 a	6 d	7 c

Exercise 2

1 take a psychometric test	4 work a probationary period
2 attend an interview	
3 shortlist a candidate	5 apply for a job

Exercise 3

1 b	2 b	3 d	4 c	5 a	6 a	7 a	8 c	9 b	10 d

Writing

● Students get further practice in writing letters.

Sample answer

Dear Mr Wilder

Thank you for coming to the interview for the post of General Manager at Fast Fitness in São Paulo.

There were many highly qualified candidates. Unfortunately, despite your skills and experience, we are unable to offer you the position at this time.

We will keep your name on file and will let you know about any future job openings in our organisation that may be of interest to you.

Sincerely

9 International markets

Vocabulary

● Students practise these important collocations (word combinations).

1 f	2 d	3 a	4 c	5 b	6 e

Conditions

● Further practice is provided with these tricky structures.

Exercise 1

1 d	2 e	3 f	4 a	5 c	6 b

Exercise 2

1 'll	2 wouldn't	3 'd	4 won't	5 'll	6 'd

Skills

● Students get another chance to practise the language of negotiating.

1 c	2 e	3 b	4 a	5 d

Cultures: Doing business internationally

● Students look again at some key cultural issues.

1 B	2 J	3 J	4 SA	5 SA	6 B	7 J	8 J	9 J, SA	10 B

Ethics

AT A GLANCE

	Classwork – Course Book	Further work
Lesson 1 *Each lesson (excluding case studies) is about 45 to 60 minutes. This does not include time spent going through homework.*	<u>**Starting up**</u> Students discuss some ethical issues. **Vocabulary: Right or wrong?** Students look at words related to honesty and dishonesty and practise using them.	**Practice File** Vocabulary (page 40) **i-Glossary** (DVD-ROM)
Lesson 2	**Reading: The ethics of résumé writing** Students read about lying on résumés. **Listening: Helping environmental research** Students listen to David Hillyard of EarthWatch, an environmental research organisation.	**Text bank** (pages 150–153) **Resource bank: Listening** (page 197) **Course Book Listening** (DVD-ROM)
Lesson 3	**Language review: Narrative tenses** Students work on the verb tenses used in narratives, listen to a conversation where they are used and apply them themselves. <u>**Skills: Considering options**</u> Students look at the language of considering options and use it themselves.	**Practice File** Language review (pages 41–42) **ML Grammar and Usage** **Resource bank: Speaking** (page 185) **Practice File** Giving advice and making suggestions (page 73)
Lesson 4 *Each case study is about 1½ to 2 hours.*	<u>**Case study: Principles or profit?**</u> Students discuss the problems in a firm facing a number of ethical dilemmas and make recommendations as to the course of action to follow.	**Resource bank: Writing** (page 213) **Practice File** Writing (pages 42–43) **Case study commentary** (DVD-ROM)

For a fast route through the unit focusing mainly on speaking skills, just use the underlined sections.

For one-to-one situations, most parts of the unit lend themselves, with minimal adaptation, to use with individual students. Where this is not the case, alternative procedures are given.

BUSINESS BRIEF

Bribery and corruption

Whether persuading key officials to give authorisation to set up in business, grant government contracts or just let your goods through customs, the alternatives for the word **bribe** are many and varied: **kickback, sweetener** (AmE), **backhander** (BrE), **baksheesh** and the **greasing of palms** (international). The law courts, if it gets that far, will refer more prosaically to **illicit payments**, and defendants in such cases may just talk about **commissions**. If payments go to a **slush fund** to finance a political party, this form of **corruption** may be referred to as **sleaze**, especially by journalists.

The corporation as good citizen

All businesses increasingly want to be perceived as **good citizens**. Different types of business face different ethical issues.

- Following the **accounting scandals** at Enron and WorldCom, which gave a false view of their profits, despite the work of their **auditors**, the outside accountants who are meant to prevent this, there has been pressure on legislators and regulators to improve **accounting standards**.

- When the strain of competing gets too much, competitors may go for the easier option of **price fixing**, so that each can maintain a reasonable profit margin. Competitors who do this form a **cartel**. This is an area where outsiders may only find out what is going on if one of the managers involved contacts the authorities. Someone doing this is a **whistleblower**.

- Financial institutions try to prevent **insider trading** by erecting notional barriers called **Chinese walls** between different departments: to prevent someone in share trading from discovering from the mergers department that a particular company is involved in merger talks and that its share price will soon rise.

- Financial institutions also have to guard against **money laundering**, where money passes through the banking system in a way that disguises its criminal origins.

- Manufacturers increasingly claim that their products are **green** or **environmentally friendly** in all stages of their production, use and disposal.

- Clothing companies claim to **trade fairly** and that their products were not made in **sweatshops** paying **subsistence wages** and using **child labour**.

- Companies in general will talk about **equal opportunities** or, in the US, their **affirmative action program**, to ensure that people are recruited and promoted on the basis of **merit** and not **discriminated against** on the grounds of race or gender. Women who get promoted so far and no further complain of the **glass ceiling**. These are part of the **social issues** of **equality and diversity**.

And, of course, the near-collapse of the banking system in 2008 was blamed by many on the greed of those who ran them, including their willingness to sell ultimately worthless securities as high-grade financial investments.

Codes of ethics and mission statements

A company's internal **code of ethics** contains its ethical credo and may cover any of the issues mentioned above. Some of the financial, environmental and diversity-related issues may also be referred to in its **mission statement**. And there may even be an **ethics ombudsman** to check that they are put into practice and deal with complaints when they are not. All the issues mentioned here are part of the wider picture of **corporate social responsibility (CSR)**. Companies have to pay attention to the **triple bottom line** of economic, social and environmental **sustainability**.

Read on

Wayne Visser *et al*: *The A to Z of Corporate Social Responsibility*, Wiley, 2007

Simon Webley and Lise More: *Does Business Ethics Pay?* Institute of Business Ethics, 2003

Doris Rubenstein: *The Good Corporate Citizen*, Wiley, 2004

LESSON NOTES

Warmer

- Get students to look at the words *ethics* and *ethical* in a good monolingual dictionary, e.g. *Longman Dictionary of Contemporary English*, or in a good bilingual one. What do they find?

Overview

- Tell students they will be looking at the subject of ethics. Tell them they may also see the terms *corporate responsibility* or *corporate social responsibility*.

- Go through the overview panel at the beginning of the unit, pointing out the sections that students will be looking at.

Quotation

- Ask students what they understand by the quote. Ask them if they agree with it, or if moral rules are universal. If you did Unit 8 with them, students will already have seen a quote from Hubbard there, too. If interested, and if students haven't already done so, they can find out more about him on Wikipedia.

Starting up

Students discuss some ethical issues, decide if the people in some jobs behave more ethically than in others and comment on the degree to which some activities in business are unethical.

A

- Get students to discuss these in pairs, then ask members of pairs to talk about their findings with the whole class. You could then do a quick survey of attitudes with a show of hands for each item.

B

- Ask students if some professions, and the people in them, are by their nature more ethical than others.

- Get them to score the professions given, where 7 is very ethical and 1 is unethical. Go round the room and help where necessary.

- With the whole class, ask for results and discuss them. You could point out that, in the UK, journalists, estate agents and politicians are at the bottom of the league in many surveys and nurses and teachers towards the top.

C

- Get students to discuss these in pairs. Go round the room and help where necessary. Explain any difficulties.

- With the whole class, ask for answers. Ask them what they think of the economist Milton Friedman, who said, 'The only social responsibility of a business is to increase its profits' – that is, to take care of its shareholders.

Vocabulary: Right or wrong?

Students look at words related to the ethics of different situations and practise using them.

A

- You could do these as a quick-fire whole-class activity or get students to work on them in small groups, following on from Exercise C in Starting up. Get students to vote on the degree of unethical behaviour in each, for example on a scale 1 to 10.

B – C 🔊 CD2.25

- Explain the activity. Get students to use a good monolingual dictionary like *Longman Dictionary of Contemporary English*, or a good bilingual one, for words that they don't know.

- Get students to do the exercise in pairs, marking the stressed syllables. Do not play the recording yet. Go round the room and help where necessary.

1	bribery and corruption	6	tax fraud
2	price fixing	7	counterfeit goods
3	environmental pollution	8	money laundering
4	sex discrimination	9	animal testing
5	insider trading	10	industrial espionage

- With the whole class, go through the answers to the word partnerships. For light relief, try to say the expressions stressing all syllables equally so as not to pre-empt the next activity.

- Play the recording and get students to check the stresses in each expression.

- Explain any remaining difficulties and work on pronunciation and stress, getting individual students to say each expression. (Don't ask them to 'think up' sentences containing them, as this is very difficult.)

D – E

- Get students to work on the questions and issues in small groups. Go round the class and assist where necessary. Monitor the language being used. Note down good points and those that need further work.

- Bring the class to order. Praise the correct language that you heard and practise points that need further work.

- Then get a member of each group to talk to about their findings, giving their reasons and being sure to incorporate the corrections that you just made.

◎ i-Glossary

Reading: The ethics of résumé writing
Students look at the issues of lying on CVs and the reasons that people do it.

A
- Explain that *résumé* is American English and *CV* is the equivalent in British English. Get students to discuss the question in small groups.
- Bring the class to order and ask students to report on their group's opinions.

B
- Get students, in pairs, to anticipate five words, some connected with dishonesty, that will appear in the article
and write them down: e.g. *mislead*, *distort*, *untrue*.
- Then get the pairs to read the article, underline expressions connected with dishonesty and see if any of their words come up. Go round the class and assist where necessary.
- Bring the class to order and check the answers. Also elicit other words that students predicted but that did not come up. Write them on the board if they are relevant.

lie, stretch the truth, deception, dishonesty

C
- Get students to look through the questions and then read the article again to find the answers.

1 Everyone else does it, companies lie about job requirements, it's hard to get a good job
2 They can lose their jobs.
3 (Ask for students' opinions.)
4 You begin to fool yourself and develop habits of distorted thinking.
5 It forces you to think clearly and creatively, it checks the accuracy of your claims, it trains your old boss in how to represent you during reference checks, your old boss may give you better ways to represent yourself.

- Explain any remaining difficulties.

D
- Get students to discuss the points in small groups, recycling vocabulary from the rest of this section. Go round the class and assist where necessary. Monitor the language being used. Note down good points and those that need further work.
- Bring the class to order. Praise the correct language that you heard and practise points that need further work.

- Then get a member of each group to talk to about their findings, being sure to incorporate the corrections that you just made.

➡ Text bank (pages 150–153)

Listening: Helping environmental research
Students listen to David Hillyard, Director of Programmes at EarthWatch, an environmental research organisation.

A ◀)) CD2.26
- With the whole class, get students to look through the text and suggest what the missing expressions might be.
- Then play the recording once or twice and elicit the answers. Get one of the students to read the whole text aloud.

1	international	5	world
2	conservation	6	scientists
3	education	7	plants
4	100	8	environment

- Work on any difficulties, e.g. the pronunciation of *enVIRonment*.

B ◀)) CD2.26
- Get students to look at the questions. Then play the recording once or twice again and explain any difficulties, but don't give away the answers, of course.
- Elicit the answers.

1 The US, the UK, India, Melbourne (Australia), Japan, China
2 So that members of the public, company employees, teachers, young people and young scientists can join researchers in the field as field assistants and collect real data that contributes to understanding what is happening.

C ◀)) CD2.27
- Get students to look at the questions. Then play the recording once or twice and explain any difficulties.
- Elicit the answers.

1 To help to reduce the environmental impact of their operations
2 To educate and engage their employees and get their employees inspired and motivated to do something in their own communities or in their workplace with respect to the environment

D ◀)) CD2.28

- Prepare your students for the final task and put them into pairs. Play the recording at least twice and get students to write their three sentences. Go round the class and assist where necessary.

- Get members of each pair to read their sentences to their partner.

- Bring the class to order. Get individual students to read their partner's sentences for the whole class.

Sample answer

EarthWatch is working with HSBC, the global bank, so that the bank's employees can work on data collection along with EarthWatch researchers.

This research is about how forests are coping with climate change and how animals and plants are affected.

This is a way of involving employees and getting them to go back into their companies so that they influence colleagues about climate change.

- Work on any remaining difficulties.

E

- Discuss this with the whole class. Perhaps your students have examples of involving employees in environmental issues. If not, get them to research the subject on the Internet and report back in the next lesson. Don't forget to follow up on this if you ask them to do this.

⮕ Resource bank: Listening (page 197)

◉ Students can watch the interview with David Hillyard on the DVD-ROM.

Language review: Narrative tenses

Students work on the verb tenses used in narratives, listen to a conversation where they are used and apply them themselves.

A ◀)) CD2.29

- Get students to look through the events a) to g) before they listen to the recording.

- Then play the recording and get them to put the events into the correct order.

- Elicit the answers and discuss why the steps are logical in this order.

b, c, f, g, d, e, a

- Go through the examples in the panel on page 100 with the whole class.

- Get individual students to call out the answers to the matching exercise.

1	Past continuous	3	Past simple
2	Past perfect	4	Present perfect

B ◀)) CD2.29

- Play the recording again, stopping after each past tense verb to allow students time to note it down.

- With the whole class, go through the answers, getting students to explain why they are correct.

a) happened, got, was, fired, said, did [...] find out, required, found out, didn't have, wasn't, cost

b) was going, was getting, was receiving, was exceeding

c) had lied, had claimed, had [...] made up, had done, had felt, had been

d) have been, 've advised

C

- Get students to work on this exercise in pairs. Go round the room and help where necessary, explaining any difficulties.

- With the whole class, go through the answers, getting students to explain why they are correct.

1 had
2 launched
3 was selling
4 were getting
5 were increasing
6 went
7 started
8 were complaining / complained
9 was using / used
10 was offering / offered
11 (was) taking / took
12 felt
13 had received
14 started
15 fired
16 have recently issued

D

- Explain the task. Tell one of the stories yourself as a model, pointing out the tenses that you are using.

- Give students time to prepare their stories individually. Go round the room and help where necessary.

- Then get some individual students to tell their stories. Insist on correct use of verb tenses.

- In a later lesson, get other students to tell their stories. This will be good revision.

Skills: Considering options

Students look at the language of considering options and apply it themselves in a role play.

A 🔊 CD2.30

- Tell students that they are going to work on the language of considering options. Get students to focus on the questions. Then play the recording once or twice.

- Elicit the answers.

1 He is sending in reports saying he's met customers when he hasn't; he is putting in false expense claims; he claims he's had meals with customers that he hasn't seen for a long time; he's rude and unco-operative with other members of the department

2 Have an informal chat, mentioning that all expense claims will be carefully checked in future, or tell him that if he doesn't change, he will be sent a warning letter than could lead to dismissal

3 Have a friendly chat with him to find out if there's a personal problem affecting his work

B

- Explain the task, talk students through the expressions in the Useful language box and practise pronunciation and intonation. Explain any difficulties.

- Then get students to call out the correct heading for each expression.

1 b   2 b   3 c   4 d   5 f   6 a   7 c

C 🔊 CD2.30

- Prepare students for the task and then play the recording once more.

- Elicit the answers and work on any remaining difficulties.

The problem is, he's a really good salesman.

There are two ways we could deal with this.

If we do that, he may come to his senses.

Let's look at it from another angle.

Let's see if we can sort this out.

I'll arrange for Tom to meet us.

D

- Ensure students understand the task.

- Put students into pairs and get them to start the role play. Go round the class and assist where necessary.

- Monitor the language being used. Note down good points and those that need further work.

- Bring the class to order. Praise the correct language that you heard and practise points that need further work.

- Then get one or two of the pairs to re-enact part of the role play for the whole class.

➡ Resource bank: Speaking (page 185)

CASE STUDY

Principles or profit?

Students discuss a number of ethical dilemmas that a drugs firm is facing. Students make recommendations as to the course of action to follow in each case.

Introduction

- Get students to focus on the case study by looking at the background.

- Write the headings on the left-hand side of the table and elicit information from students to complete the right-hand side.

Company	Universal Pharmaceuticals (UP)
Based in	Atlanta, Georgia
Earlier performance	Highly successful thanks to the effective treatments it developed for people suffering from diabetes and Parkinson's Disease
Recent performance	Less good – withdrawal of its asthma drug (harmful side-effects)
Image	Damaged by articles on its sales methods – questioned whether the company was living up to its mission statement that it was an 'ethical company which will always put principle before profit'

Ethical dilemmas 🔊 CD2.31

- Say that students will hear information about the first of three ethical dilemmas in the recording. Play the recording once or twice and explain any difficulties.

- Elicit the answer.

Sample answer

The ethical dilemma the company must deal with is whether to invest a lot of money in a drug that will potentially cure a fatal disease but will not produce much profit for the company.

Discussion topics for the management meeting

- Get students to read about the other two dilemmas individually or in pairs and make written notes on them.

- Bring the class to order and get individual students to talk about the dilemmas, based on their notes.

Task

- Explain the task to the whole class. Get students to work on it in fours, and appoint a chair for each group. Start the task. Go round the room and monitor the language being used. Note down strong points and points that need correction or improvement.

- When most groups have finished, bring the class to order. Praise some of the good language points that you heard and work on half a dozen others that need improvement, getting individual students to say the correct thing.

- Then get representatives from each group to say what they decided about the action to take in relation to each dilemma. Encourage whole-class discussion.

One-to-one

Work on the background to the dilemmas, as above.

Run the task. Monitor the language that you both use. After the activity, underline some of the language that you chose to use and some that your student used correctly and work on five or six points from what they said that need improving.

◎ You can also refer to the *Case study commentary* section of the DVD-ROM, where students can watch an interview with a consultant discussing the key issues raised by the case study.

Writing

- Explain the task. Emphasise the need for a summary of the discussion and the reasons for each decision, then get your students to write a short report of 200–250 words in class or for homework.

➡ Resource bank: Writing (page 213)

➡ Writing file, page 130

AT A GLANCE

	Classwork – Course Book	Further work
Lesson 1 *Each lesson (excluding case studies) is about 45 to 60 minutes. This does not include time spent going through homework.*	**Starting up** Students discuss the factors that make great leaders, as well as some of their less attractive qualities. **Vocabulary: Character adjectives** Students look at some expressions relating to leaders' characteristics and discuss which characteristics are most typical.	**Practice File** Vocabulary (pages 44) **i-Glossary** (DVD-ROM)
Lesson 2	**Listening: Qualities of leadership** An executive search consultant talks about the characteristics of good leaders. **Reading: Leading L'Oréal** Students read about Sir Lindsay Owen-Jones, Chairman of L'Oréal.	**Resource bank: Listening** (page 198) **Course Book Listening** (DVD-ROM) **Text bank** (pages 154–157)
Lesson 3	**Language review: Relative clauses** Students look at relative clauses and develop their ability to use them. **Skills: Presenting** Students looks at some tips and expressions for making presentations and put them into practice.	**Practice File** Language review (page 45) **ML Grammar and Usage** **Resource bank: Speaking** (page 186)
Lesson 4 *Each case study is about 1½ to 2 hours.*	**Case study: Lina Sports** Students suggest solutions for the future strategy and leadership of a declining sports goods company.	**Resource bank: Writing** (page 214) **Practice File** Writing (pages 46–47) **Case study commentary** (DVD-ROM)

For a fast route through the unit focusing mainly on speaking skills, just use the underlined sections.

For one-to-one situations, most parts of the unit lend themselves, with minimal adaptation, to use with individual students. Where this is not the case, alternative procedures are given.

BUSINESS BRIEF

Some organisations *are* their leaders. Amazon is identified with Jeff Bezos, eBay with Pierre Omidyar and Google with Larry Page and Sergey Brin. **Entrepreneurs** and founders of their organisations, they are perceived to have visionary leadership qualities. They are often asked to pronounce on the issues of the day. They are often held up as **role models**.

The mercurial leadership that is characteristic of many entrepreneurs means that they might found and then sell a series of start-ups, not guiding them to the next, more **mature** stage themselves. In the examples above, there are leaders who have made that transition and gone beyond to create multi-billion dollar corporations that operate on a global scale and of others who prefer to leave the day-to-day management of their companies to professional managers as their organisation matures.

Companies may become large by being successful, but they may also become **bureaucratic** and **conservative**. It's a cliché that in successful companies, change is a precondition of continued success, and the people who can lead that change are key. Formulating **strategy** is a question of making choices (often described as 'difficult'), of deciding to do x rather than y with **resources** that are, by definition, limited. The people who can make the right choices about how to use those resources are highly rewarded. (The people who make the wrong choices are also sometimes highly rewarded with generous **severance packages**, but that's another story.)

Failing companies require yet another kind of leadership: the type of leader who can **turn** them **round**, and this third species of leader may not be suited to managing other types of change, preferring to move on to another company in crisis.

Companies are increasingly thinking about how to nurture future leaders. In the US, **corporate governance** – the way that a company is run at the highest level – has become a key issue with shareholders. They have rejected the previous cosy arrangements, where **directors** appointed people they knew to the **board**, and now shareholders demand much greater scrutiny over who is chosen and how.

This is part of the process of recognition that companies are led by *teams* of key managers. The qualities of the **chief executive** cannot be seen in isolation. There must be the right chemistry between the chief executive and other top people and they must have the right mix of complementary skills.

Even so, picking the **successor** to the current **CEO** (**Chief Executive Officer**) is an extremely sensitive task. Will it be someone from within the company, perhaps someone groomed to take over by the current boss? Or do you use **headhunters** (specialised, highly paid recruiters) to track down someone, perhaps from a completely different industry, and bring them in to shake up the existing order? If your new CEO leaves after six months in the job, perhaps after what the papers describe as 'irreconcilable differences' or as a **boardroom battle**, the company and perceptions of it will suffer, and so, probably, will its share price.

There is debate about whether leadership can be taught and about whether reading about the lives and methods of great leaders, business and non-business, can help to develop business leadership skills.

Leadership and your students

Discuss with your in-work students what they look for in a good manager. (Tactfully, as ever, and perhaps best to be avoided if managers are present!) It may be easier to talk to pre-work students about leaders in history.

Read on

Daniel Goleman *et al.*: *The New Leaders*, Time Warner, new edition, 2003

John P. Kotter: *What Leaders Really Do*, Harvard Business School Press, 1999

John Adair: *The Inspirational Leader: How to Motivate, Encourage and Achieve Success*, Kogan Page, new edition, 2005

Warmer

- Get students to brainstorm all the words they know for *leader* in different contexts. Students call out words out or come up one by one to write them on the board. For example: *boss, captain, chairman, chief, coach, foreman, general, king, manager, monarch, president, principal, queen.*

- Discuss with students which words are used in which contexts.

Overview

- Tell students they will be looking at the subject of leadership.

- Go through the overview panel at the beginning of the unit, pointing out the sections that students will be doing.

Quotation

- Ask students what they think of the quotation. To get them thinking and talking, you could ask them if leadership in a company is like leadership in the army, or not. (Blanchard is the co-author of famous management books such as *One-Minute Manager* and *Who Moved my Cheese*? Your students may have heard of these.)

Starting up

Students discuss the factors that make for great leaders, as well as some of their less attractive qualities.

A

- Go through the questions and explain any vocabulary difficulties.

- Get students to discuss the questions in pairs. Go round the room and help where necessary.

- Bring the class to order. Get individual students to talk about their findings. As ever, be tactful, especially when students are talking about their bosses!

B

- Get students to discuss in small groups. Go round the room and help where necessary.

- Bring the class to order and get individual students to discuss the points that were made in their groups. As ever, be tactful.

Vocabulary: Character adjectives

Students look at some vocabulary relating to leaders' characters and discuss which characteristics are most typical.

A – B

- Some of this vocabulary will probably already have come up in the Starting up session. This is a good opportunity to consolidate it.

- Go through the two boxes of adjectives, explaining any difficulties. Or get students to work in pairs on them with a monolingual or bilingual dictionary.

- Bring the class to order and practise stress and pronunciation, e.g. *deCIsive.*

- Elicit the answers.

> **Exercise A**
>
> cautious/decisive; casual/formal; idealistic/realistic; assertive/diffident, encouraging/critical
>
> **Exercise B**
>
> dynamic/laid-back; radical/conservative; ruthless/principled; distant/approachable

- As an additional activity, you could get students to discuss and report back on the following questions:
  - Are there any leaders which you think have any of these qualities?
  - Which of the adjectives would you use to describe an ideal business leader? Give reasons for your choice.
  - What adjectives would you add to the list?

C

- Do as a quick-fire whole-class activity, getting students to say why they chose the adjective in each case.

1	cautious	5	ruthless
2	critical	6	approachable
3	formal	7	conservative
4	idealistic	8	principled

D – E

- Get students to work on these in pairs. Go round the class and assist where necessary.

- Bring the class to order. Elicit the answers.

Exercise D
1 e **2** b **3** a **4** f **5** d **6** c

(Some other pairs are possible, e.g. 1b, 4c, 5a, but the ones above are the most likely.)

Exercise E
a) 4 **b)** 5 **c)** 6 **d)** 1 **e)** 2 **f)** 3

F

- Again, get students to discuss these questions in pairs. Monitor the language being used. Note down good points and those that need further work.

- Bring the class to order. Praise the correct language that you heard and practise points that need further work.

- With the whole class, get some of the pairs to give and justify their opinions, paying special attention to the vocabulary that you have covered in this section.

◎ i-Glossary

Listening: Qualities of leadership
An executive recruitment consultant talks about the characteristics of good leaders.

A ◀)) CD2.32

- Tell students that they are going to listen to Elizabeth Jackson, Managing Director of an executive recruitment company, an organisation that finds people to fill high-level jobs.

- Get students to look at the question. Then play the recording once or twice and explain any difficulties without giving away the answers.

- Elicit the answers.

A sense of direction, courage, communication, respect, emotional intelligence

B ◀)) CD2.33

- Again, get students to look at the questions. Get them to note the expression *natural born leader*.

- Then play the recording once or twice and explain any difficulties without giving away the answers.

- Elicit the answers and work on any difficulties, e.g. the pronunciation and meaning of *charisma*.

1 Charisma, intelligence, ability to influence people
2 Not usually

C ◀)) CD2.34

- Get students to look at the statements.

- Then play the recording once or twice and explain any difficulties without giving away the answers.

1 False: '...my husband is a few years older than me'
2 False: He has 'the ability to fight like a cornered rat when he needs to' but there is no mention of boxing.
3 True
4 True
5 True

- Work on any remaining difficulties.

⇨ Resource bank: Listening (page 200)

◎ Students can watch the interview with Elizabeth Jackson on the DVD-ROM.

Reading: Leading L'Oréal
Students read about Sir Lindsay Owen-Jones, Chairman of L'Oréal.

A – B

- Ask students in small groups to write down four things that they know about L'Oréal. Go round the class and assist where necessary.

- Then get them to read through the article to see if any of them are mentioned.

- With the whole class, get a member of each group to say which of their ideas were mentioned. (One of the things they may know is that their English slogan is *Because you're worth it*, but this is not mentioned in the article. Ask students if the same slogan is used in their own languages.)

C

- Before going any further, explain any difficulties of meaning or pronunciation. Then get students, still in the same groups, to match the items.

- With the whole class, elicit the answers.

1 a **2** b **3** a **4** a **6** a **7** c **9** a **10** d
5 and **8** are not mentioned.

D

- Tell students they are going to give a short presentation about L'Oréal and get them to make notes.

- Put students into pairs and tell them that they will hear their partner give a presentation about L'Oréal and they need to ask a question at the end of the talk.

- Get students to give their presentations and ask their questions in parallel pairs. Monitor the language being used. Note down good points and those that need further work.

- Bring the class to order. Praise the correct language that you heard and practise points that need further work.

- With the whole class, get a couple of students to give their presentations again, paying special attention to the improvements you discussed.

E

- Get students to close their books and do this as a quick-fire whole-class activity. Elicit the answers.

1	from	**4**	up
2	down from; over; to	**5**	of
3	with		

- Underline particularly the leadership-related vocabulary *step down* and *hand over*.

F

- Again, get students to discuss these questions in small groups. Monitor the language being used. Note down good points and those that need further work.

- Bring the class to order. Praise the correct language that you heard and practise points that need further work.

- With the whole class, get some of the pairs to give and justify their opinions, paying special attention to the vocabulary that you have covered in this section.

➡ Text bank (pages 154–157)

Language review: Relative clauses

Students look at relative clauses and develop their ability to use them.

- Talk students through the commentary and the examples in the panel. Write the examples on the board as you explain them. Bring students' attention to the extra information in the Grammar reference section on page 151 of the Course Book and ask them to study it for homework.

A – **B**

- Do as quick-fire whole-class activities. Explain any difficulties.

Exercise A

1	which/that	**5**	who
2	which/that	**6**	who
3	who	**7**	which/that
4	who		

Exercise B

1	which/that; where	**4**	who/that
2	who/that	**5**	who/that
3	which/that		

C

- Get students to work on this exercise in pairs. Go round the class and assist where necessary.

- With the whole class, elicit the answers, getting students to explain why they have chosen them.

We now need to encourage investment in new high-technology industries such as clean energy and environmental technology. These are sectors **where** we have lacked political leadership not just recently, but for decades.

The Internet, **which** enables the open and free exchange of information, is critical to our future economic growth. It has already proved to be vital to entrepreneurs and America's small businesses, **which** generate up to 80 per cent of new jobs in the US. But continuing this record will require a strong federal commitment to keeping the Internet open.

Technologies such as the Internet can also help make our government more open and responsive to citizens. But even those of us **who/that** are technology's biggest enthusiasts must recognise its limitations. In the end, it is people **who/that** have to make the decisions.

More than ever, we need a leader **who/that** will look beyond the old thinking and orthodoxies and **who** understands the importance of investment in ideas and technology for our future.

This article expresses the personal opinion of Eric Schmidt, **who** is the Chief Executive of Google.

Skills: Presenting

Students looks at some tips and expressions for making presentations and put them into practice.

A

- Explain the task and get students to do it in pairs.

- Go through the answers with the whole class, encouraging discussion. Where your students are from more than one country, there may be a variety of responses.

Suggested answers

a) 2, 10   **b)** 1, 3, 4, 5, 6, 8   **c)** 7, 9

1   Can be a good way of building rapport, but be careful in unfamiliar cultures with the use and type of humour in particular contexts. If in doubt, it is best avoided. Serious subjects require a serious approach.

2   But not too slowly – it can sound condescending. (Teach this word.) However, do try to vary the speed at which you speak.

3   Occasionally, perhaps, but don't overdo it.

4–5 Involve the audience by giving a presentation that they can relate to and are interested in, but you may want them to keep questions to the end to avoid digressions.

6   You may have to adapt if necessary, but if you have researched the audience and what they expect, this should not be necessary.

7   Try not to wander around too much, but occasional movement helps the audience to concentrate.

8   This is partly cultural – some cultures use more gesturing than others. Do what comes naturally to you, but don't overdo it.

9   Probably not a good idea – it will sound monotonous. But there may be key sections, quotations, etc., that it is good to have written down. If so, read out as spontaneously as possible.

10   Usually advisable, but it depends on the size of the audience. If there are 100 people or the setting is formal, definitely stand up. With a small audience in an informal setting, it's sometimes OK to sit down. Standing in front of a small audience can seem intimidating to them.

B

● Ask the whole class for their ideas and discuss them.

Possible ideas

Appearance

● Be careful about how you are dressed. This can play an important part in the overall effect. Think about the level of formality required. In some cultures, it's not a good idea to loosen your tie or to take off your jacket, even if it's quite hot.

Visual aids

● Make your visual aids as professional-looking as possible.

● Be careful about equipment and possible back-ups: if a particular audience requires a particular approach, for example with PowerPoint slides, it will probably be difficult to improvise anything that is satisfactory if the equipment does not work. If you don't have a back-up computer and projector, bring the slides also in the form of overhead transparencies.

● If you have spent hours developing slides and these are necessary for your presentation, it's probably not a good idea to leave them in your hotel room.

Timing

● Do not run over the allotted time. The question-and-answer session is often where this happens, so allow plenty of time for it. In a large room, repeat the questioner's question, so that everyone can hear it. Answer the question as politely as possible, but if you think the answer is not of much interest to the rest of the audience, tell the questioner that you can discuss it with them afterwards, one to one.

● Make it clear when the presentation is over by saying *Thank you very much* or *Thank you for listening* in a final sort of way, otherwise things can drag on and people start leaving the room not knowing if it's over or not.

C ◀)) CD2.35

● Go through the expressions in the Useful language box with the whole class.

● Explain the task and play the recording once or twice.

Good morning, everyone.

I'm going to divide my talk into four parts.

First, I'll give you … . After that, … . Next, … . Finally, … .

I'll give you some background.

As you know, …

To sum up, …

Well, that's all I have to say. Thank you for listening.

● If necessary, play the recording again and work on any other difficulties.

D – **E**

● Get students to look through the points that they will be assessing in the presentations.

● Then get students to choose one of the topics and prepare their presentations. You could get students to do this for homework.

● When students are ready, or in the next session(s) if you have given the task for homework, get students to give their presentations to each other in groups of three. In smaller classes, they could give the presentation to the whole class. Make sure that the other participants assess the presentation on the criteria given.

● Monitor the language being used. Note down strong points and points that need correction or improvement.

● When students have given their presentations, praise strong points that you heard and work on points that need correction or improvement, getting students to say the correct thing, especially in the area of language used for presentations.

● Then get other students to give their assessments and explain their reasons. Encourage them to be honest but tactful!

Resource bank: Speaking (page 186)

CASE STUDY

Lina Sports

Students suggest solutions for the future strategy and leadership of a struggling sports goods company.

Background, problems and possible strategies

- Get students to focus on the case study by looking at the background information.
- Write the headings on the left-hand side of the table and elicit information from students to complete the right-hand side.

Company	Lina Sports (LS)
Based in	Italy
Products	Originally specialised in tennis shoes, but later diversified into football, athletics, tennis and volleyball clothing.
Founded	In 1978 by Franco Rossi
Chief Executive	Still Franco Rossi, but he would like to hand over to one of the present directors and become Chairman.
Results	Disappointing: falling profits, rising costs
Possible takeover	By French retailer, but only if 'friendly', i.e. with agreement of Lina board
Problems	Launched too many product lines, spent too much on expensive endorsements with top sports people, suffered from fierce competition from stronger competitors, lost its reputation for innovation.
Possible strategies	LS could ... • merge with, or be taken over by, a larger, financially stronger company. • acquire a number of smaller companies and focus more on making sports accessories. • grow organically by revising its organisation, product ranges and marketing strategy.

Task

- Explain the task.
- Get students to work in groups of five or six, with the three Lina directors making up Group A and the two or three (non-presenting) directors making up Group B. Be clear about who is who in each group, and which non-presenting director is going to chair the session, but don't let them turn to their respective pages yet.
- Then get students to turn to the page with their information. Ensure that they turn to the correct page.
- Give students plenty of time to absorb their information. Go round the class and assist where necessary.
- When students are ready, get them to start the activity. Monitor the language being used. Note down good points and those that need further work.
- Bring the class to order. Praise the correct language that you heard and practise points that need further work.
- Get a member from each group to say who they chose as Rossi's successor and why.

One-to-one

Work on the background to bring out the key points about the company.

Run the task with your student taking the part of one of the presenting directors. Monitor the language that you both use.

After the activity, underline some of the language that you chose to use and some that your student used correctly and work on five or six points from what they said that need improving. (If there is time and interest, you could get your student to make another presentation using the information for another of the directors and paying particular attention to the points you raised.)

You can also refer to the *Case study commentary* section of the DVD-ROM, where students can watch an interview with a consultant discussing the key issues raised by the case study.

Writing

- Get your students to write an e-mail of about 200 words from the Chairman of Lina Sports to the Head of JPS Consultants, briefly summarising the three business strategies and indicating which one has been chosen, giving reasons. Students could do this for homework or in pairs in class.

Resource bank: Writing (page 214)

Writing file, page 127

AT A GLANCE

	Classwork – Course Book	Further work
Lesson 1 *Each lesson (excluding case studies) is about 45 to 60 minutes. This does not include time spent going through homework.*	**Starting up** Students do a questionnaire to see how competitive they are. **Vocabulary: Competition idioms** Students look at competition idioms originating in sport and use them in context.	**Practice File** Vocabulary (pages 48–49) **i-Glossary** (DVD-ROM)
Lesson 2	**Reading: Head-to-head competition** Students read about the current rivalry between Starbucks and McDonald's and how each company is planning for future success. **Listening: The Competition Commission** Rory Taylor, Media Relations Manager for the UK's Competition Commission, talks about its work.	**Text bank** (pages 158–161) **Resource bank: Listening** (page 199) **Course Book Listening** (DVD-ROM)
Lesson 3	**Language review: Passives** Students look at passives and practise using them in a series of exercises. **Skills: Negotiating** Students look at some diplomatic and less diplomatic negotiating language and hear it being used in context. They then use it themselves in a role play.	**Practice File** Language review (pages 49–50) **ML Grammar and Usage** **Resource bank: Speaking** (page 187)
Lesson 4 *Each case study is about 1½ to 2 hours.*	**Case study: Fashion House** Students negotiate details of a new contract that a jewellery retailer wants to agree with its suppliers.	**Resource bank: Writing** (page 215) **Practice File** Writing (page 51) **Case study commentary** (DVD-ROM)

For a fast route through the unit focusing mainly on speaking skills, just use the underlined sections.

For one-to-one situations, most parts of the unit lend themselves, with minimal adaptation, to use with individual students. Where this is not the case, alternative procedures are given.

BUSINESS BRIEF

Michael Porter was the first to analyse systematically the **competitive forces** that operate in a particular industry. He found that in any given industry there are:

- **cost-leaders**: **low-cost producers** with a **broad scope** and **cost advantage**, appealing to many industry **segments**: many different types of buyers, each with different needs;

- **differentiators**, appealing to buyers who are looking for particular **product attributes** (characteristics) and **positioning** themselves as the most able to meet those needs;

- **focusers**, concentrating on one particular segment who try to find **competitive advantage** by satisfying the needs of buyers in that segment better than anyone else.

These are the available choices, according to Porter, that a commercial organisation has if it wants to compete effectively and not get 'stuck in the middle'.

Competition between companies can be **tough, aggressive**, even **ferocious** or **cut-throat**. Firms may price aggressively in order to build **market share**, perhaps selling at a loss. They hope to recoup their losses later when, having established themselves to benefit from **economies of scale** (producing in larger quantities so that the cost of each unit goes down), they are able to charge **market prices** with a healthy **profit margin** on each unit sold. This is one way of becoming a cost leader.

Competition can also be **gentlemanly** or even **cosy**. Companies of similar size in a particular industry may have similar costs and charge similar prices. But then one competitor reduces its prices, hoping to increase its **unit sales** (the number of goods it sells), bringing in more money to cover its **fixed costs** and thereby increase profit. Other competitors follow suit, each reducing its prices in a **price war**. This happened in the UK quality-newspaper market, but there was no clear winner, especially as the overall market was shrinking.

Competitors may enter into forms of **co-operation**, such as **joint ventures** for specific projects. They may even talk about **strategic alliances**. But these can go wrong and lead to recrimination between the **partners**.

Emerging industries are very attractive. Companies want to get in before the rules of the game become set in stone and be able to influence how they are fixed. A **start-up** has the advantage of building its own **corporate culture**: its own way of doing things. An **established company** may buy firms in **unrelated industries**, including start-ups in emerging industries, hoping that some of their acquisitions will turn out to be leaders in their fields and become money-spinners. But it may just end up as a **conglomerate** of more or less profitable companies and some unprofitable ones, with different and perhaps **incompatible cultures**.

These are the $64,000 questions in competitive strategy: Which are the industries to stay in, invest in and develop? Which are the new ones to get into? Which are the ones to get out of? Answering these questions is not easy: multi-billion dollar mistakes are easy to make.

Competition and your students

All your students should find it easy to relate to competition as consumers buying competing products. In-work students will be able to talk about competitors in their own industry: it's often interesting to see how they perceive the 'culture' of competing companies in relation to their own company.

Read on

Porter's ideas referred to above were developed in the 1980s and are still influential. These are recent editions of his two seminal books:

Michael E. Porter: *Competitive Strategy: Techniques for Analyzing Competitors and Industries*, Free Press, 2004

Michael E. Porter: *Competitive Advantage*, Simon and Schuster, 1998

Also recommended are:

Henry Mintzberg *et al.*: *Strategy Safari: The Complete Guide Through the Wilds of Strategic Management*, FT Prentice Hall, 2008

W. Chan Kim and Renée Mauborgne: *Blue Ocean Strategy: How to Create Uncontested Market Space and Make the Competition Irrelevant*, Harvard Business School Press, 2005

LESSON NOTES

Warmer

- Write these words on the board and get students to say how they are pronounced, especially in relation to stress. Get them to say which syllables should be underlined to indicate stress.

> compete   competitor   competition
> rival   rivalry

- Then get students to look up the words in a good monolingual dictionary, such as *Longman Dictionary of Contemporary English*, or a good bilingual one.

- Get them to tell you something that the dictionary says about each word, e.g. '*compete* is followed by *with*, *competition* can be countable or uncountable, *rival* is another word for *competitor*, etc.'

Overview

- Tell students they will be looking at the subject of competition.

- Go through the overview panel at the beginning of the unit, pointing out the sections that students will be looking at.

Quotation

- Get students to look at the quotation and see if they agree with it. (Probably they will know about Darwin, his theory of evolution and the 'survival of the fittest' – only the animals, or in this case the businesses, most suited to their environment will continue to exist.)

Starting up

Students do a questionnaire to see how competitive they are.

A

- With the whole class, ask if students think they are competitive. Ask them if they consider that they come from a competitive educational background or profession. Treat the ensuing discussion tactfully, of course.

B

- Get students to ask each other the questions in pairs and to note the answers. Go round the room and help where necessary, e.g. with the meaning of *flashy* (item 3c).

- When most students have finished, bring the class to order and get a member of some of the pairs to say what they each replied.

- Students score their answers by looking at page 140 of the Course Book.

- With a show of hands for each answer, get the class to decide if they are, on the whole, competitive or not.

Vocabulary: Competition idioms

Students look at some sports-related competition expressions and use them in context.

A – B

- Explain the tasks and get students to do them in pairs. Go round the room and help where necessary.

- Bring the class to order and explain anything that has caused general difficulty. Get individual students to call out the answers.

> 1 field (football) – a
> 2 seat (motor racing) – h
> 3 neck (horse racing) – c
> 4 horse (horse racing) – e
> 5 player (football, baseball) – j
> 6 goalposts (football) – g
> 7 ball (tennis or any ball game) – f
> 8 game (any sport) – b
> 9 race (horse racing) – d
> 10 ropes (boxing) – i

C

- Get students to work on the exercise individually or in pairs.

> 1 playing field
> 2 a one horse race
> 3 flogging a dead horse
> 4 in the driving seat (You could also accept *ahead of the game*.)
> 5 neck and neck
> 6 major players

D

- Get students to discuss the questions in pairs. Go round the room and help where necessary.

- Bring the class to order and ask individual students from some of the pairs to summarise the things they came up with under each point.

 i-Glossary

Reading: Head-to-head competition

Students read about the current rivalry between Starbucks and McDonald's and how each company is planning for future success.

A

- In small groups, get students to say what they know about and think of Starbucks and McDonald's.
- Then, with the whole class, get members of different groups to say what their findings were.

B

- Ask students to read the article specifically for this piece of information.

Starbucks

C

- Get students to find the answers to these questions individually or in pairs. Go round the class and assist where necessary.
- With the whole class, elicit the answers.
- Deal with any vocabulary difficulties that have been causing general problems.

| 1 M | 2 S | 3 S | 4 M | 5 S | 6 S | 7 M | 8 M | 9 M |

D – E

- Do as quick-fire whole-class activities.

Exercise D

1	up	4	on
2	by	5	on
3	out to		

Exercise E

a)	lose out to	d)	replace (by)
b)	take on	e)	stir up
c)	focus on		

F – G

- In order to vary the approach, get students to work in pairs. Go round the class and assist where necessary.
- With the whole class, elicit the answers.

Exercise F

1 c   2 a   3 b   4 e (as in *take out a loan*)   5 d

Exercise G

1	take on	4	take out
2	taken over	5	take off
3	taken aback		

H

- Do as a quick-fire whole-class activity. Get students to justify their answers.

Optional extra activity

Get students to work in groups on this situation.

You have won a competition to take over a small café in your town for a year. An entrepreneur has given you the premises for free and €200,000 as start-up capital. She wants you to compete against the local Starbucks and McDonald's. Brainstorm how you would redesign the café and the products you would offer.

- Explain the situation and start the groupwork. Go round the class and assist where necessary.
- Monitor the language being used, especially language related to competition. Note down good points and those that need further work.
- Bring the class to order. Praise the correct language that you heard and practise points that need further work.
- Then get representatives from one or two groups to summarise their ideas.

➡ Text bank (pages 158–161)

Listening: The Competition Commission

Rory Taylor, Media Relations Manager for the UK's Competition Commission, talks about its work.

A 🔊 CD2.36

- Without pre-empting the first question too much, say that the Competition Commission is an official UK organisation that looks at competition between companies.
- Play the recording once or twice and get students to answer the questions. Explain any difficulties.

1 It carries out investigations into particular mergers and markets in the UK and into regulated industries.

2 To see if the ownership structure is in the interests of consumers (i.e. to see if it is a competitive market)

B 🔊 CD2.37

- Get students to look through the statements. Explain any difficulties, e.g. *static*.
- Then play the recording once or twice. Elicit the answers.

1   False: 'It's actually a matter of … not so much looking at the number of competitors or providers in a particular market so much as looking at the dynamics of that market.'

2   True

3   True

4   False: '… after in-depth investigation, it was clear that this is a market where these companies are competing actively with each other.'

C ◀)) CD2.38

- Get students to look through the text, predicting what might be in the gaps.

- Then play the recording and elicit the answers.

1	static	4	prices
2	switching	5	innovation
3	competing	6	choice

- Explain any remaining difficulties.

▸ Resource bank: Listening (page 199)

◉ Students can watch the interview with Rory Taylor on the DVD-ROM.

Language review: Passives

Students look at passives and practise using them in a series of exercises.

- Talk students through the commentary and the examples in the panel.

- Bring students' attention to the extra information in the Grammar reference section on page 151 of the Course Book and ask them to study it for homework.

A

- Get students to work on the sentences in pairs. Go round the room and help where necessary.

- Check the answers with the whole class and explain any difficulties.

1   Correct

2   The leadership contest was depended on the boardroom vote.

3   Where were you when the president was be shot?

4   Correct

5   They are **depending** on the CEO to show strong leadership.

6   Correct

7   Correct

8   Correct

9   Problems may **occur** after the leadership vote.

10 Correct

11 Correct

12 The audience **consists** largely of senior executives.

B

- Get students to look through the entire minutes before doing the exercise individually or in pairs. Go round the class and assist where necessary.

- Elicit the answers.

1   was held

2   was attended

3   was / had been circulated

4   was / had been intended

5   was (being) forced

6   had been cut

7   had been increased

8   had been commissioned

9   was informed

10 had been reached

11 were being investigated

12 was being / had been implemented

13 were being / had been considered

Optional extra activity

Explain the task below and write the prompts 1 to 12 on the board (or photocopy this page and hand it out, being careful not to hand out the answers too!).

A large automobile company is feeling the pressure from its competitors and has decided to launch a new car. Use the notes below to describe the stages in the launch. Include passive and active structures and use words like *first*, *next*, *then*, *after that*, *following that* and *finally*.

1   designer – choose

2   design – produce

3   model – build

4   modifications – R&D department engineers – make

5   design – modify

6   prototype – build

7   new engine – use – or existing engine develop – can be very costly

8   new model – test – special roads

9   deal with problems – costly if problems serious

10 journalists – invite – test-drive model

11 reviews – write – by journalists – major newspapers and car magazines

12 model – display – famous motor exhibition – Geneva or Earl's Court MotorShow

- Get students to work on the task individually or in pairs. Go round the class and assist where necessary.

- Bring the class to order and elicit the answers.

Sample answers

1 First, a designer is chosen.
2 Then he or she produces a design.
3 Next a model is built.
4 After that, the R&D department engineers make modifications.
5 Following that the design is modified.
6 Then a prototype is built.
7 The company can use a new engine or an existing engine. A new engine can be very costly to develop.
8 Following that the new car is tested on special tracks or roads.
9 Next they have to deal with any problems. This can be costly if the problems are serious.
10 The next step is to invite journalists to test-drive the new model.
11 Then reviews are written by journalists from major newspapers and car magazines.
12 Finally, the model is displayed at a famous motor exhibition like the Geneva or the Earl's Court Motor Shows.

Skills: Negotiating

Students look at some diplomatic and less diplomatic negotiating language and hear it being used in context. They then apply it themselves in a role play.

A ◀)) CD2.39

- Tell students they will be looking at the language of negotiations, first of all in the situation of an Italian bicycle manufacturer who wants to get into the Swedish market.
- Get students to look at the questions.
- Then play the recording once or twice and elicit the answers.

1 a, b   2 To make it profitable

B

- Talk about the importance of knowing the difference between direct and indirect language.
- Do the exercise as a quick-fire whole-class activity.
- Elicit the answers.

1 e   2 d   3 c   4 b   5 a

- Work on the intonation of the direct and indirect utterances, getting students to exaggerate both (i.e. the directness of phrases 1 to 6 and the indirectness of phrases a to f).

C ◀)) CD2.40

- Tell students that they are going to hear some negotiating expressions that they have to complete.
- Play the recording once, or more if necessary, and get students to complete the sentences.
- Elicit the answers with the whole class.
- Students will probably have already understood that some expressions are diplomatic and others are non-diplomatic. With the whole class, get individual students to say which are which.

1	would be perfect (D)	6	could help (D)
2	no good (ND)	7	will you pay us (ND)
3	far better (ND)	8	talk about (ND)
4	suggest (D)	9	To be honest (D)
5	want at least (ND)	10	must be (ND)

- As in Exercise B above, get students to read the utterances in a slightly exaggerated way.

D

- Explain the task and divide the class into pairs.
- Start the role play and go round the room and help where necessary. Also monitor the language being used. Note down strong points and points in the area of diplomatic negotiating language that need correction or improvement.
- When most pairs have finished, bring the class to order.
- Praise strong points that you heard and work on points that need correction or improvement, getting students to say the correct thing.
- Get students to read out the expressions in the Useful language box as a recap of this section.

➡ Resource bank: Speaking (page 187)

CASE STUDY

Fashion House

Students negotiate details of a new contract that a jewellery retailer wants to agree with its suppliers.

Background

- Get students to focus on the case study by looking at the background information.

- Write the headings on the left-hand side of the table and elicit information from students to complete the right-hand side.

Company	Fashion House
Based in	Miami, Florida
Activity	Chain of stores selling high-class jewellery products, including necklaces, bracelets, earrings
Profit margin	At least 80 per cent on most products
Date now	1 October
Delivery deadline	5,000 necklaces and bracelets and 3,000 earrings to be delivered by 15 November
Confident of selling	3,000 necklaces and bracelets and 2,000 earrings; more if the prices are competitive and the demand strong
Cashflow	Temporarily problematic, wishes to pay as late as possible
Possible suppliers	Three companies in India, Peru, Chile
Objective	Long-term relationship with new supplier

Task

- Explain the task. Get students to look through the information about the three suppliers and point out potential problems, e.g. Supplier 1 may be unable to deliver required quantities on time, demands 50 per cent deposit upfront (teach this expression), which is not good from the cashflow point of view, etc.

- Point out that each buyer will have to obtain the missing information from the supplier that they deal with

- Divide the class into groups of six. Allocate buyer roles to three of the students and a different supplier role to each of the other three. Make sure that each student is looking at the correct page.

- When students are ready, get them to start role-playing the negotiations in pairs. Go round the room and monitor the language being used. Note down strong points and points that need correction or improvement, especially in the area of the language of negotiation.

- When most pairs have finished, bring the class to order.

- Praise strong points that you heard and work on points that need correction or improvement, getting students to say the correct thing.

Conclusion

- Tell the buyers and the suppliers in each six to get together in two separate groups and discuss the negotiation that they just had.

- Point out that the buyers exchange information about the suppliers they spoke to and decide which one to use. Suppliers discuss how they feel about the negotiation. What were they happy or unhappy about? What would they do differently?

- When most supplier and buyer groups have finished, bring the class to order and ask the buyers to announce their decision and the reasons for it, and the suppliers to say what they would have done differently.

- To round off, ask what students have learned about the negotiating process in general.

One-to-one

Work on the background to bring out the key points about the situation.

Run the task, doing the buyer–supplier negotiations for each supplier. Change roles so that your student is sometimes the buyer and sometimes the supplier.

Monitor the language that you both use. After the activity, underline some of the language that you chose to use and some that your student used correctly and work on five or six points from what they said that need improving.

After the negotiations, both you and your student come out of role, discuss what happened with each supplier and which one the buyer would choose.

◎ You can also refer to the *Case study commentary* section of the DVD-ROM, where students can watch an interview with a consultant discussing the key issues raised by the case study.

Writing

- Get your students to write an e-mail of about 250 words to their opposite number confirming the details of your negotiation and any outstanding points to be decided on. Students could do this for homework or in pairs in class.

⇨ Resource bank: Writing (page 215)

⇨ Writing file, page 127

Communication styles

Introduction

This Working across cultures unit looks at the ways that people communicate, not only through language, but also in other ways.

A

- Introduce the idea of communication styles by getting students to look through points 1 to 4.

- Start the discussion in small groups. Go round the class and assist where necessary.

- Get representatives of each group to say what their findings were.

---

1   Different cultures have different ideal distances when people are speaking. This will depend on how well people know each other and other factors. But some research has shown that, typically, two English speakers talking across a table think that 8 feet (just over 2 metres) is a comfortable distance.

2   This could be quite personal. Some people hold eye contact for longer than others even within the same culture, for reasons of shyness, outgoingness, etc.

3   In some cultures, such as Finland and Japan, silence means that you are considering carefully what the other person has said. The English-speaking world, on the whole, is not comfortable with too much silence.

4   English speakers would probably say that it is rude to talk 'over' someone before they have finished speaking but recordings of meetings, etc., would probably prove otherwise! Some other cultures are more comfortable with this.

B 🔊 CD2.41

- Tell students about what they are going to hear: someone giving a workshop about communication styles and cultural awareness.

- Get students to look through the table and help with any difficulties, e.g. the meaning of *proximity*. Get students to start to anticipate the cultures that might be in the gaps.

- Play the recording and see if students' expectations are confirmed or not. (Explain that East Asia refers primarily to China, Japan and Korea.)

---

1   East Asians, (North) Americans, Northern Europeans
2   Southern Europeans, Latin Americans
3   East Asians
4   Latin cultures of Europe and Latin America
5   Venezuelans
6   Arab and Latin cultures
7   North Americans and Northern Europeans
8   East Asians

- Discuss with the whole class whether they agree with the information or not.

C 🔊 CD2.41

- Get students to look through the items 1 to 7. (Explain *rhetorical question* if necessary: one where the speaker does not expect an answer.) You could play the recording again with students looking at the audio script.

- Elicit the answers.

---

1   How close do you like to be when speaking with a business colleague?
    How much eye contact are you comfortable with?
    Are you comfortable with long periods of silence?
    And how do you feel about interruptions?

2   **These are some of the questions we will be looking at** in today's workshop on communication styles and cultural awareness.

3   **I've had** 12 overseas postings, including Brazil, Russia, China and India, and I speak four languages.

4   **By the end of the workshop today, you'll have** a better understanding of communication styles in your own culture and an introduction to those styles in other cultures ... and this is the starting point for learning how to deal with cultural differences.

5   It's **worth bearing in mind** that ...

6   **Let me tell you briefly what we are going to cover today. I'll get the workshop going with** a brief talk. **Firstly, I'm going to talk about** some ways in which we use verbal communication and **I'll look at** two areas. **Then I'm going to look at** non-verbal communication, again looking at two areas. **And after that, we'll** do some activities looking at communication styles in your own culture.

7   **Can you put up your hands if** you've already had an overseas posting?

- Go over the language in bold above, underlining how it is used, in preparation for the next activity.

D

- Get students to discuss this in small groups. (In multinational classes, put different nationalities in each group as far as possible, so that they can share experiences.)

- Go round the class and assist where necessary. If they are short of ideas, you could suggest they think about eye contact (is looking away from someone considered rude or polite?), body language (is leaning back in one's chair acceptable?), interruptions (perhaps interrupting someone means that you are very interested in what they are saying and that you want to respond immediately, which in some cultures is not considered rude), etc. However, try not to pre-empt the Task activity that follows too much.

- Bring the class to order. Get a representative from each group to say what its findings were.

Task

- Get students to look through the Task description. Emphasise that they should only look at four areas of etiquette in their presentations and that they must use the structure that is outlined.

- Get them to start preparing their presentations, writing notes rather than a full script. Go round the class and assist where necessary. (In large classes, get students to prepare presentations in small groups. Tell students that only one member of each group will have to present, but they won't know in advance who it will be!)

- When most students are ready, get one student to give their presentation. Tell the other students in the class to monitor it, checking that the presenter is following the required structure, and monitor it yourself too. Note down good points and those that need further work.

- When the presentation is over, get the other students to say how closely the presenter followed the structure.

- Then praise the correct language that you heard and practise points that need further work.

- If you run out of time, get students to do some more presentations in later classes.

UNIT **D** Revision

This unit revises and reinforces some of the key language points from Units 10–12 and from Working across cultures 4. Links with those units are clearly shown. You can point out these links to your students.

10 Ethics
Vocabulary

- These exercises provide further practice in vocabulary related to ethical issues.

Exercise 1

money laundering

sex discrimination

animal testing

counterfeit goods

price fixing

Exercise 2

1	price fixing	4	counterfeit goods
2	animal testing	5	sex discrimination
3	money laundering		

Narrative tenses

- Students complete a text using the correct narrative tenses.

1	started	6	had tested
2	heard	7	were losing
3	was causing	8	realised
4	were doing	9	decided
5	was happening		

Skills

- Students get practice in error-spotting.

1 Please find attached the expenses claim form that you <u>sent</u> to our Accounts Department last

2 week. I <u>am</u> afraid we cannot process it as it is, because it is incomplete.

3 Firstly, we need to know the names of the customers that you <u>took</u> for lunch on May 12, as

4 well as the name of the restaurant <u>where</u> you took them. We also need to know the reason for

5 the £60 that you <u>entered</u> under 'sundry expenses'. Finally, we would like to remind you that all

6 expenses <u>have</u> to be authorised by your manager.

11 Leadership
Vocabulary

- Students get further practice in the vocabulary of personality and phrasal verbs.

Exercise 1

1	approachable	4	diffident
2	encouraging	5	Ruthless
3	idealistic	6	conservative

Exercise 2

1	be up to	4	come in for
2	hand in	5	deal with
3	take on	6	put forward

Relative clauses

- Students get more practice with relative clause structures.

1 We went to the workshop <u>that Li had recommended to us</u>.

2 Most of the proposals <u>that/which we had put forward</u> were eventually accepted.

3 The firm, <u>which organised business travel for top executives</u>, went bankrupt last month.

4 What's the title of the talk <u>that/which you are going to attend</u>?

5 Mrs Martens, <u>who is fluent in four languages</u>, heads our translation service.

6 Two of the speakers <u>that/who (or whom) we had invited</u> were unable to come.

7 My favourite manager was a young man <u>who came from Brazil</u>.

8 Where is the report <u>that/which was on my desk this morning</u>?

12 Competition

Vocabulary

- Students get further practice with sport-related idioms.

1	horse	**5**	neck
2	field	**6**	seat
3	goalposts	**7**	ball
4	game		

Passives

- Students get more practice with these structures.

Exercise 1

1 are tested
2 is read
3 will be met
4 must be reviewed
5 have been closed
6 is (...) being developed

Exercise 2

1 have (...) been accused
2 is being/will be sold, is estimated
3 are owned
4 was founded
5 is (...) known, are (...) supplied
6 is (...) being discussed

Writing

- Students work on the cohesion of a written text.

Exercise 1

1 f   2 e   3 d   4 a   5 c   6 b

Exercise 2

2, 3, 5, 4, 6, 1

Cultures: Communication styles

- Students get further practice in the language used to talk about styles of communicating.

Exercise 1

1 How close do you like to be when speaking with a business colleague?
2 How much eye contact are you comfortable with?
3 How comfortable are you with prolonged periods of silence?
4 How do you feel about being interrupted?

Exercise 2

Ensure that students' presentations are to the point and cover all four issues above.

Text bank

TEACHER'S NOTES

Introduction

The Text bank contains articles relating to the units in the Course Book. These articles extend and develop the themes in those units. You can choose the articles that are of most interest to your students. They can be done in class or as homework. You have permission to make photocopies of these articles for your students.

Before you read

Before each article, there is an exercise to use as a warmer that helps students to focus on the vocabulary of the article and prepares them for it. This can be done in pairs or small groups, with each group then reporting its answers to the whole class.

Reading

If using the articles in class, it is a good idea to treat different sections in different ways, for example reading the first paragraph with the whole class, and then getting students to work in pairs on the following paragraphs. If you're short of time, get different pairs to read different sections of the article simultaneously. You can circulate, monitor and give help where necessary. Students then report back to the whole group with a succinct summary and/or their answers to the questions for that section. A full answer key follows the articles.

Discussion

In the Over to you sections following each article, there are discussion points. These can be dealt with by the whole class, or the class can be divided, with different groups discussing different points. During discussion, circulate, monitor and give help where necessary. Students then report back to the whole class. Praise good language production and work on areas for improvement in the usual way.

Writing

The discussion points can also form the basis for short pieces of written work. Students will find this easier if they have already discussed the points in class, but you can ask students to read the article and write about the discussion points as homework.

STORE BRANDS

Before you read

Do you buy store brands (ones owned by the chain store selling them) when food shopping? Why? / Why not?

Reading

Read this article from the *Financial Times* and answer the questions.

FT

LEVEL OF DIFFICULTY ● ● ○

Real chief says own brand is the way ahead

by Gerrit Wiesmann in Neuss, Germany

Joël Saveuse walks across the Real hypermarket in northern Germany in search of 'those little biscuits'. Moving from toys to the freezer section, the 55-year-old, who runs the country's biggest food retailer, finds what he is looking for in aisle 45. 'This is my favourite product,' Mr Saveuse says, holding a packet of chocolate-filled Mini Double Biscuits. 'Look, here's a simple picture of the contents,' he says as his finger moves across the packaging, 'and top left is the "Real Quality" logo.'

Together with a handful of rivals, the Frenchman is starting a small revolution in Germany by replacing its different in-house brands with a single own brand that links the retailer with a product range. The aim is to raise in-house brand sales from 15 per cent up to 25 per cent of food sales in two to three years' time. Mr Saveuse says that customers get top quality for at least 15 per cent less than they would pay for a name brand – and Real gets a better profit margin.

Such logic has seen Real's foreign rivals push true own-brand lines for decades. Real reckons up to 60 per cent of Tesco's UK sales come from its three Tesco brands, and Carrefour is aiming for a 30-per-cent quota, up from 25 per cent now.

After working on the concept for the last year, Real introduced 850 Real Quality items this September – coincidental but 'absolutely perfect timing' for the economic downturn that followed the banking crisis, the Real head says. Although Mr Saveuse says that shopping habits at Real have not yet been affected by economic woes, he stresses that next year could see shoppers buying more own brands as they look for more value for money. 'Crisis doesn't just bring disadvantages,' he says.

Given the power of own brands in good times and bad, it is surprising that German retailers only launched distinctive lines last year. The cause lies with Germany's powerful discounters. Aldi and Lidl have in the past generation helped corner 40 per cent of the food retail market – as against 6 per cent in the UK – by selling little else than a small range of own brands, a move copied by Real, with, say, its low-cost 'Tip' range.

'But we're internationalising now,' Mr Saveuse says. 'In Poland and Turkey, we're competing against Carrefour and Tesco, in Russia and Romania against Carrefour – that has forced us to focus on true own-brand as a way of building our presence.' Strengthening the Real brand is key to reviving the chain. A format held back by discounters, Mr Saveuse reckons the German hypermarket has a future. He should know. Until 2005, he was second-in-command at hypermarket pioneer Carrefour.

1 **Look through the whole article to find the following information about Joël Saveuse.**

  a) His nationality

  b) His age

  c) His job

  d) The organisation that he worked for before

2 **What two phrases are used in paragraph 2 for a brand owned by the store selling it?**

3 **Use information from the first three paragraphs to complete the table. If the information is not given, write *not given*.**

	Real	Tesco (UK)	Carrefour
Percentage of own-brand food products now			
Company's objective for percentage of its own-brand food products in its shops in 2–3 years from now			
Typical price of a store-brand product as a percentage of the price of a name brand for the same type of product			

4 **Match the words to make expressions from paragraphs 4 and 5.**

1	banking	a)	downturn
2	economic	b)	habits
3	perfect	c)	timing
4	shopping	d)	discounters
5	economic	e)	crisis
6	powerful	f)	woes

5 **Match the expressions in Exercise 4 to their meanings.**

  i) retail organisations that sell cheap products and have a lot of influence on the market

  ii) where, when, how, etc. people usually buy things

  iii) when financial institutions were in extreme difficulty

  iv) when the time to do something is just right

  v) when sales, profits, etc. go down

  vi) when the economy is in difficulties

6 **Why have own brands not been as important in Germany as elsewhere? (paragraph 5)**

Over to you 1

In your experience, are own brands less good than name brands for these products?

- food
- cleaning products
- over the counter medicines (e.g. aspirin)

Over to you 2

Do name brands have a future in the face of store brands in your country? Why? / Why not?

BRAND LOYALTY IN CHINA

Before you read

Are you loyal to particular brands? Or are brands not important to you?

Reading

Read this article from the *Financial Times* and answer the questions.

FT

LEVEL OF DIFFICULTY ● ● ○

TEXT BANK

Chinese shoppers focus more on prices

by Patti Waldmeir in Shanghai

Chinese consumers are becoming more price-conscious, less brand-loyal and generally harder to please, according to a McKinsey survey that suggests competitive pressures are increasing in the Chinese consumer goods market. The report comes at a time when many multinational companies are counting on strong Chinese domestic demand to make up for global economic weakness.

Last month, retail sales in China grew by 23 per cent year-on-year, and consumer activity remains 'buoyant', despite signs of a slowdown in sales of some items such as cars, says Jing Ulrich of JP Morgan Securities. But consumer-goods companies will have to work harder to satisfy 'increasingly sophisticated' Chinese consumers, the report says. 'This is not an easy market,' says Max Magni of McKinsey in Shanghai, one of the authors.

'China is still a gold mine, but now there are thousands and thousands of miners that have discovered it.' The conventional wisdom that Chinese consumers are more brand-driven than shoppers in more developed markets remains true. 'But the importance of brands, and brand loyalty specifically, is falling as the choices facing consumers multiply,' the report said. Chinese shoppers are markedly more value conscious than last year, and loyalty to particular brands is declining: the proportion of consumers who said they would continue to buy their existing food and beverage brand has halved.

But the weakening of brand loyalty could be good news for foreign companies, the report says, because shoppers are less nationalistic in choosing a brand: a small majority of those surveyed showed no clear preference for brand origin. And premium brands could also benefit from a willingness to pay more for high-end products. The top 15 per cent of consumers will pay 60 per cent more for high-end consumer electronics and 300 per cent more for some personal care products.

If the trend continues, 'it will lead to the kind of polarised consumption patterns familiar in the West', between 'no-frills' goods and high-end products, the report says. Companies should compete at one or both ends of the market but avoid being stuck in the middle, it advises. Companies needed to differentiate more between regions too, the report says, noting that the traditional marketing strategy of classifying consumers by the size of the city they live in may no longer work.

1 Read paragraphs 1 and 2 and decide if these statements are true or false.

a) Competition in the Chinese consumer-goods market is weakening.

b) Multinationals are relying on sales in China to make up for lower sales elsewhere.

c) Sales of consumer goods in China are increasing for all types of product.

d) Max Magni compares China to a gold mine.

e) He says that sellers of consumer goods in China will find it easier to make money in the future.

2 Find expressions from paragraphs 3 and 4 that mean the following.

a) generally accepted ideas

b) influenced by brands

c) when someone buys the same brand each time

d) aware of value for money

e) putting one's country first

f) the most expensive and prestigious

g) top-of-the-range

3 Complete the definitions of the expressions in italics from paragraphs 4 and 5 by choosing the correct alternative.

a) The *origin* (line 54) of a brand is ...
   i)   who buys it.
   ii) where it comes from.
   iii) who sells it.

b) An example of *consumer electronics* (lines 59–60) is ...
   i)   TV sets.
   ii) furniture.
   iii) household goods.

c) An example of a *personal care product* (line 61) is ...
   i)   washing powder.
   ii) clothing.
   iii) cosmetics.

d) If a situation is *polarised* (line 63), it has ...
   i)   no extremes.
   ii) two extremes.
   iii) three extremes.

e) *No-frills* (line 65) products ...
   i)   have lots of special features.
   ii) are basic and cost less.
   iii) cost more than other products.

f) If a company is *stuck in the middle* (lines 69–70), it ...
   i)   makes lots of money from the mid-market.
   ii) can't move to more profitable areas.
   iii) doesn't serve any part of the market very well.

g) If a company *differentiates* (line 71) between different regions, it ...
   i)   treats them differently.
   ii) treats them the same.
   iii) treats them indifferently.

4 Items a)–e) are short summaries of the paragraphs in the article. Put the summaries in the correct order.

a) High demand, but consumers more sophisticated and competition very strong

b) Trends for the future in two areas

c) Main findings of a McKinsey report on brand loyalty in China

d) Brand loyalty falling, but good outlook for expensive brands

e) Brand loyalty falling and consumers more price-conscious

Over to you 1

What are the current consumer trends in your country? Are consumers becoming more price-conscious, or is brand loyalty more important?

Over to you 2

Describe some of the regional differences in consumer tastes and behaviour in your country.

TEXT BANK

BUILDING HOTELS FAST

Before you read
Would you stay in a hotel made of modified shipping containers?
Why? /Why not?

Reading
Read this article from the *Financial Times* and answer the questions.

FT

LEVEL OF DIFFICULTY ● ● ○

Hotel changes the landscape of building

by Robert Cookson

The biggest hotel to be constructed from shipping containers opens in London this week. Travelodge, the budget hotel chain, imported the containers from China – complete with bathrooms, plastering and air conditioning units – then stacked them into a 300-room hotel near Heathrow in just three weeks. The steel modules are made by Verbus Systems, a London-based company that designs, manufactures and supplies what it calls a 'Lego kit' for developers.

'Our proposition is absolutely unique,' Paul Rollett, director of Verbus, says. Verbus supplies oversized shipping containers – as much as five metres wide – that are strong enough to build high-rise buildings anywhere in the world. It has provided a developer in Liverpool with two modules that came fully finished, with pillows on the beds.

For medium-sized hotels – those with more than 200 rooms and six storeys – Verbus claims its modules are up to 20 per cent cheaper and 50 per cent faster than traditional building systems. 'It cannot be beaten,' says Mr Rollett. The Heathrow Travelodge took 58 weeks from start to finish – 16 weeks faster than a conventional build would have been. During one evening, an entire floor of 60 rooms was lifted into place in three hours.

Travelodge plans to expand aggressively over the next decade and expects to use containers in many of its larger hotels. The containers can be stacked 17 storeys high without the need for additional support. They can also be recycled. 'We could unbolt this building, take it down, refurbish the rooms and move it to Sydney,' Mr Rollett says.

It remains to be seen whether developers will break with convention and adopt steel modules over bricks, concrete and timber en masse. But Mr Rollett argues that containers are the most reliable option, as well as the cheapest, especially in extreme environments.

He cites Canada, where construction must be rapid because of permafrost; west Africa, 'where you can't build timber-frame hotels because the termites eat them'; and the United Arab Emirates, where cities are springing up in the desert.

The future imagined by Mr Rollett, with buildings worldwide made from identical metal blocks, would require a profound shake-up of the established order and, in its most extreme form, would cause nightmares for traditional builders and architects. But as Mr Rollett says, industrialisation is a powerful force. 'If Henry Ford in 1903 had started making houses and not cars, the world would be a completely different place. I just can't understand why buildings aren't made in factories.'

1 Look through the first four paragraphs and match the figures to the things that they refer to.

1	3	a)	the number of rooms in a new Travelodge near Heathrow
2	5	b)	the number of weeks saved on building the Heathrow Travelodge
3	16	c)	the number of storeys that can be built without additional support using the system
4	17	d)	the width in metres of some shipping containers
5	20	e)	the percentage by which Verbus's buildings can be built faster than others
6	50	f)	the number of weeks it took to stack the containers to build the Heathrow Travelodge
7	60	g)	the percentage by which Verbus's building system is cheaper than others
8	300	h)	the number of rooms on one hotel floor that was lifted into place in one evening

2 Find the answers to these questions in paragraphs 1 and 2.
   a) Where are the containers made?
   b) What do they come with?
   c) Is there another supplier for this system?
   d) Are there limits as to where it can be used?
   e) Can they be delivered fully finished and equipped?

3 Give the infinitive form of verbs in paragraphs 4 and 5 that mean the following.
   a) start using
   b) make bigger
   c) take from one place to another
   d) use again
   e) improve something to its original state
   f) pile one on another
   g) take apart

4 Find expressions in paragraphs 5 and 6 to complete these statements.
   a) Places where the climate is very hot or cold have ....
   b) If you start to doing something in a new way, you ....
   c) If people or organisations start doing something in large numbers, they do it ....
   d) The best way of doing something is ....
   e) If houses or towns start to be built quickly in a place where there were none before, they .... there.
   f) If it's too early to say definitely if something will happen, you can say ....

5 Find the answers to these questions in paragraphs 6 and 7. Start your answers with *Because* ...
   a) Why must buildings go up very quickly in Canada?
   b) Why are wood-frame buildings unsuitable for Africa?
   c) Why is Verbus suitable for the United Arab Emirates?
   d) Why will it not be easy to change traditional building methods around the world?
   e) Why is Paul Rollett optimistic about his vision of for the future?

Over to you 1

'If Henry Ford in 1903 had started making houses and not cars, the world would be a completely different place. I just can't understand why buildings aren't made in factories.' Do you agree? Why? / Why not?

Over to you 2

Go back to the answer you gave in Before you read on page 118. Would it still be the same? Why? / Why not?

TEXT BANK

VIDEOCONFERENCING

Before you read

Do you consider the environmental effects of travel when planning:

a) business trips?

b) private trips and holidays?

Why? / Why not?

Reading

Read this article from the *Financial Times* and answer the questions.

LEVEL OF DIFFICULTY ● ● ●

TEXT BANK

Reluctant users slow to take up videoconferencing

by Danny Bradbury

The public relations executive was enthusiastic on the phone. The IT company he represented had started installing green data centres and energy-efficient computers. Would I like to fly to California to see for myself? That would be a 2,500-mile round trip from my home in midwestern Canada. According to the online calculator from Terapass, the trip would release 1,132 pounds (about 500 kilos) of CO_2 into the atmosphere. 'If you're really into green technology, couldn't we do a videoconference instead?' I asked. 'Sure,' said the PR person. 'We are totally into green issues.' He promised to arrange it. Months later, nothing had happened.

The high-tech industry is quick to praise the benefits of flexible communication, but videoconferencing is one area where things have failed to live up to the hype. 'Videoconferencing has not significantly displaced travel,' says Frank Modruson, CIO for global technology consulting firm Accenture. As the IT sector continues to push its green values, this mismatch between rhetoric and reality is becoming harder to ignore. So why are relatively few people using videoconferencing?

Andrew Davis, managing partner at online collaboration market research firm Wainhouse, says the technology is let down by usability. For many people, videoconferences are just too difficult to set up. This is why Nortel is emphasising the services side. 'The barrier isn't the technology. It's the services around that technology,' says Dean Fernandes, the company's General Manager of Network Services.

Nortel is one of several companies getting into a relatively new segment of the videoconferencing market called telepresence. Specially equipped rooms enable people to appear as if they are sitting across the table, with life-size video representations of remote colleagues in high-definition video. Customers pay to use Nortel's facilities, which can also handle video filming, enabling the room to double as a production facility for corporate TV, for example. Nortel will also handle post-production tasks such as editing. Accenture, on the other hand, opted for the capital investment route. Mr Modruson said it is installing telepresence systems, creating rooms in Chicago and Frankfurt, and hopes to roll out another 11 cities in the next few months.

1 Look through the whole article and match the people to their jobs.

1	the writer of the article	a)	Chief Information Officer, Accenture
2	the public relations executive	b)	a partner at Wainhouse, a market research firm
3	Frank Modruson	c)	a journalist interested in environmental issues
4	Andrew Davis	d)	someone representing an IT firm

2 Choose the best summary of the first paragraph, a or b.

a) An IT company said it was developing environmentally friendly services. The writer asked its public relations representatives to organise a videoconference in order to talk about its latest services, but nothing happened. Perhaps this was because it was too complicated to arrange.

b) Videoconferences are good in theory, but it's better to travel to see someone, even if the environmental cost is high, as nothing can replace face-to-face communication.

3 Look at the expressions in italic. True or false?

If ...

a) something does not *live up to the hype* (lines 25–26), reality is just as good as what people say about it.

b) something *displaces* (line 27) something else, they both exist together.

c) someone *pushes* (line 31) a particular idea, they encourage people to believe in it, use it, etc.

d) there is a *mismatch between rhetoric and reality* (lines 32–33), people don't do what they say they do.

e) you are *let down by the usability* (lines 40–41) of something, you can rely on it.

f) something is *difficult to set up* (line 43), it is hard to arrange.

g) you *emphasise* (line 44) something, you say that it is important.

h) there is a *barrier* (line 45) to using something, it is easy to use.

4 Match the two parts of these expressions from paragraph 4.

1	corporate	a)	representations
2	high-definition	b)	tasks
3	life-size video	c)	video
4	post-production	d)	facility
5	production	e)	colleagues
6	remote	f)	market
7	videoconferencing	g)	TV

5 Now match the expressions in Excerise 4 to their meanings.

i) people in your company who work in another place

ii) electronic pictures of people that are as big as in real life

iii) the things that have to be done on a film before it can be shown

iv) the place where the things in iii, above, are carried out

v) very high-quality electronic pictures

vi) the organisations that might use this sort of system and similar systems

vii) television programmes made and shown within an organisation

Over to you 1

Would you like to talk to a life-size video representation of a colleague sitting opposite you across the table instead of going to see them face to face?
Why? / Why not?

Over to you 2

Have you tried using a webcam camera and microphone on a PC to talk to friends or colleagues? If so, describe the experience. If not, what do you think it would be like?

TEXT BANK

THE INEVITABILITY OF CHANGE

Before you read

Do you find it easy to make changes in:

a) your personal life?

b) your professional life?

Give some examples.

Reading

Read this book review from the *Financial Times* and answer the questions.

FT

LEVEL OF DIFFICULTY ● ● ○

Changeability

by Morgan Witzel

Why Some Companies are Ready for Change – and Others Aren't
(by Michael Jarrett; published by Pearson Education)

'Change is inevitable,' said British prime minister Benjamin Disraeli in 1867. 'In a progressive country, change is constant.' In his new book, Michael Jarrett puts it another way: 'Change is inevitable, like death and taxes.' And, just as we fear death and taxes, many of us fear change. We hope that if we resist for long enough, the need for it will go away and we can carry on as before. But even when companies accept the need for change and set out to achieve it, they often fail. Jarrett, an expert in organisational behaviour at London Business School, believes that 70 per cent of all change-management programmes fail.

Why? Jarrett argues that managers often mistake the nature of change. They see it as something logical that can be solved using step-by-step approaches. They are wrong. 'There is no simple recipe for organisational change,' he says. 'There is no one single way that will deliver change.' But there are some basic principles that most managers can adopt. First, they need to make certain that the internal organisation is in a position to make changes and that people support them fully. Second, they need to make sure that they understand the environment around them.

In other words, rather than developing change-management strategies, companies should first find out whether they are capable of change at all. Do their internal systems and culture support change? If not, these too must change. 'Readiness for change' is far more important than actual planning or implementation, says Jarrett. To all the various words that have already been coined in order to describe this state of readiness, such as 'flexibility' and 'adaptability', Jarrett adds another: 'changeability'. He de-

fines this as 'the sum of leadership, internal routines and organisational capabilities that make companies ready for change'.

A few years ago, for instance, McDonald's Europe faced declining sales and market share. Denis Hennequin, the new president, redesigned restaurants to make them more appealing and began sourcing food locally. Market share and profits rose. Dell, too, aware that its competitors were beginning to catch up with its original low-price model, embarked on a programme of market research. The information it gathered was analysed with a view to spotting emerging and future customer needs. The most dangerous state for a business, says Jarrett, is the steady state. Companies that resist change – he cites the pharmaceutical industry – run a greater risk of failure.

1 **Look through the whole article and answer these questions.**

a) Who is Michael Jarrett?

b) What is:

   i) his subject?

   ii) his speciality?

2 **Look at how the expressions in italic are used in the article. True or false?**

a) A *progressive country* (lines 3–4) is one where people are willing to adapt and change.

b) If something is *constant* (line 4), it happens only sometimes.

c) If something is *inevitable* (line 7), you can avoid it.

d) If you *resist* (line 10) something, you do it.

e) If you *carry on* (lines 12–13) doing something, you continue to do it.

f) If you *set out* (line 15) to do something, you finish doing it.

g) If you *achieve* (line 15) something, you reach a particular objective.

h) If you *fail* (line 16) to do something, you succeed.

3 **Find expressions in paragraph 2 that mean the following.**

a) reasonable and sensible (1 word)

b) an easy series of instructions, used for example in cooking (2 words)

c) ways of doing things one at a time (4 words)

d) a unique method (3 words)

e) the most important ideas, etc., about something (2 words)

f) the structure of a company, department, etc., rather than the way it relates to the outside world (2 words)

g) the outside world (1 word)

4 **Complete the table with words from paragraph 3. (Complete the last line of the table with two words, both from the same part of the article, that are related in the same way.)**

adjective	noun
adaptable	……… a)
changeable	……… b)
flexible	……… c)
……… d)	organisation
ready	……… e)
……… f)	……… g)

5 **Which of the words above has Michael Jarrett added to discussion about change? What meaning does he give it?**

6 **Complete the table with information from paragraph 4. If there is no information for a particular point, write *not given*.**

company	president	problems	change	results

7 **Which industry is Michael Jarrett pessimistic about in relation to its attitude to change?**

8 **Items a)–d) are short summaries of the paragraphs in the article. Put the summaries in the correct order.**

a) Examples and counter-examples

b) Mistaken ideas about change

c) Readiness for change

d) The inevitability of the need for change

Over to you 1

How do you rate your own organisation (school or company) on its changeability on a scale of 1 to 10 in relation to other similar organisations?

Over to you 2

Describe some actual examples of change (or resistance to it!) in your organisation, how they were put into action, and what their results were.

TEXT BANK

MANAGING CHANGE SUCCESSFULLY

Before you read

What is the reputation of the legal profession in your country in terms of its attitude to change?

Reading

This article from the *Financial Times* is about a competition to find the best ways of introducing change in the management of law firms. Read the article and answer the questions.

FT

LEVEL OF DIFFICULTY ● ● ●

TEXT BANK

Law firms get into shape

by Laura Empson

Until quite recently, even the largest UK-based law firms were fairly loose organisations where partners had considerable personal
5 autonomy. When important management decisions needed to be made, the partners could rely on their shared educational and social backgrounds and their
10 long years of working together to help them reach a common understanding of what needed to be done. This represented the 'glue' that held the firms together.
15 This glue does not work properly any more. In the past 10 years, the leading law firms have expanded rapidly and have grown to accommodate different
20 kinds of lawyers, doing different kinds of work in different ways, with different expectations of their careers and their firms.

Law firms have responded
25 to the challenge by developing and implementing more explicit methods of management that can accommodate this new-found complexity. Senior managers
30 have introduced a range of new management systems and structures and have expanded the teams of business services staff to support these initiatives.

35 All of these schemes, while necessary steps on the road to professionalised management, have challenged the traditional bonds that have held these
40 partnerships together. Five to 10 years ago, even the largest law firms were no more than adolescents in the area of management, with
45 ambitious ideas about their futures and vast amounts of energy but very limited expertise in developing and executing systematic, long-term strategies.
50 In spite of (or perhaps because of) this, the leading law firms have been extremely successful. They have made plenty of mistakes, but have
55 expanded at a phenomenal pace while maintaining profitability.

These firms have not simply grown – they have grown up.

The successful entries in the
60 competition this year represent a wide variety of initiatives, showing increasing sophistication. Some entries relate to current hot topics in law-firm management.
65 For example: market entry strategy in China (Lovells); retaining and promoting women lawyers (Latham & Watkins); and new models of
70 service delivery (iLaw).

And lastly, spare a thought for the partners of Baker & McKenzie on their 'Fit for Life' programme. The firm has
75 introduced a scheme to help its lawyers perform at their best, including a complete review of their well-being – emotionally, physically and mentally. While
80 all law firms must be aware of the need to get into shape to survive the tough times ahead, Baker & McKenzie seem to have taken the advice literally.

1 **Read paragraphs 1 and 2 and decide if these statements are true or false.**

a) Until recently, UK law firms were highly structured.

b) Each partner had a lot of independence.

c) Partners made management decisions by bringing in outside consultants.

d) Partners found it difficult to take decisions because they came from different backgrounds and did not understand each other.

e) The 'glue' that held firms together refers to the shared values of the people working there.

f) Law firms have grown quite slowly in the last decade.

g) People working for law firms are now looking for different things in their careers.

2 **Match the verbs with the nouns that they go with in paragraph 3.**

1	respond to	a)	complexity
2	implement	b)	new management systems
3	accommodate	c)	a challenge
4	introduce	d)	initiatives
5	expand	e)	methods of management
6	support	f)	teams of business services staff

3 **Now use the verbs 1–6 from Exercise 2 to complete these definitions.**

If you …

a) .... something, you bring it into use for the first time.

b) .... something difficult, you are able to deal with it.

c) .... something, you make it bigger.

d) .... something, you help it.

e) .... something, you do something as a reaction to it.

f) .... something, you put it into action.

4 **Find adjectives in paragraphs 4 and 5 that mean the following.**

a) done in a proper, serious way (16 letters)

b) done in a structured way (10 letters)

c) done in the old way (11 letters)

d) determined to be successful (9 letters)

e) very big (4 letters)

f) designed to last well into the future (4 letters, 4 letters)

g) extremely fast (10 letters)

h) the biggest and most successful (7 letters)

5 **Why are law firms described as *adolescents* in line 43?**

6 **Which of these examples of change management are *not* mentioned among the competition entries?**

a) promoting people from ethnic minorities

b) promoting women

c) introducing flexible ways of working

d) offering years off for study and personal development

e) finding ways of getting into new markets

f) finding new ways of providing services

7 **Baker & McKenzie *seem to have taken the advice* (on complete emotional, physical and mental well-being) *literally* (lines 83–84). Which of these alternatives is the most probable explanation for the author writing this? She's suggesting that the firm …**

a) does not really believe in its initiative, even if it pretends to and carries out a lot of activities that are not really useful.

b) is doing something (perhaps something not mentioned here) that shows they are taking ideas on change management too far.

c) has not taken ideas on change management far enough, despite putting a number of measures into action.

Over to you 1

Imagine a competition in your company or industry, or one you would like to work for, to find the best initiative in change management. Who would win, and what would these initiatives be?

Over to you 2

Is it the job of organisations to take care of their employees' complete emotional, physical and mental well-being? Why? / Why not?

TEXT BANK

COLLECTIVE INTELLIGENCE

Before you read
Will large companies still exist 100 years from now? Why? / Why not?

Reading
Read this article from the *Financial Times* and answer the questions.

FT

LEVEL OF DIFFICULTY ● ● ●

Looking to Wikipedia for answers
by Thomas Malone

To understand how large-scale work was organised during the past 100 years, the best models were traditional hierarchical organisations such as General Motors, IBM and Wal-Mart. But to understand how large-scale work will be organised in the future, we need to look at newer examples such as Wikipedia, eBay and Google.

In Wikipedia, for instance, thousands of people from across the globe have collectively created a large and surprisingly high-quality intellectual product – the world's largest encyclopaedia – and have done so with almost no centralised control. Anyone who wants to can change almost anything, and decisions about what changes are kept are made by a loose consensus of those who care. Wikipedia is a remarkable organisational invention that illustrates how new forms of communication, such as the Internet, are making it possible to organise work in new and innovative ways.

Of course, new ways of organising work are not desirable everywhere. In many cases, traditional hierarchies are still needed to capture economies of scale or to control risks. But in an increasing number of cases, we can have the economic benefits of large organisations without giving up the human benefits of small ones – freedom, flexibility, motivation and creativity.

These human benefits can provide decisive competitive advantages in knowledge-based and innovation-driven work. During the coming decades, we can expect to see such ideas in operation in more and more parts of the economy. These new practices have various names, but the phrase I find most useful is 'collective intelligence'.

What if we could have any number of people and computers connected to, for instance, care for patients in a hospital? Or designing cars. Or selling retail products. We might find that the best way to do a task that today is done by five full-time people would be to use one part-time employee and a host of freelance contractors each working for a few minutes a day.

One important type of collective intelligence is 'crowd intelligence', where anyone who wants to can contribute. Sometimes, as in the case of Wikipedia or video-sharing website YouTube, people contribute their work for free because they get other benefits such as enjoyment, recognition or opportunities to socialise with others. In other cases, such as online retailer eBay, people get paid to do so.

These changes will not happen overnight, but the rate of change is accelerating, and businesspeople a hundred years from now may find the pervasive corporate hierarchies of today as quaint as we find the feudal farming system of an earlier era.

TEXT BANK

1 Look through the whole article and find:

a) three traditional companies.

b) four Internet companies.

2 Read paragraph 2 and decide if these statements are true or false.

Wikipedia ...

a) entries can only be changed by the person who wrote them.

b) has no central control at all.

c) is the largest encyclopaedia in the world.

d) is of high quality.

e) copies existing ways of working.

3 Look at paragraph 3 and find:

a) two benefits of large organisations.

b) four benefits of small ones.

4 Now match the expressions in Exercise 3 to their definitions.

a) when people have new ideas

b) the ability to work 'as your own boss'

c) to limit the effect of unexpected events

d) when people work with enthusiasm and a sense of purpose

e) the ability to work when and where you want to

f) when high levels of production result in lower costs per unit produced

5 Read paragraph 4. In which areas will the benefits of small organisations be most useful?

6 Find the name the writer prefers for this new way of working in paragraph 4.

7 Which of these areas is *not* mentioned in paragraph 5 in relation to the potential application of collective intelligence?

a) healthcare   b) wholesale   c) retail   d) design

8 What three benefits do people get from contributing to crowd intelligence websites, apart from money? (paragraph 6)

9 Use correct forms of expressions from paragraph 7 to complete these statements.

a) If something exists in a lot of different places, it is ....

b) A social system with aristocrats and almost powerless farmers is ....

c) If something doesn't happen immediately, it doesn't happen ....

d) Something that is strange and old-fashioned is ....

e) If a process speeds up, it ....

Over to you 1

Do you share the writer's optimism about the potential of collective intelligence? Why? / Why not?

Over to you 2

Could collective intelligence be used in your own industry, or one that you would like to work in?

INSIDERS AND OUTSIDERS

Before you read

Some organisations recruit graduates and prepare them over time for senior positions, rather than recruiting senior managers directly from outside. What are the benefits and disadvantages for organisations of this approach?

Reading

Read this article from the *Financial Times* and answer the questions.

FT

LEVEL OF DIFFICULTY ● ● ○

Graduate recruitment

by Stephen Overell

It is part of the mythology of the modern world of work that the days when it was possible to enter a big company as a graduate
5 fresh from college and stay there for 20 years, provided one was not incompetent, are long gone and will never return. Today, the world changes too fast, it is
10 sometimes alleged. People are more likely to hop between jobs. How reassuring, then, to learn that many big companies are still keen to catch graduates young,
15 shape them over a long period and turn them into executives.

At AstraZeneca, the pharmaceuticals company, graduates can choose between
20 several different specialist schemes, such as in engineering, finance and product strategy. At any one time, 15 people are on a three-year course working
25 towards qualifications as chartered management accountants. The explicit intention, says David Powell, Audit Director for Global Operations who manages the

30 scheme within the company, is to 'bring people on to be future finance directors and finance vice-presidents'.

Could the company not
35 recruit qualified management accountants on the open market? Mr Powell says it could and sometimes does. But he argues that the virtue of a formal
40 graduate scheme is that trainees experience life in different business units during the training and acquire contacts which serve them well in the future.

45 Paul Farrer, Chief Executive of the Graduate Recruitment Company, a division of recruitment company PFJ, notes that graduate management
50 trainee-schemes are heavily over-subscribed by applicants because they understand the nature of the future marked out for them if they are successful; every
55 position has about 30 applicants. During their time on a management scheme, graduates will be rotated through various business units, get

access to high-profile people in
60 the organisation, gain broad skills and be handed opportunities to work their way up. 'Organisations are hoping to get their CEOs of the future from these
65 schemes,' he says. That is not to say they don't also recruit outside them, but, for people who come in from outside, there is less certainty, less of a definite
70 future within the company.

With graduate trainees, the aim is to turn them into business unit managers in seven or eight years. Organisations
75 differ widely in how successful they are in this aim.

At the top of the retention league are employers in the public sector, information
80 technology and oil. At the bottom are construction and retail companies. Some employers manage to lose half their graduate intake in the first year.

1 Look through the whole article to find the names of the following.

a) an employer of graduates
b) someone who works there, and their job
c) a recruitment organisation
d) the group of which that recruitment organisation is a part
e) its Chief Executive

2 Choose the alternative with the closest meaning to the expression in italic.

a) It is part of the *mythology* of the modern world of work ... (lines 1–2)
  i) ideas about ancient Greece and Rome
  ii) ideas that may or may not be true
  iii) ideas that are interesting
b) ... that the days when it was possible to enter a big company as a graduate fresh from *college* and stay there for 20 years, ... (lines 2–6)
  i) secondary school
  ii) postgraduate institution
  iii) university or equivalent
c) ... provided one was not *incompetent*, are long gone and will never return. (lines 6–8)
  i) unable to do one's job
  ii) skilled at doing one's job
  iii) overqualified for one's job
d) Today, the world changes too fast, it is sometimes *alleged*. (lines 8–10)
  i) accused   ii) claimed   iii) denied
e) People are more likely to *hop between jobs*. (lines 10–11)
  i) change jobs frequently
  ii) change jobs infrequently
  iii) never change jobs
f) How *reassuring*, then, to learn that many big companies ... (lines 12–13)
  i) sad to know   ii) good to know
  iii) uninteresting to know
g) ... *are still keen to* catch graduates young, shape them over a long period, and turn them into executives. (lines 13–16)
  i) are still unwilling to
  ii) are still undecided about   iii) still want to

3 Read paragraphs 2 and 3 and decide if these statements are true or false.

The three year course ...
a) takes place in a company that produces drugs and medicines.
b) is part of the specialist scheme in engineering.
c) leads to a professional qualification that is recognised outside the company.
d) is managed by someone who only deals with the UK.
e) is designed to produce senior managers in the future, but this is not stated anywhere.
f) produces all the senior managers that the company needs.
g) gives trainees experience in working in different parts of the company.
h) allows trainees to meet people whom it will be useful for them to know later.

4 Complete these statements with expressions from paragraphs 4 to 6.

a) In-company programmes for graduate development are referred to here as *graduate management trainee* .... (1 word)
b) If too many people apply to be on a programme like this, it is ....-...................... . (1 word)
c) The people who want to participate in these programmes are referred to as .... (1 word)
d) If what you are expected to do is planned beforehand, it is .... for you. (2 words)
e) If you are given different jobs to do, you are .... them. (2 words)
f) If you get general abilities, useful in different parts of the organisation, you .... (3 words)
g) If someone, thanks to their own efforts, is promoted to increasingly senior jobs in an organisation, they .... their way .... (2 words)
h) People not recruited for a job from within an organisation .... (4 words)
i) A list of companies and how good they are at keeping graduate recruits is referred to as the .... (2 words)
j) People working for the state are in the .... (2 words)
k) The number of people who join a company straight from college in a particular year is its .... (2 words)

5 Which statement best summarises the article? Choose the correct alternative.

a) Companies' graduate schemes for recruiting people who will become senior managers are becoming rarer and will eventually disappear.
b) Organisations often combine graduate schemes with recruitment from outside, and the outside recruits feel just as certain of their place there.
c) Despite what many people think, some organisations still have graduate schemes for recruiting people who will become senior managers.

Over to you 1
How good is your organisation, or one you would like to work for, at keeping its graduate recruits?

Over to you 2
'... for people who come in from outside, there is less certainty, less of a definite future within the company.' Is this true of your organisation, or one you would like to work for?

INTERNET ADVERTISING

Before you read

Do you look at advertising on the Internet or do you ignore it? Why?

Reading

Read this article from the *Financial Times* and answer the questions.

FT

LEVEL OF DIFFICULTY ● ● ○

TEXT BANK

Advertisers try the soft sell as TV drifts online

by Joshua Chaffin

Visitors to Hulu, the online video site jointly owned by NBC Universal and News Corp, can do something that television viewers would never have imagined just a few years ago: choose their own advertising. When, for example, an advertisement sponsored by a carmaker pops up, viewers might be asked to click on a sports car, a pick-up truck or a family sedan, depending on their preference, and watch a corresponding message. (Skipping past, unfortunately, is not an option.) 'It's choose-your-own-adventure advertising,' says Jean-Paul Colaco, Hulu's Senior Vice-President of Advertising, who is hoping to reduce the friction between audiences and marketers by making advertisements less intrusive for the former and more efficient for the latter.

The Ad Selector, as Hulu calls it, is just one example of a burst of innovation in online advertising. As audiences increasingly move to the web to consume video – be it full-length television episodes or short clips – media companies and advertising agencies are rushing to develop new and more effective advertising strategies in the hope of creating a profitable business.

They are eager to harness the interactive possibilities that differentiate the Internet from the more passive experience of traditional television. In a marketer's dream scenario, consumers who see a message for a product that interests them might pause a video, click through to a website and even make a purchase. But that same interactive power can also be a curse for marketers because it makes it easy for viewers to jump to other websites if they feel bombarded by irritating and irrelevant advertisements.

'Internet video is a lean-forward experience. The audience is watching with their hand on the mouse, ready to click away as soon as they lose interest,' says Matt Cutler, Vice-President of Visible Measures, a company that tracks online behaviour. He estimates that more than 30 per cent of consumers abandon an online video within the first 10 per cent of its stream.

Solving those problems is vital for media companies. While they were once content merely to collect clicks on their web pages, they are now desperate to retain viewers for longer periods. 'Advertisers are less interested in general impressions. They want engagement,' explains Patrick Keane, Chief Marketing Officer at CBS Interactive, promising more innovative advertising formats in the future.

1 Use the correct form of verbs from paragraphs 1 to 3 to complete these statements.

If …

a) an advertisement appears suddenly on your screen, it ....

b) you 'jump' past an advertisement without watching it, you .... it.

c) an advertiser pays for an advertisement on a website, on TV, etc., they .... it.

d) someone makes conflict, disagreement, etc. less strong, they .... it.

e) you watch video, you .... it.

f) you start something from nothing, you .... it.

g) you exploit the power of something, you .... it.

h) make something different from something else, you .... the two things.

i) you feel that you're watching too many advertisements, you feel .... by them.

2 Look at paragraphs 1 to 3 and find:

a) a noun that describes the relationship between advertisers and Internet users.

b) two adjectives that describe advertisements from the point of view of many users.

c) one adjective that describes how users relate to advertisements in a way that can be good or bad for advertisers.

d) a noun that relates to the bad effect of the adjective in c above.

3 How is the Internet experience described in relation to traditional television?

4 How quickly do nearly a third of users stop watching an Internet video on average? What do they do when this happens?

5 What, in a word, do advertisers want from users that they didn't have before? How will this be achieved?

6 Which of these statements sums up the article best?

Internet advertisers …

a) are only interested in the number of people who click on advertisements.

b) don't know how to avoid users 'clicking away' from advertisements.

c) are looking at ways of engaging users so that they do not click away from advertisements.

Over to you 1

Will Internet advertisers ever find a way of retaining the attention of users? Why? / Why not?

Over to you 2

Can you imagine clicking on an advertisement and making a purchase in one process? If so, what product or service might you buy in this way?

TEXT BANK

SHOCK ADVERTISEMENTS

Before you read

Where are pharmaceuticals (medicines) sold in your country, apart from in pharmacies or chemists? Is their sale strictly controlled?

Reading

Read this article from the *Financial Times* and answer the questions.

FT

LEVEL OF DIFFICULTY ● ● ○

Pfizer uses big screen to fight counterfeit drugs

by Andrew Jack

Pfizer, the world's largest pharmaceuticals company, has launched a hard-hitting cinema advertising campaign to warn
5   consumers of the medical dangers of counterfeits when illegally purchasing prescription medicines on the Internet. The advert, to be shown in 600 cinemas around
10 the UK, is best seen before filmgoers dig into their popcorn. It shows a middle-aged man spitting up a rat after swallowing a tablet delivered by post.

15 The campaign reflects growing safety concerns – and commercial losses for the drug industry – caused by a rise in unregulated Internet sales of medicines.

20 It also marks an extension of advertising by drug companies to raise their public profile, in spite of tight restrictions on the marketing of prescription
25 medicines to consumers.

The film contains no reference to Pfizer's medicines, but shows the corporate logo alongside that of the Medicines and
30 Healthcare Products Regulatory Agency, the UK organisation that co-ordinates an increasing number of investigations of counterfeiters. It agreed to a
35 pioneering partnership with the company.

Pfizer has raised its public image in its fight against counterfeits, warning of
40 health risks and calling for action against parallel traders.

These are the intermediaries that buy medicines abroad for resale at higher prices in the
45 UK. Pfizer argues that parallel trading risks allowing fakes into pharmacies.

But the overall level of counterfeit medicines in the
50 developed world is estimated at only about 1 per cent, with most sold via the Internet rather than through normal supply chains. A recent Pfizer poll suggested
55 10 per cent of men purchased prescription-only medicines via unregulated sources, including the Internet. Pfizer is one of the hardest hit by Internet sales
60 of medicines, since it produces a fifth of the top-selling prescription medicines in the UK by sales. The campaign, which includes a website, cost
65 nearly £500,000 ($731,000).

The cinematic rat was inspired by the discovery of rat poison in a counterfeit version of a Pfizer blood pressure drug.
70 Pfizer said the rats it used in the advert were supplied by trained specialists and not killed during filming.

1 **Look at the headline. Which of these words means the same as *counterfeit*?**

a) authentic   b) fake   c) substitute   d) similar

2 **Read paragraph 1. What is the purpose of Pfizer's campaign?**

a) To promote its products

b) To advertise popcorn

c) To dissuade people from buying drugs that may harm them

3 ***The advert ... is best seen before filmgoers dig into their popcorn.* (lines 8–11) Why?**

4 **Match the two parts to make expressions from paragraphs 2 to 4.**

1	safety	a)	sales
2	commercial	b)	restrictions
3	unregulated	c)	profile
4	public	d)	partnership
5	tight	e)	losses
6	corporate	f)	concerns
7	pioneering	g)	traders
8	parallel	h)	logo

5 **Now match the expressions in Exercise 4 to their meanings.**

i)   when unauthorised products are sold

ii)   when two organisations do something for the first time

iii) worries about the dangers of something

iv) a symbol used by a company

v)   when no profit is made in selling something

vi) strict rules

vii) unauthorised sellers

viii) the ideas that people have about an organisation

6 **Why does Pfizer object to unauthorised distributors selling its products in the UK?**

a) lost profit   b) safety   c) other reasons

7 **What do these figures refer to?**

a) 1 per cent (line 51)

b) 10 per cent (line 55)

c) a fifth (line 61)

d) 500,000 (line 65)

e) 731,000 (line 65)

8 **Why were rats used in making the advertisement?**

Over to you 1

Do you think that shock advertisements such as this work? Give your reasons.

Over to you 2

Think of other examples of parallel trading. What steps, if any, do manufacturers and retailers take to prevent them?

FINANCIAL REPORTING

Before you read

Which is the biggest retailer in your country?

Reading

Read this article from the *Financial Times* and answer the questions.

FT

LEVEL OF DIFFICULTY ● ● ○

Wal-Mart profits reach $13bn

by Jonathan Birchall

Wal-Mart, the world's largest retailer, beat expectations after its US discount stores accounted for about 50 per cent of all US retail growth last year – while its full-year global sales passed $400bn (€318bn) for the first time and profits hit $13.4bn.

Mike Duke, Chief Executive, said the fourth quarter and full-year results showed that Wal-Mart had gained 'momentum' during the year in all of its markets, in spite of the tough economic environment. 'We are doing all the right things to continue our momentum and to widen the gap between the competition and us. We finished January strong, and February is off to a good start.'

The results again underlined the retailer's ability to generate cash in a recession and to use the money to invest in its business at a time when most of its rivals are cutting back. Wal-Mart has been able to make acquisitions, concluding a $2.6bn deal in January for a controlling share of D&S, the largest retailer in Chile.

It is continuing to invest in its stores with a big remodelling programme, called Project Impact, now underway in the US. With this programme, Wal-Mart expects to significantly boost the sales per square foot of its more than 3,000 supercentres and discount stores.

Total net sales at Wal-Mart USA rose 6 per cent on the last quarter to $71.5bn, although higher than expected expenses, including healthcare costs, led to its operating income growing more slowly than sales, up 2.2 per cent to $5.4bn.

Internationally, the strong dollar weighed on earnings, with the value of sales down 8.4 per cent from the last quarter to $24.7bn and operating income down 14.3 per cent at $1.5bn. At constant currencies, international operating income would have been up 5.1 per cent and net sales up 9 per cent.

The retailer highlighted the performance of its Asda stores in the UK, which gained market share with increased customer traffic and average purchases made.

In Japan, Wal-Mart reported that comparable sales at its Seiyu stores fell 0.5 per cent from the last quarter, but were positive in November and December.

TEXT BANK

1 Match the verbs with the nouns to make expressions from paragraphs 1 to 3.

1	beat	a)	the gap
2	gain	b)	momentum
3	widen	c)	momentum
4	generate	d)	expectations
5	make	e)	cash
6	continue	f)	acquisitions

2 Now match the expressions from Exercise 1 to their meanings as they are used in the article.

i) become more successful

ii) continue success

iii) make money

iv) increase a difference in performance

v) buy other companies

vi) exceed forecasts

3 Look at paragraphs 1 to 4 and decide if these statements are true or false.

In its latest financial year, Wal-Mart …

a) performed worse than had been expected.

b) was responsible for half the growth of all US retailers.

c) had sales of more than $400 billion for the first time.

d) had profits of less than $10 billion.

e) had a better financial performance, even though the general economic conditions were not good.

f) performed better than its competitors by the same amount as before.

g) had good sales in January, but less good in February.

h) was able to buy a company in Chile only by increasing its borrowing.

i) is putting more money into its US stores.

4 Complete the information about the last three months of Wal-Mart's financial year using information from paragraphs 5 and 6.

a) International sales: $ . . . .

b) Operating income from international operations: $ . . . .

c) Increase (+)/decline (–) in international sales in dollar terms: . . . . %

d) US sales after costs: $ . . . .

e) Increase (+)/decline (–) in US operating income after costs: . . . . %

f) US operating income: $ . . . .

5 Which store chains does Wal-Mart own in the UK and Japan? How did they perform?

Over to you 1

Look at Exercise 4. Find similar information for a company you are interested in, perhaps by looking at its website.

Over to you 2

Which is the biggest retailer in your country? How is it currently performing in relation to its competitors?

SHORT SELLING

Before you read

Is it acceptable to be able to sell something that you do not own?

Reading

Read this article from the *Financial Times* and answer the questions.

Are short sellers necessary?

by William Leith

Short selling is not like making a normal investment. When you make a normal investment, you buy something, hoping it will be more desirable in the future. This type of investment – 'going long' – seems to be about optimism and hope. With short selling, you look for something that you think is going to decline in value. Then you borrow some shares in that thing. Next, you sell those shares to someone who is more optimistic, or less discerning, than you. If you're right, and the shares plummet, you can buy them back for less than you sold them. If you're wrong, and they treble in value, you're bust, because you still owe the shares to their original owner.

Imagine if I go to a shop and see a big shelf of expensive handbags. Let's say I look at these handbags for a while and come to believe they're not worth anything like the price on the label. To me, they look like rubbish handbags. So I go to the owner of the store and ask him, for a small fee, to borrow these handbags for a week. Then I take the bags out of the store and sell them to a trader for a fraction less than the price on the label. He's happy – he thinks he can make a profit.

Six days later I go to see him. I was right – the handbags were rubbish. He hasn't sold a single one. So I make a deal – I'll buy them back for half of what I sold them for. Now he's happy to get rid of them. The next day, I go back to the store and return the bags to the owner. He's happy, but maybe a little suspicious. That's short selling.

So what's actually happened? I, the short seller, have spotted that somebody is charging a lot of money for handbags that are rubbish. Next, I've found somebody who is prepared to sell any old rubbish as long as he thinks there's something in it for him.

Now, who are these short sellers? What sort of people are they likely to be? Well, they are people who see things that look good on the surface but are actually rubbish. They are people, in other words, who see the difference between the appearance and the reality. They are the first to notice when something is a con. Short sellers, in fact, reveal the problem. It was short sellers, apparently, who made people realise that Enron was a rubbish product. No, the problem is not the short sellers. It's the world of empty promises and false values that enables them to thrive. To ban them is to shoot the messenger.

1 Choose the correct alternative to complete these statements about the expressions in italic.

a) In *short selling* (line 1), you expect that the value of something will …
i) fall.   ii) stay the same.   iii) rise.

b) If you *go long* (line 6), you buy something expecting that its value will …
i) fall.   ii) stay the same.   iii) rise.

c) If someone is *optimistic* (line 14), they think the future will be …
i) worse.   ii) the same.   iii) better.

d) If someone is *discerning* (line 14), their judgement is …
i) bad.   ii) good.   iii) mistaken.

e) If the value of something *plummets* (line 16), it falls …
i) a little.   ii) an average amount.   iii) a lot.

f) If something *trebles* (line 19) in value, it is worth …
i) twice as much.
ii) three times as much.
iii) four times as much.

g) If someone is *bust* (line 20), they have …
i) made a lot of money.
ii) sold their shares in something.
iii) lost a lot of money.

2 Look at paragraphs 2 to 4 and find:

a) a noun used before another noun to say that something has very little value.

b) an expression meaning that goods are not nearly as valuable as the price shown.

c) a noun meaning an amount that someone pays for a particular service.

d) a noun referring to someone who buys and sells things.

e) an expression meaning that an amount is slightly lower than another amount.

f) an expression to emphasise that someone has not sold anything at all.

g) an expression used to talk about finding a way to 'lose' something that you no longer want.

h) an adjective describing someone who does not trust someone else.

i) an expression meaning that someone will benefit from a particular situation.

3 Which three sentences in the article sum up the purpose of the story about the handbags in the context of the whole article?

4 True, false or not mentioned in the last paragraph of the article?

Short sellers …

a) are immoral.

b) are useful because they show the real value of things.

c) were useful in revealing the Enron scandal.

d) were useful in revealing other scandals at the time of the Enron scandal.

e) are only able to do to well because people make false promises.

f) should be banned.

g) are like messengers.

Over to you 1

Go back to the answer you gave in Before you read. Is it the same now that you have read the article? Why? / Why not?

Over to you 2

Financial authorities ban the short selling of shares in some situations. Should they do this, or should short selling be allowed at all times?

TEXT BANK

THE PLACE OF ENGLISH

Before you read
What is the place of the English language in your country? How many people speak it? Who uses it?

Reading
Read this article from the *Financial Times* and answer the questions.

FT

LEVEL OF DIFFICULTY ● ● ○

The difficulties of cross-cultural communication

by William Barnes

English has frequently been compared to Latin, which flourished for centuries as an international language, even after
5 the collapse of the Roman Empire, becoming a shared resource for much of the globe. English is rapidly becoming an international lingua franca, as it becomes the
10 essential skill of any manager with ambition. It is a language that in some ways is becoming separated from its origins. One consequence is that non-native speakers may
15 be better at using English with each other than native speakers.

David Graddol, an applied linguist and consultant, observes: 'Conventional wisdom has it
20 that native speakers must be best at communicating in English. That may not be true. In fact, native speakers may be poor at using English as an international
25 language. What is more, the presence of native speakers may hinder communication within a group of non-native speakers.'

Mr Graddol says research
30 shows that, whereas intelligibility is the most important thing for non-native speakers, native speakers – who have never been challenged to acquire the ability
35 to make themselves clear to 'foreign' speakers – may struggle to overcome what may be, by international norms, their personal usage. It is likely that any manager
40 working in Asia will agree that merely speaking a common language does not amount to mutual comprehension, let alone a guarantee of trust or friendship.

45 It used to be thought in the high days of the British empire that everything worth knowing could be known in English. We are more likely to feel these days
50 that a language carries with it certain cultural baggage, ways of thinking that cannot be expressed well in another language.

A man who runs a design
55 company in Bangkok thinks that foreign-educated Thais often do not fit well into his work teams. 'They think that because they are fluent in the "global language",
60 they somehow know all the secrets of the world. In acquiring an "international" culture, they have lost some of their cultural yardsticks and consequently

65 often don't communicate as well as they think they do,' says this continental European, who has worked in Asia for more than 30 years. They are, he explains, Thais
70 who have forgotten how to switch between their social personalities.

As a first language, English has already peaked – the number of native speakers is growing, but
75 not nearly as fast as non-native speakers. There are many experts who say that the future of English is uncertain, as the economic centre of the world shifts east.

80 Nevertheless, its current global use appears as strong as ever. China alone adds 20 million to the global community of English speakers every year. Many
85 native English speakers who have worked in Asia will not necessarily accept Mr Graddol's warning about the 'native-speaker problem', while accepting
90 his idea that cross-cultural communication is a tricky thing. A matter of more than just language.

1   Look at how the expressions in italic are used. True or false?

a)   If something *flourishes* (line 3), it is successful.

b)   A *shared resource* (line 6) can only be used by one person.

c)   A *lingua franca* (line 9) is only spoken by a small number of people in one country.

d)   The *origin* (line 13) of something is where it comes from.

e)   A *native speaker* (line 16) of a language learns it as their first language.

f)   *Conventional wisdom* (line 19) consists of opinions that only a few people believe.

g)   Someone's *presence* (line 26) in a place refers to the fact that they are there.

h)   If something *hinders* (line 27) something else, it helps it.

2   Complete the table with words from paragraphs 2 and 3, and related words.

adjective	noun
.... a)	convention
present	.... b)
intelligible	.... c)
able	.... d)
.... e)	native
.... f)	person
.... g)	foreigner
comprehensible	.... h)

3   Now match the adjectives in Exercise 2 to their meanings.

a)   understandable (2 expressions)

b)   usual

c)   relating to an individual

d)   referring to someone from a particular place

e)   not from the speaker's country

f)   not absent

g)   capable

4   What is the most important point in paragraphs 1 and 2? Choose the best summary.

a)   English is like Latin, as it is now spoken everywhere and is used as a language of international communication.

b)   Most people think that native speakers are the best speakers of English, but this may not be true when considering English as a language for international communication.

c)   Some native speakers make great allowances when they speak with non-native speakers and are careful to avoid using unusual expressions.

5   Find two-word expressions in paragraphs 4 and 5 that mean the following.

a)   countries that used to belong to the UK

b)   ways of thinking that belong to a particular country, group, etc., that might not be helpful in another country, etc.

c)   a language spoken all over the world

d)   way of judging things in a particular country, group, etc.

e)   someone from Europe but not the UK or Scandinavia

f)   the way someone behaves differently depending on the context

6   What, according to someone in paragraph 5 who manages a team of them, is the problem for the members of a particular national group who speak good English?

7   Answer these questions using the words given and information from paragraphs 6 and 7 of the article. (The first one has been done for you as an example.)

Is ...

a)   the number of English speakers rising as fast as it was? – No, it *has peaked*.

b)   the centre of economic power moving? – Yes, it ....

c)   English declining as a world language? – No, its ....

d)   the number of English speakers in China rising? – Yes, it ....

e)   David Graddol right about the 'native-speaker' problem? – Not necessarily, but it's true that ....

Over to you 1

'Non-native speakers may be better at using English with each other than native speakers.' Do you agree? Why? / Why not?

Over to you 2

How long will it be before English is replaced as the world's *lingua franca*? What will replace it? Give your reasons.

TEXT BANK

TEXT BANK

LIVING AND WORKING ABROAD

Before you read

Would you find it easy to live and work in another country?
Why? / Why not?

Reading

Read this article from the *Financial Times* and answer the questions.

FT

LEVEL OF DIFFICULTY ● ● ○

Moving experiences

by Pauline Harris and Simon Kuper

I once travelled around Japan with a British friend who was living there. Each new Japanese problem – why was it impossible
5 to find any address in Tokyo? – made me want to go home. But my friend would look up from the Japanese grammar book that he carried everywhere, try to
10 understand the Japanese reasoning and then interpret it in the most generous way possible. He treated the whole country as a friend he had yet to make. I now see that he
15 was the perfect expatriate. Many years later, he is still happy in Tokyo.

About 200 million people, or 3 per cent of the world's population,
20 already live outside their home countries, and relocation continues to rise. Each country presents its own oddities. In Germany, childcare is hard to come by. In
25 the Netherlands, it's hard to arrange for cooked dinners to be delivered. In the US, without an American credit history, you might not get a credit card, and
30 without a credit card, you will not exist. To survive, you should emigrate with more official documents than you could possibly need and hire a relocation
35 agent, especially if your company is paying. These people can do everything from putting your new apartment in their names to sitting with you at your rented kitchen
40 table as you burst into tears.

'You will do things wrong; it's normal,' says Soledad Aguirre of Statim Relocation in Madrid. 'In our intercultural training
45 programmes, there's a classic curve at two or three months, when the excitement has died down and people find themselves in this hole,' adds Cathie Estevez
50 of Swift Relocation Service in Munich. 'The difficulties of life in a new country have become a reality and they feel they've made a bad mistake. But
55 after seven or eight months, people tend to start feeling at home again. Knowing that this will come and that it happens to a lot of people should help you
60 get through it.

'The language is fundamental,' says Martine Ruiz, Manager of MRI Relocation in Lyons, France. Otherwise even calling
65 a plumber will be a torment. How to learn it? Make a lot of time. Take a course before you leave. Invest in audio or video tapes. Find a small, local language
70 school, many of which are quite good. Hire a personal tutor. Carry a bilingual dictionary every where. Some French teachers in Paris also recommend the
75 *école horizontale*, or 'horizontal school'; in other words, living with a local. This is also an instant route to meeting native friends, your partner's
80 irritating work colleagues and potential mothers-in-law.

1 **Look through the whole article for people who are mentioned. True or false?**

   a) The name of the British person living in Japan is not given.

   b) Soledad Aguirre works for an organisation in Spain that helps people to move to other countries.

   c) She thinks that people should be careful not to make mistakes in other countries from their first day onwards.

   d) Cathie Estevez works in Germany for another organisation offering intercultural training programmes.

   e) Martine Ruiz works for the same organisation.

   f) Her advice is specifically about learning the local language.

2 **What is the main message of paragraph 1? Choose the best one.**

   a) Finding addresses in Tokyo is difficult, so you should always carry a street map with you.

   b) Japanese is difficult, so you should always carry a grammar book with you.

   c) Adapting to a new culture is difficult, but you should always be as open as possible.

3 **Find nouns in paragraphs 1 and 2 that mean the following.**

   a) someone who lives and works abroad

   b) moving to live and work somewhere different

   c) things that are strange

   d) the services of people, organisations, etc. that look after children

   e) someone's record of repaying loans

   f) someone whose job is to help people to move abroad

4 **Which of these are *not* mentioned in paragraph 2?**

   Cultural difficulties relating to ...

   a) financial services.

   b) food.

   c) finding work.

   d) childcare.

   e) finding somewhere to live.

   f) meeting people.

5 **Use the expressions in the box to replace those in italic in the extract so as to keep the same meaning.**

   - be officially recognised as living in the country
   - use the services of
   - start crying
   - be able to live
   - difficult to obtain
   - move to the new country

In Germany, childcare is *hard to come by*[a)]. In the Netherlands, it's hard to arrange for cooked dinners to be delivered. In the US, without an American credit history, you might not get a credit card, and without a credit card, you will not *exist*[b)]. To *survive*[c)], you should *emigrate*[d)] with more official documents than you could possibly need and *hire*[e)] a relocation agent, especially if your company is paying. These people can do everything from putting your new apartment in their names to sitting with you at your rented kitchen table as you *burst into tears*[f)].

6 **Answer these questions using the words given and information from paragraph 3 of the article.**

   When you move abroad, ...

   a) will it be possible to do everything right? – No, you will ....

   b) how might you feel after two or three months? – In a .... This is all part of the .... that people follow.

   c) will you definitely feel, after a few months, that you've done the right thing? – No, you might ....

   d) how will you feel after a few more months, if your experience is typical? – At ....

   e) how will knowing what other people feel about the experience help you? – It should ....

7 **In which order is this advice given in paragraph 4?**

   a) Buy a self-study language course.

   b) Find a language school.

   c) Find a one-to-one teacher.

   d) If you don't learn the language, even calling someone to make repairs to your house or flat will be very difficult.

   e) You will meet other people as well!

   f) Moving in with someone might be the best way of learning the language.

   g) Take a dictionary everywhere you go.

   h) Learning the language is extremely important.

Over to you 1

Give some advice to someone coming to live and work in your country.

Over to you 2

What advice would you give to someone learning your language:

a) in your country?   b) outside it?

THERAPEUTIC CONSULTANCY

Before you read

Are there any easy ways of telling employees that they are being fired?

Reading

Read this article from the *Financial Times* and answer the questions.

FT

LEVEL OF DIFFICULTY ● ● ○

Helping workers manage bad news

by Emma Jacobs

'Anxiety' and 'paralysis' were two words that came to mind when Professor Binna Kandola, a business psychologist, visited an
5 engineering services organisation that was making redundancies. 'Everybody was frozen, the employees and the managers,' he remarks.
10 Such a response is common, he says. When managers announce redundancies, 'people tend to imagine that they'll lose their job, their home, then their
15 marriages will fall apart. Uncertainty is stressful. A lot of mental energy goes into worry – energy that is diverted from our job.'
20 So how can managers support the workforce through an economic downturn? Therapeutic consultancies in the UK, such as the Grubb Institute of
25 Behavioural Studies and the Tavistock Consultancy Service, offer some interesting answers and are reporting increased demand for their services.
30 'Managing a fearful workforce is one of the greatest problems for companies in the current economic climate,' says Dr Bruce Irvine, Executive Director
35 of the Grubb Institute. He says that, if organisations do not manage anxiety in tough trading conditions, employees will not work effectively and performance
40 will suffer at a time when every penny of revenue counts.

'In times of recession, people can behave defensively in order to avoid reality,' says Judith Bell,
45 Director of the TCS. 'We try to get teams to address some of the difficulties that lie under the surface and prevent people from getting on with the task in hand.'
50 Described as the 'coaches in white coats' by one investment bank, TCS draws on therapeutic models to examine employees' behaviour at work. It has worked
55 with organisations ranging from government bodies to Mars, the food group, and Morgan Stanley, the investment bank.

Ms Bell says that, in highly
60 stressful conditions, people often believe that 'aggressive or bullying behaviour is justified'.

In fact, she suggests, leaders may need to take more care
65 to understand why people are not performing well and work harder to motivate them.

Dr Irvine agrees. He has witnessed organisations take
70 fright at the economic downturn and simply repeat behaviour that has been shown not to work rather than examine ways to improve. 'Team
75 leaders may just go back to a tried-and-tested approach.'

Sebastian Parsons, Chief Executive of Elysia, the UK distributor of Dr Hauschka
80 beauty products, will be using the Grubb Institute to help him motivate his staff and survive the downturn. The challenge is to come up with new ways of
85 marketing to customers with less money to spend. Aggressive methods may be counter productive and cause suspicion of management – many of his
90 employees have left companies that 'treated them like a machine'.

1 Look through the whole article to find the names of:

a) a business psychologist.

b) two therapeutic organisations.

c) the Executive Director of one of these organisations.

d) another director in this organisation.

e) a company and the name of a bank.

f) a company head, and the name of his company.

2 Complete the table by finding grammatically related words in paragraphs 1 to 4 of the article.

noun	adjective
.... a)	anxious
.... b)	paralysed
.... c)	redundant
.... d)	stressful
.... e)	energetic
therapy	.... f)
.... g)	uncertain
fear	.... h)

3 Now match the adjectives in Exercise 2 to these definitions.

a) out of work

b) not sure

c) causing worry, tiredness, etc.

d) very worried (2 adjectives)

e) unable to act

f) curing an illness, bad situation, etc.

g) active and hard-working

4 Read paragraphs 1 to 4 and decide if these statements are true or false.

When redundancies are announced, employees ...

a) think it won't happen to them.

b) have extreme psychological reactions.

c) are unable to do their jobs properly and the organisation's financial results suffer.

d) bring in therapeutic consultants to help resolve the difficulties.

5 Choose the correct alternative. *Coaches in white coats* (lines 50–51) implies that each consultant is a combination of:

a) a bus driver and a surgeon.

b) a butcher and a dentist.

c) a trainer and a psychologist.

6 Read paragraphs 8 and 9 and answer these questions.

a) What is the danger for team leaders in an economic downturn?

b) Why will Elysia be using the Grubb Institute?

7 What is the key message of the article? Choose the best summary.

Therapeutic consultancy is used ...

a) for people who are being made redundant.

b) to assist organisations get through an economic downturn by helping employees deal with the psychological challenges.

c) to help managers to make employees redundant without psychological problems for the managers or the employees.

Over to you 1

Is it always possible to change the attitudes of people in difficult situations such as redundancy? Give some examples to support your opinion.

Over to you 2

What sort of consultancy or coaching would be the most suitable for improving conditions in your own organisation? Why?

HUMAN CAPITAL PLANNING

Before you read

What's the best way of finding the right person for a particular job?

Reading

Read this book review from the *Financial Times* and answer the questions.

FT

TEXT BANK

The right people for the right jobs
by Morgan Witzel

The Differentiated Workforce: Transforming Talent into Strategic Impact
(by Brian Becker, Mark Huselid and Richard Beatty; published by Harvard Business Press)

For years, there has been much talk about the 'war for talent'. The idea was that talented people were a scarce resource for which companies had to compete. But hiring talented people is only half the battle. They must be found jobs where they can be truly effective. If they are given the wrong jobs, with the wrong things to do, they will be square pegs in round holes, no matter how much potential talent they have. The authors argue that hiring and promoting people on the basis of past experience and past performance is not enough.

Instead, companies would be better advised to plan more rigorously, identify where and when particular talents and skills will be needed and then find, train and develop the right people for the right posts.

This is neither quick nor easy. The authors cite a senior executive at one IBM division as saying it takes at least two years to prepare an employee to fill a responsible position in a complex working environment.

The book starts from the premise that human resources requirements must follow on from strategy. The first step is to identify the business's goals and the strategy for reaching them. The next is to prepare a 'human capital plan' that indicates what kinds of people with what kinds of talents will be able to carry out the strategy.

The book's main impact is to raise the idea that human capital needs to be planned and treated systematically. Out-of-date HR policies mean too many businesses end up following the 'Peter Principle', promoting employees to the level of their incompetence – or they end up full of clones where every employee is recruited and trained according to a set pattern.

Differentiating among employees and investing in the key ones means that talent should operate in the right place at the right time. This can have a powerful impact on a business. According to the authors, Sears, the US retailer, measures its human capital carefully and believes its levels of human capital are responsible for both customer satisfaction and overall financial performance. It even believes its method has some predictive value of financial performance in the future.

At Microsoft, the case is put still more strongly. The authors quote Nathan Myhrvold, the company's former Chief Scientist, as saying that 'the top software developers are more productive than average software developers not by a factor of 10 times or 100 times or even 1,000 times, but by 10,000 times'. As the authors comment: 'Few jobs show the enormous variation in performance cited by Microsoft, but differences in performance of 20- to 50-to-one are common, especially in knowledge-intensive roles.'

1 Find expressions in paragraph 1 to complete these statements.

a) Someone or something useful that is hard to find is a ....

b) Conflict among companies to recruit the best people is referred to as ....

c) When a particular effort is only part of what is required to reach a particular goal, it is only ....

d) People in the wrong jobs are ....

e) What people have done in previous jobs and the way they have done it is their ....

2 Put these steps into the correct order according to paragraphs 2 to 4 of the article.

Companies should ...

a) train and develop the people who have been found.

b) plan human resource requirements carefully.

c) identify the business's goals and the strategy for reaching them.

d) find the right people for the right posts.

3 Choose the correct alternatives to replace expressions in italic so as to keep the closest meaning in the context.

a) The book's main *impact* ... (line 43)
   i) collision
   ii) hit
   iii) message

b) ... is to *raise* the idea ... (lines 43–44)
   i) lift
   ii) examine
   iii) hoist

c) ... that human capital needs to be planned and treated *systematically*. (lines 44–46)
   i) methodically
   ii) superficially
   iii) subjectively

d) *Out-of-date* HR policies ... (lines 46–47)
   i) fashionable
   ii) contemporary
   iii) no longer relevant

e) ... mean too many businesses end up following the 'Peter Principle', promoting employees to the level of their *incompetence* ... (lines 47–50)
   i) corruption
   ii) inability to perform
   iii) irrelevance

f) ... or they end up full of *clones* where every employee is recruited and trained according to a set pattern. (lines 51–53)
   i) people who are quite like each other
   ii) people who differ from each other
   iii) people who are exactly the same as each other.

4 Find adjectives in paragraphs 6 and 7 that mean the following.

a) very big (8 letters)

b) forecasting the future (10 letters)

c) relating to money (9 letters)

d) strong (8 letters)

e) frequent (6 letters)

f) doing a lot of work (10 letters)

g) relating to jobs where information is important (9 letters-9 letters)

h) producing a particular result (11 letters)

5 Decide if these statements are true or false according to the article.

a) Companies should train and develop all their employees in the same way.

b) Sears studies its human resource function closely.

c) The review gives figures about the benefit of human resource planning at Sears.

d) The figures for Microsoft show that the best programmers are slightly better than average.

e) Other companies find differences in performance that are similar to those at Microsoft.

Over to you 1

What are the arrangements for human capital planning in your organisation, or one you would like to work for?

Over to you 2

... differences in performance of 20- to 50-to-one are common, especially in knowledge-intensive roles (lines 82–85). Do you agree with this? Give some examples to support your ideas.

GETTING INTO NEW MARKETS

Before you read

What are the leading brands of white goods (refrigerators, washing machines, etc.) in your country?

Reading

Read this article from the *Financial Times* and answer the questions.

FT

Panasonic enters European white goods market

by Robin Harding in Tokyo

To enter a mature and notoriously competitive market during a recession might seem foolish, especially when that market
5 loads its washing machines from the front, not the top. Yet Panasonic's launch of large white goods such as washing machines and refrigerators on the European
10 market reflects the Japanese electronics group's willingness to take risks. The products had to be completely redesigned to meet European tastes.

15 The arrival of such a deep-pocketed competitor will shake up a market dominated by European brands such as Electrolux and Bosch and is set
20 to be the first of many new areas that Panasonic invades. That Panasonic is able to make such moves reflects the transformation that the company, which sells
25 almost every electrical and electronic product imaginable in Japan, has undergone over the past 10 years.

'In the past, we had a strict
30 division system, but we were not good at co-ordinating divisions,' said Hitoshi Otsuki, the Director of Panasonic's overseas operations. Overseas sales companies were
35 fed products, not always suitable, from a number of divisions in Japan. After 2000, Panasonic radically changed its structure to cut overlap and
40 focus on profitability – it now closes any business that has not made money for the past three years – and the company is on the offensive abroad again.

45 The sale of white goods in Europe is on the direct instructions of Fumio Ohtsubo, Panasonic's President. In the revamped company, the project has gone
50 from conception to launch in only 18 months. The move to sell white goods in Europe is backed by Panasonic's belief that it has an edge in green
55 technologies, such as low power consumption, that will appeal

to Europeans. 'We don't just introduce ordinary products. In this case, we have environmental
60 technologies,' said Mr Otsuki.

In the context of Panasonic's expected turnover of ¥7,750bn ($80bn) this financial year – and its forecast net loss of
65 ¥380bn – European appliance sales are unlikely to make much difference. The company's goal is to double current sales of €260m ($331m) over the next five years.

70 However, Panasonic sees Europe as a stepping stone for white-goods sales in Russia and the Middle East, on top of its markets in Asia. Mr Otsuki said
75 the company was also considering the launch of other products abroad, such as hearing aids in China and other Asian markets, while there was interest from
80 buyers, including in the UK, for its new fuel cell-based systems that generate heat and power at home.

TEXT BANK

1 Look through the whole article to find two businessmen. Who are they, and what are their jobs?

2 Use appropriate forms of expressions from paragraph 1 of the article to complete the answers to these questions.

a) Is it easy to make money in the European white-goods market? – No, it's very ....

b) Is it wise to try to enter this market? – No, it may be ....

c) Is this market growing fast? – No, it's ....

d) Does Panasonic avoid taking risks? – No, it has a ....

e) Do most Europeans prefer top-loading washing machines? – No, they ....

f) Is Panasonic going to sell the same products as in Japan? – No, the products ....

3 Choose the alternative with the closest meaning to the expression in italic.

a) The arrival of such a *deep-pocketed* competitor ... (lines 15–16)
   i) well-dressed
   ii) long-established
   iii) well-funded

b) ... will *shake up* a market ... (lines 16–17)
   i) stabilise
   ii) transform
   iii) grow

c) ... *dominated* by European brands such as Electrolux and Bosch ... (lines 17–19)
   i) where European brands sell the most
   ii) where European brands are less successful
   iii) where only European brands are sold

d) ... and is set to be the first of many new areas that Panasonic *invades*. (lines 19–21)
   i) withdraws from
   ii) starts to sell to in large quantities
   iii) does research in

e) That Panasonic is able to make such moves *reflects* the transformation that the company, ... (lines 21–24)
   i) shows
   ii) denies
   iii) contradicts

f) ... which sells almost every electrical and electronic product imaginable in Japan, has *undergone* over the past 10 years. (lines 24–28)
   i) imposed
   ii) overcome
   iii) been through

4 Read paragraph 3 and answer these questions.

a) Why was Panasonic less competitive globally?

b) What did it do to compete more effectively?

5 Read paragraphs 4 and 5 and decide if these statements are true or false.

a) Panasonic's Overseas Sales Director decided to sell white goods to Europe.

b) The project took one and a half years to put into action.

c) Panasonic's managers think that it is better at producing environmentally friendly products than some other companies.

d) Panasonic's President is quoted talking about these technologies.

e) One example given of an environmental technology is in relation to the amount of electricity that their products use.

f) Panasonic thinks it might be difficult to attract Europeans to these products because tastes are different there.

g) The company is expected make a loss this year but it will be less than a tenth of sales revenue.

h) In five years, the company hopes to have sales of about €520 million in Europe.

6 Find expressions in paragraphs 5 and 6 with these meanings.

a) an intermediate stage (two words)

b) devices to help people to hear better (two words)

c) devices to produce energy (four words)

d) electricity (one word)

e) in addition to (three words)

f) objective (one word)

g) selling products for the first time (one word)

h) to produce (one word)

Over to you 1

What other consumer goods are modified to reflect different tastes around the world? (Product size, characteristics, etc.)

Over to you 2

What information and advice would you give to a white-goods manufacturer trying to sell in your country for the first time? (Main competitors, sales outlets, pricing, etc.)

BUSINESS-TO-BUSINESS E-COMMERCE

Before you read

How important is e-commerce in your country for:

a) consumers (for example, eBay and Amazon)?

b) business-to-business?

Reading

Read this article from the *Financial Times* and answer the questions.

FT

LEVEL OF DIFFICULTY ● ● ○

Alibaba

by Kathrin Hille

Every time a salesperson at online trading site Alibaba signs up an important new account, the entire sales department cheers in
5 triumph. But today they have been asked to keep the noise down, as Jack Ma, founder and chairman of the world's largest online trading platform for businesses,
10 is being interviewed in the open-plan office. If Mr Ma feels most comfortable next to his sales force, it is because their work comes closest to what the 44-year-old
15 has been doing over the past 15 years: preaching the importance of the Internet and convincing companies to pay for offering their products on Alibaba's business-
20 to-business e-commerce website.

Today, Alibaba has 36 million registered users worldwide and generated revenues of 2.2bn renminbi ($322m) in the first nine
25 months of last year – 43 per cent up from the previous year. The group employs 12,000 people and intends to hire another 4,500 this

year. It also controls Yahoo China
30 and Taobao, China's leading consumer e-commerce platform, which Mr Ma founded in 2003.

The key to Alibaba's business model is the assumption that
35 small and medium-sized enterprises (SME) are those that can benefit most from the Internet because it gives them access to buyers they would otherwise only
40 meet at trade shows. With access to a wider pool of customers, it also reduces their dependency on market-dominant clients.

'Companies like Wal-Mart,
45 these big-size buyers, killed a lot of SME buyers,' says Mr Ma. 'But now most of the SME buyers and sellers started to do business throughout the world
50 because of the Internet. So I think the world has moved. I strongly believe small is beautiful.'

Although China's economy is so far faring better than
55 others, domestic trade has slowed, affecting a large chunk

of Alibaba's business – 28.7 million of its registered users are in its home market. To soften
60 the blow, Alibaba has provided loans in excess of Rmb1bn to SMEs that would otherwise have struggled to get money.

But a bigger change for Mr Ma's
65 company is the group's shifting geographic focus. 'Before this financial crisis, we were helping China's products abroad. Now we are thinking about helping
70 SMEs in the other parts of the world. Help them sell across the nations. Help them to sell to China,' he says. 'In the next 10 years, we are moving from a
75 pure China exporting centre to a global platform for SMEs to exchange products.' In the past six months, Alibaba has made a big push in this direction
80 with a programme called Export to China, which offers non-Chinese sellers virtual Chinese-language storefronts.

1 Look through the whole article and match the figures to the things that they refer to.

1 12,000   **a)** Jack Ma's age

2 15   **b)** the number of employees at Alibaba

3 28.7 million   **c)** the number of years Alibaba has existed

4 44   **d)** the number of people to be recruited by Alibaba this year

5 4,500   **e)** the number of Alibaba's registered users in China

6 36 million   **f)** Alibaba's revenues for the first three quarters of last year

7 $322 million   **g)** the number of Alibaba's registered users worldwide

2 Find expressions in paragraph 1 of the article that mean the following.

a) workplace without walls
b) telling people about the benefits of something
c) shout with joy
d) relaxed
e) persuading
f) between companies rather than consumers
g) group of salespeople
h) get a new customer
i) be quieter than usual

3 Read paragraphs 2 to 4 and decide if these statements are true or false.

a) Alibaba's revenues for the whole of last year will be less than Rmb2 billion.
b) There are nearly seven renminbi (Rmb) to the dollar.
c) The increase in revenue in relation to the previous year is more than 40 per cent.
d) By the end of this year, Alibaba will employ nearly 17,000 people.
e) Jack Ma's group only deals with business-to-business e-commerce.
f) Alibaba gives small businesses access to a larger number of customers.
g) The customers that SMEs can find on Alibaba are the same ones that they would meet at trade fairs.
h) SMEs until now have relied on a few, very large customers.
i) Large buyers in the past pushed out smaller ones.
j) The world has changed, according to Mr Ma.

4 Replace each expression in italic in the extract below with an appropriate form of one of the expressions in the box.

- supply
- reduce the negative effects
- perform
- part
- internal (used twice)
- find it difficult

Although China's economy is so far *faring*a) better than others, *domestic*b) trade has slowed, affecting a large *chunk*c) of Alibaba's business – 28.7 million of its registered users are in its *home*d) market. To *soften the blow*e), Alibaba has *provided*f) loans in excess of Rmb1bn to SMEs that would otherwise have *struggled*g) to get money.

5 Combine the words in the box below to make expressions from paragraph 6 that refer to the following.

a) websites in Chinese for companies outside China who want to sell there (4 words)
b) suppliers not based in China or run by Chinese people (3 words)
c) changing emphasis on different parts of the world (3 words)
d) a website that has users all over the world (2 words)
e) a website used only by companies based in China that want to sell abroad (4 words)
f) a period when banks do not lend, businesses go bust, people lose their jobs, etc. (2 words)

virtual	storefronts	shifting	sellers
pure	platform	non-Chinese	language
global	geographic	centre	financial
exporting	crisis	Chinese	China
focus			

Over to you 1

Imagine that you work for an SME. Would you use the Internet to buy supplies, equipment, etc. from another SME that you had never heard of in another country? What guarantees would you require?

Over to you 2

In what ways has the Internet made it easier for small companies to do business, apart from e-commerce?

ETHICAL CVS

Before you read

In some places, employers are using Google to check the information in job applicants' CVs. Is this reasonable? Why? / Why not?

Reading

Read this article from the *Financial Times* and answer the questions.

FT

LEVEL OF DIFFICULTY ● ● ○

Beware the risky business of résumé fraud

by Jonathan Guthrie

Recent research by the Chartered Institute of Educational Assessors found that 30 per cent of job applicants embellished the truth or lied on a curriculum vitae. The level of lying is increasing as unemployment increases and competition for jobs rises. It was the same during the downturn of the early 1990s. A journalist colleague admitted to me then that his degree from a top university was entirely fake. Another friend explained a year of total inactivity by telling possible employers that he had been writing a guide to the wild flowers of the Pyrenees.

Charles Thomas of Kroll, a company whose services include background checks on job applicants, says that inaccuracies on CVs divide into three main groups. First, there are honest mistakes, typically made when candidates mix up dates. Second, there is deliberate lying about qualifications. Mr Thomas says: 'A lie told 20 years ago to get a job can become part of the liar's reality. So he tells it again when he switches jobs, even though he has become a successful finance director.' Third, applicants close up suspicious gaps in their employment history. In one case investigated by Kroll, a candidate turned out to have spent a three-month gap in prison for fraud.

How can the honest candidate compete? A newspaper job advertisement can attract up to 700 applicants, reports Owen Morgan of Penna, a human resources consultancy. A junior HR officer will typically reduce these to a long list, spending no more than 15 seconds examining each CV. Or they may simply do a keyword search on CVs submitted electronically. Kerwin Hack, a counsellor at HR consultancy Fairplace, therefore suggests using phrases from the job ad in the CV.

When I last encountered Mr Hack, he was discouraging a redundant investment banker from using the words 'I really need the money' in an application for a new job. There are other elements applicants may safely leave out. Date of birth is one. If you are over 40, you will increase your chance of an interview by leaving this out. You will not get the job, but at least there will be free coffee and biscuits.

What troubles me most about lying on résumés is that those who have done it are often very good at their jobs. The academic qualifications of Patrick Imbardelli, Asia boss of InterContinental Hotels, were exposed as false only during routine checks when he was promoted to the board. Colleagues described Neil Taylor, whose fake degree got him a £115,000 salary as the Chief Executive of a large UK hospital group, as 'highly competent'.

1 **Look through the whole article and find these expressions related to lying.**

a) Someone who tells lies is a l.........................

b) If someone 'improves' their exam results, previous job performance, etc., they
e......................... t.........................
t.........................

c) Something that is not true or genuine is
fa......................... or fa.........................

d) A period on a CV that is not explained may look like a s......................... g......................... .

2 **Look through the whole article again and find six examples of lying on CVs and the people responsible for them.**

3 **Look at paragraph 1. Why is the amount of lying on CVs increasing?**

4 **Read paragraph 2 and answer these questions.**

a) What are the three types of false information on CVs?

b) Which of these involve actual lies?

c) What can be done to see if lying has occurred (two possible expressions of two words each)?

5 **Read paragraph 3 and decide if these statements are true or false.**

a) A newspaper job advertisement might get over 700 applications.

b) All the applications are looked at in detail.

c) The applications are reduced to a long list.

d) The CVs in the applications may only by looked at by doing word searches on a computer.

e) It isn't good to use expressions from a job advertisement in the application.

6 **Read paragraph 4. What two things should applicants leave out from their CV?**

7 **Use appropriate forms of the expressions in the box to replace those in italic in the extract below so as to keep the same meaning.**

- university
- make (someone) a director
- show to be
- bother
- extremely good at (one's) job

What *troubles*[a] me most about lying on résumés is that those who have done it are often very good at their jobs. The *academic*[b] qualifications of Patrick Imbardelli, Asia boss of InterContinental Hotels, were *exposed as*[c] false only during routine checks when he was *promoted to the board*[d]. Colleagues described Neil Taylor, whose fake degree got him a £115,000 salary as the chief executive of a large UK hospital group, as '*highly competent*'[e].

Over to you 1

Is it acceptable in your country to leave out one's date of birth and marital status (single, married, divorced, etc.) from your CV? Why? / Why not?

Over to you 2

How much should employers take account of each of the following when considering someone for a job?

a) The overall look of their CV

b) Their experience

c) Their qualifications

d) Their performance at the job interview

Give your reasons.

TEXT BANK

WHISTLEBLOWERS

Before you read

A whistleblower is an employee who tells the authorities about wrongdoing in their organisation.
What cases of whistleblowing have you heard about or could you imagine in these industries?
a) airlines   b) chemicals   c) cars   d) banking

Reading

Read this article from the *Financial Times* and answer the questions.

FT

LEVEL OF DIFFICULTY ● ● ○

TEXT BANK

What whistleblowers should know

by Michael Skapinker

The House of Commons Treasury Committee has been examining the management of UK banks leading up to the banking crisis.
5 In evidence to the committee, Paul Moore spoke publicly for the first time of his warnings three years ago to HBOS, the UK bank, that it was expanding too fast.
10 Mr Moore's evidence to the committee quickly led to the resignation of Sir James Crosby as Deputy Chairman of the Financial Services Authority, the regulator
15 of the UK banking industry. It was Sir James, at that time HBOS Chief Executive, who had forced Mr Moore out of his job at the bank.
20 Few whistleblowers enjoy such sweet revenge. The Government Accountability Project, a US organisation that supports whistleblowers, has a message
25 for anyone else thinking of exposing an employer's wrongdoing: think hard before you do because you are going to suffer. It warns that whistle-
30 blowers 'pay an enormous professional and personal price for their actions – often a price

they did not expect. Long after the public has forgotten your
35 brave actions, your former bosses will remember what you did to them.'
Mr Moore was in a far stronger position to blow the whistle
40 than most. He was not just any HBOS employee. He was Head of Group Regulatory Risk. That meant that it was his job to point out the risks the bank
45 was running. HBOS made him redundant after a restructuring. He sued for unfair dismissal under whistleblower protection laws and reached a 'substantial'
50 settlement. He had agreed to a gagging order that prevented him talking publicly about what had happened, but gagging orders against whistleblowers
55 have no force under the UK's Public Interest Disclosure law.
Whistleblowers are essential in pointing out cases of corruption or incompetence, but they need
60 to know how to go about it. Whistleblowers can be extremely bitter about their experiences. The Government Accountability Project recognises the dangers.

65 It advises whistleblowers on how to deal with the media: 'Do not talk about all the injustices you have been through. Be an advocate for the story, not for yourself.'
70 Mr Moore followed that advice, which is why his intervention at the Treasury committee was so devastating. But he made plenty of enemies along the way. A
75 previously unpublished review of his departure by accountants KPMG accused him of 'stating matters in an overly dramatic way'. Mr Moore's response:
80 'Well, they would say that, wouldn't they?'
The first lesson of whistle-blowing is that people will try to discredit you so, hard as
85 it is, keep your cool. The second is: after every discussion, e-mail a note repeating your concerns. The lesson for corporate management is even clearer.
90 When you start receiving polite e-mails telling you the company is doing something wrong, pay attention. You may see the same words in a parliamentary
95 report.

1 Look through the whole article and match the people and organisations to their descriptions.

1 Paul Moore
2 Sir James Crosby
3 House of Commons Treasury Committee
4 HBOS
5 the FSA
6 the Government Accountability Project
7 KPMG

a) a body in the UK parliament that looks at problems in the economy and finance industry
b) an accountancy firm who wrote a report about Mr Moore's actions at HBOS
c) the Chief Executive of HBOS and then Deputy Chairman of the FSA before he had to resign
d) the bank where Mr Moore worked
e) Head of Group Regulatory Risk at HBOS until he was made redundant
f) the organisation in the UK that oversees banks to make sure that they are managed properly
g) a US charity that supports whistleblowers

2 Answer the questions using information from paragraphs 1 to 4 and the words shown.

a) What did Paul Moore warn HBOS management about three years ago? – That it was ....
b) What happened to him? – He was forced .... ; he was made ....
c) Where did he give evidence about his experiences? – To the ....
d) How did he get his revenge? – His former boss at HBOS .... from his job at the FSA.
e) What happens to most whistleblowers? – They .... for their actions and pay an ....
f) What happens in the long run? – People forget ...., but the whistleblower's bosses ....

3 Decide if these statements are true or false.

If …

a) a company undergoes *restructuring* (line 46), it reorganises.
b) an employer *sues for unfair dismissal* (line 47), they lose their job without getting extra money.
c) someone in a legal dispute *reaches a substantial settlement* (lines 49–50), they get a little money.
d) there is a *gagging order* (line 51) after an agreement between two sides, the people involved cannot talk about it.

4 Look at paragraphs 5 to 7 and find:

a) a noun used to talk about someone not doing their job properly.
b) an adjective describing the negative feelings of many whistleblowers.
c) a plural noun referring to the bad treatment that they often receive.
d) a noun meaning someone who expresses a particular opinion.
e) a formal noun referring to a time when someone speaks at a meeting, etc.
f) an adjective to say that something is very effective.
g) an adverb to say that something is done too much, too intensely, etc.
h) a verb used to say that someone should not be believed.

5 Look at paragraphs 5 to 7 again and find three pieces of advice for being an effective whistleblower.

Over to you 1
What sort of legal protection do whistleblowers receive in your country?

Over to you 2
Why are whistleblowers so often badly treated by their colleagues, even if everyone knows that the company is doing something wrong?

THE NORDIC LEADERSHIP STYLE

Before you read

Which one of each of these pairs of characteristics do you associate with a Nordic or Scandinavian style of leadership?

a) high-profile/low-profile

b) consultation before making decisions / telling people what to do without consulting them

c) symbols of power such as large offices / modest lifestyle

Reading

Read this article from the *Financial Times* and answer the questions.

FT

LEVEL OF DIFFICULTY ● ● ○

TEXT BANK

Jorma Ollila

by Richard Milne

Despite chairing two of Europe's largest companies and heading a group of the continent's leading industrialists, Jorma Ollila is hardly a household name. This suits the operational style of the 58-year-old Finn, who is Chairman of both Nokia, the world's largest mobile phone company, and Royal Dutch Shell, Europe's biggest oil group. He is also Head of the European Roundtable of Industrialists, a grouping of the continent's leading 50 or so chief executives or chairmen. 'We like to work in the background,' says Mr Ollila, in what could almost be his mission statement.

As well as masking his level of influence today, his low-key style contrasts sharply with his record. During his 15 years as Chief Executive of Nokia, he turned what was once a struggling industrial conglomerate into a global mobile phone powerhouse.

He has long had a focus on the social aspects of business. Indeed, Mr Ollila says he is most of all 'a people manager'. For example, although Nokia was in trouble when he took over as the company's CEO in 1992, he still found time to set out values on how the group should behave, treat its people and deal with internal conflicts. He argues that management has to take such a task seriously, instead of making it 'an annexe in the annual report'. As CEO, he felt his role was 'to get everybody involved, create a sense of urgency, who does what, and then: run'.

Mr Ollila was helped at the start by the fact that nobody expected much. 'We could work for the first two years without anybody expecting anything other than survival at best.' Most fondly, however, he talks of his time as part of a team with an average age under 40 who then turned Nokia around. 'It was an entrepreneurial task. It was extremely rewarding,' he says.

The concern for what he calls 'the human role' above things like skills and strategy comes across in his passion for the Nordic approach to business. He echoes Jack Welch, the former boss of General Electric, in criticising some companies' sole focus on shareholder value. 'The current crisis will lead to a rethink in the corporate world. It is not just about short-term, mid-term or long-term profitability but it is also about certain values.'

Values are not the only Nordic thing Mr Ollila thinks the world should adopt. He argues that the Nordic way of capitalism – being open to globalisation but protecting people from its negative aspects and providing everyone with a good education – provides the answers that are needed.

1 Find expressions in paragraphs 1 and 2 that refer to the following.

a) the way that someone works

b) someone who is very well known

c) heads of companies

d) behaviour that is not meant to be noticed

e) an unsuccessful group of companies

f) a very important business person working in industry

g) a sentence that describes a company's main purpose

h) a dynamic company

2 Decide if these statements are true or false.

If …

a) something *suits* (line 6) something else, it helps it to succeed.

b) you *work in the background* (line 17), you want to be seen.

c) something *masks* (line 20) something else, it hides it.

d) something *contrasts with* (line 22) something else, they are the same.

e) you *turn* something *into* (lines 25–26) something else, you transform it.

3 Look at paragraph 3. What did Jorma Ollila focus on at Nokia?

a) stechnical skills

b) people management

c) competitive strategy

4 Which of these management tasks is *not* mentioned in paragraph 3?

How a company should …

a) decide salary levels.

b) treat its people.

c) manage disagreements.

d) involve people.

e) create a sense that things had to be done quickly.

f) pay performance-related bonuses.

g) allocate tasks.

5 Complete these sentences with appropriate forms of words used in paragraphs 4 to 6 of the article. The first one is done for you as an example.

a) Nobody expected Nokia to do more than *survive*, at best.

b) Mr Ollila talks of his time as part of a team with f.........................

c) He approached the work like an e.........................

d) He talks about the Nordic approach to business with p.........................

e) What he says about business is an e......................... of what Jack Welch has said.

f) Companies should not f......................... s......................... on shareholder value.

g) The way that companies are managed needs to be r.........................

h) We need to think less about how to make a p......................... and more about the a......................... of human values.

i) There should be o......................... towards globalisation but we should give p......................... to people against its negative effects.

Over to you 1

Would it be easy to apply similar Nordic approaches to management in your country? Why? / Why not?

Over to you 2

Is it always possible for managers to work in the background? Why? / Why not?

TEXT BANK

LEADERSHIP IN DIFFICULT TIMES

Before you read

What should leaders do and say during difficult times for their company? Should they tell their employees how bad things are, or should they sound optimistic?

Reading

Read this article from the *Financial Times* and answer the questions.

FT

LEVEL OF DIFFICULTY ● ● ●

TEXT BANK

The challenges facing leadership

by Rob Goffee and Gareth Jones

Leadership is more important than ever. Organisations that are well led have a much better chance of surviving in difficult times. This is not the occasion to take your eye off critical processes of leadership development – and smart organisations know this. First, since leadership is always contextual – leading in a pharmaceutical company is different from leading in a shipyard – the ability to adapt is vital. Effective leaders have a real sense of what is going on in their company. The old idea of 'managing by walking around' contained one great truth: you need to be in a position to collect soft data, to know what is happening on the shop floor before the management information system tells you.

Business leaders will also be tested by their capacity to make sense of a difficult situation. Rudolph Giuliani, Mayor of New York at the time of the terrorist attacks of 2001, was not only in the right place at the right time, he also offered New Yorkers hope for the future – he assured them that New York would be back.

In much the same way, Andrew Higginson, Finance Director of UK retailer Tesco, recently said that the unpopularity of the retail banks represented an opportunity for them to further develop their popular brand in the financial services business. Michael O'Leary, Chief Executive of low-cost airline Ryanair, goes even further. He welcomes the recession. In his view, it will kill off poor operators and show what a great business Ryanair is.

Each of these examples demonstrates that effective leaders both read context and rewrite it. In difficult times, the danger is that business leaders are trapped and become entirely reactive. Skilled leadership involves not just reacting but proactively and constructively reshaping events.

Second, a strong focus may be a required for survival. Leaders will need to be focused on hard-nosed, tough prioritisation, including cutbacks and cost control. These actions are likely to be painful. But they should not come at the expense of team or organisational cohesion. If people must leave, they must leave with dignity.

Finally, sensing situations and building team cohesion will require social closeness to ensure a company-wide sense that 'we are all in this together'. The criticism targeted at some senior business leaders, for example, stems from the fact that they continue to pay themselves bonuses while others suffer. But strong 'identification with the troops' should not limit the ability of leaders to step back and see the bigger picture.

1 There are three main points in the article. Look through the whole article and find the first word that introduces each point.

2 Match the adjectives (1–6) to the nouns (a–f) that they relate to in the article.

1 vital   a) processes
2 soft   b) leadership
3 smart   c) data
4 critical   d) organisations
5 effective   e) ability to adapt
6 contextual   f) leaders

3 Now match the phrases from Exercise 2 to their meanings.

i) related to the human or emotional rather than the factual or statistical
ii) extremely important capacity to change
iii) extremely important ways of doing things
iv) ways of leading that depend on when or where something occurs
v) leaders who produce results
vi) intelligent companies, etc.

4 Look at paragraphs 2 and 3 and find three leaders, their jobs and their organisations.

5 Now match the leaders in Exercise 4 to their ideas.

a) He thinks that declining economic activity is a good thing as it will eliminate the weaker companies in his industry.
b) He said that the city would recover.
c) He says that the banking crisis is good for his company because it will be more able to offer financial services.

6 Look at paragraph 4. Which adjective refers to someone who only acts following events, and which adverb describes the actions of someone who tries to anticipate events? What expression is used in relation to each of these types of leadership?

7 Complete the table with words from paragraphs 5 and 6 and related words.

noun	adjective
focus	.... a)
toughness	.... b)
pain	.... c)
.... d)	dignified
.... e)	cohesive
organisation	.... f)
.... g)	close

8 What is the danger when a leader is too close to the workforce?

Over to you 1
Think of someone who provided leadership through difficult times. What was the most important aspect of their leadership style?

Over to you 2
What, if anything, should be done about leaders who continue to receive bonuses even when their organisations are in trouble?

TAKING ON COMPETITORS

Before you read

Think of situations where a new competitor might be able to do better than existing companies. For example, what improvements could a new competitor bring to the way these products and services are sold?

a) fast food   b) cars   c) consumer electronics

Reading

Read this article from the *Financial Times* and answer the questions.

FT

LEVEL OF DIFFICULTY ● ● ○

Best Buy's competitive threat to rivals

by Tom Braithwaite in London

Best Buy, the world's largest electronics retailer, has sent a shockwave through the troubled European market with a plan to
5 open stores across the continent. The US group will take on brands such as Germany's MediaMarkt and France's Fnac, as well as Currys and Comet in the UK,
10 at a time when the retailers are struggling with depressed margins and worries over consumer spending. However, it will be some time before
15 Best Buy's European operation is firing on all cylinders.

By announcing a tie-up with Carphone Warehouse in the UK, the US group's £1.1bn purchase
20 of a 50-per-cent share in the joint venture will open up a new avenue of growth for a company that has 923 stores in the US, as well as smaller operations in Canada
25 and China, and plans to open up in Mexico and Turkey. Over the next three months, Carphone will start to stock laptops at each of its 2,400 stores, following
30 its successful entry into the PC market last year. The new joint venture will inherit Carphone's stores, which will continue to operate under the Carphone
35 brand.

Plans for the roll-out of Best Buy's trademark 'big box' format, with stores trading under its own name, were being made by Brad
40 Anderson, Chief Executive of the US retailer, and Charles Dunstone, his counterpart at Carphone. The UK will be the launchpad next year, although both men
45 have dodged questions as to how many Best Buy-branded stores the joint venture would open. Mr Anderson did acknowledge there was an 'incentive to develop a
50 meaningful business in Europe as rapidly as we possibly can'.

But he was keener to talk about the less tangible aspects of selling consumer electronics – which lie
55 at the heart of the deal. 'I think that our industry is not doing a terribly good job for the consumer,' said Mr Anderson. After consumer research in the
60 US and the UK, he was struck by the 'tech stress' suffered by shoppers, attempting to buy and link together increasingly complicated electronic products:
65 'Except for the accent, we couldn't tell the difference between the people we were talking to in Minnesota and the people we were talking to in London.'
70 Mr Dunstone, who has already brought Best Buy's successful Geek Squad, a team of roaming technical service specialists, to the UK, added: 'Consumers
75 in Europe are really ready for someone to come and try to do a better job.'

1 Look through the whole article and match each company (1–7) to its description (a–f).

1	Best Buy	a)	a French retailer of consumer electronics
2	Carphone Warehouse	b)	a German retailer of consumer electronics
3	MediaMarkt	c)	a US company that wants to get into the European market
4	Comet	d)	a team of technical experts who travel round fixing computers, etc.
5	Currys	e)	a UK company that is in a joint venture with Best Buy
6	Geek Squad	f)	a UK retailer of consumer electronics (two companies)
7	Fnac		

2 Look at how the expressions in italic are used in the article. True or false?

If …

a) an event *sends a shockwave* (lines 2–3) through a place, it has a big effect.

b) a competitor *takes on* (line 6) others, it competes with them for the first time.

c) you *struggle* (line 11) with something, it is hard to do.

d) margins are *depressed* (line 11), the profit for each product sold is more than before.

e) there are *worries* (line 12) over something, people are optimistic.

f) something is *firing on all cylinders* (line 16), it is working less well than it could.

3 Look at paragraphs 2 and 3 and answer the questions.

a) Will the joint venture involve building new stores immediately?

b) Will the joint venture operate under the Best Buy brand?

c) Will it extend this activity?

d) Why has Best Buy entered into a joint venture?

e) How much is Best Buy investing and what does this give them?

f) How are Best Buy and Carphone going to work together in the UK?

g) Has Carphone Warehouse already started selling PCs?

h) Does Best Buy already have stores in Mexico and Turkey?

4 Now put your answers to the questions in Exercise 3 in the correct order to make a summary of that part of the article.

5 Find these expressions in paragraph 3.

a) an adverb meaning 'fast'

b) an adjective used to say that something is worth doing

c) a verb meaning 'avoid' (give the infinitive)

d) a verb meaning 'admit'

e) a noun used to talk about someone in an organisation with the same job as someone in another

f) a noun referring to the size and shape of something

g) a noun referring to the first stage in a process

h) a noun used to talk about a reason for doing something

i) a noun referring here to the introduction of a new chain of stores

6 Find expressions in paragraphs 4 and 5 that mean the following.

a) travelling

b) more willing

c) concrete characteristics

d) complex

e) are the main reason for

f) anxiety when dealing with electronic products

7 Which of these possible reasons for the joint venture are *not* given in the article?

Best Buy …

a) can offer lower prices than competitors.

b) thinks that some European competitors may go out of business soon.

c) thinks it can offer a better service to people who are confused when buying electronics.

d) wants to expand in Europe.

e) wants to use the UK as a launchpad for new stores in Turkey.

Over to you 1

Do you suffer from 'tech stress' when buying electronic products? If so, what are the main causes?

Over to you 2

Retailers often have trouble breaking into new markets. What are some of the possible reasons for this?

TEXT BANK

BREAKING UP MONOPOLIES

Before you read

Think of two or three important industries in your country. What is the competitive situation in each? Are there any monopolies (situations where there is only one possible supplier)?

Reading

Read this article from the *Financial Times* and answer the questions.

LEVEL OF DIFFICULTY ● ● ○

TEXT BANK

Tide slowly begins to turn against private monopolies

by Adam Thomson

Try asking for a foreign beer in any fine restaurant in Mexico and the chances are that it will not stock a single one. Instead, the restaurant will offer you a beer from just one of the two big Mexican brewers – and almost never from both. Television is dominated by TV Azteca and Televisa, the two big media companies. Telecommunications is still largely in the hands of Telmex in the case of fixed-line services, and Telcel in the case of cellular telephony. The paint market is overwhelmingly associated with just one name: Comex. Build a house, and it is difficult not to hand money over to Cemex, the cement giant.

Almost everywhere you look in Mexico, competition is notoriously absent, and economists say that it has become one of the principal reasons for the country's relatively low growth over the past decade. It has also led to unnecessarily high prices and a lack of innovation, they say.

As Claudia Shatan, an investigator at the Economic Commission for Latin America and the Caribbean (Eclac), put it in a recent interview: 'The distortions in the Mexican economy that result from the lack of competition are overwhelming.' One of the problems, argues Ms Shatan, has to do with the way more than 1,000 state-owned companies were privatised in the late 1980s and early 1990s at a time when public finances were in a very bad state. 'Raising money was almost the only consideration,' she says. 'Not much thought was given to how they were going to behave and operate afterwards.'

In practice, these state-owned companies simply passed into private hands, in many cases keeping their monopolistic status At the same time, regulations and regulators governing strategic sectors of the economy were only set up as an afterthought. Academics say that the result today is often one of institutional weakness.

Even Luis Téllez, the govern-ment's telecommunications and transport minister, agrees. In an interview last year, he told the FT: 'The regulators have been captured by the regulated,' he said. 'They do not always respond to the public interest.' So what, if anything, has changed since then? Surprisingly, perhaps, some observers are starting to see small but important improvements.

One example is the banking sector. Changes in the law have forced banks to stop bundling products together and now obliges them to provide information in a way that allows potential customers easily to compare products between banks.

Another area is portability in telecommunications, the ability of customers from one company to switch providers while retaining the same number. This year, Cofetel, the telecoms regulator, finally forced all providers to introduce the change, potentially creating far more competition between carriers.

1 Look through the whole article to find names of companies in these industries in Mexico. (In some cases, no company is named.)

a) cement

b) banking

c) paints

d) mobile telecommunications

e) fixed-line telecommunications

f) beer

g) television

2 Look at how the expressions in italic are used. True or false?

a) If something is *notoriously absent* (line 23), people don't mind about it not being there.

b) The *principal* (line 25) reasons for doing something are the main ones.

c) A *decade* (line 27) is a period of 20 years.

d) If prices are *unnecessarily high* (lines 28–29), there is no way of avoiding this.

e) When there is a *lack* (line 29) of something, there is a lot of it.

f) *Innovation* (line 30) is the development of new ideas, products, etc.

3 Complete the table with expressions from paragraph 3 and related expressions.

noun	verb
.... a)	distort
privatisation	.... b)
.... c)	compete
.... d)	consider
behaviour	.... e)
operation	.... f)

4 Now match the nouns in Exercise 3 to their meanings.

a) the way people act

b) the way something works

c) when state-owned businesses are sold off

d) when thought is given to something

e) when something does not work as it normally would because of a negative influence

f) when companies try to be more successful than others in a particular market

5 Replace the words in italic with nouns from Exercise 3.

a) *It* was when state companies were bought by investors.

b) There hasn't been enough *of it*, and the Mexican economy is suffering.

c) Not much *of this* was given to how companies would act after they were sold by the state.

d) *This* and *this* were not in people's minds when the companies were sold off.

e) *They* have led to the market not being as efficient as it should be.

6 Find words or expressions in paragraphs 4 and 5 that mean the following.

a) when you think of something that you should have thought of earlier

b) when the situation gets better

c) when systems, organisations, etc. do not work effectively

d) what is best for people as a whole

e) researchers and teachers in universities and similar institutions

f) rules for effective competition

g) people whose job is to ensure that there is effective competition

h) people who watch a particular situation

i) groups of industries that make up the economy as a whole

j) companies whose behaviour is governed by particular rules

7 Which two improvements for consumers are mentioned in paragraphs 6 and 7?

Over to you 1

How easy is it to transfer a mobile phone number between networks in your country? What do you have to do? Has it become easier?

Over to you 2

Are there activities where a monopoly might be the best solution? (Railways, healthcare, etc.)

TEXT BANK KEY

Unit 1

Store brands

1 a) French
 b) 55
 c) Head of Real
 d) Carrefour

2 own brand, in-house brand

3

	Real	Tesco (UK)	Carrefour
Percentage of own-brand food products now	15%	60%	25%
Company's objective for percentage of its own-brand food products in its shops in 2–3 years from now	25%	not given	30%
Typical price of a store-brand product as a percentage of the price of a name brand for the same type of product	85% (15% less than name brand)	not given	not given

4–5

 1 e iii   2 a v   3 c iv   4 b ii   5 f vi   6 d i

6 The power of the discounter chains has meant that own brands have not been as successful in Germany as elsewhere.

Brand loyalty in China

1 a) False
 b) True
 c) False
 d) True
 e) False

2 a) conventional wisdom
 b) brand-driven
 c) brand loyalty
 d) value conscious
 e) nationalistic
 f) premium
 g) high-end

3 a) ii   b) i   c) iii   d) ii   e) ii   f) iii   g) i

4 c, a, e, d, b

Unit 2

Building hotels fast

1 1 f   2 d   3 b   4 c   5 g   6 e   7 h   8 a

2 a) China
 b) Bathrooms, plastering and air-conditioning
 c) No
 d) No
 e) Yes

3 a) adopt
 b) expand
 c) move
 d) recycle
 e) refurbish
 f) stack
 g) unbolt

4 a) extreme environments
 b) break with convention
 c) en masse
 d) the most reliable option
 e) spring up
 f) it remains to be seen

5 Because...
 a) of the permafrost. (The ground is frozen all the time.)
 b) of the termites (a type of ant).
 c) buildings need to go up fast there.
 d) it would need a big change in the usual way of doing things.
 e) when industrialisation in a particular area takes off, things can change quickly.

Vidoeconferencing

1 1 c   2 d   3 a   4 b

2 a

3 a) False   b) False   c) True   d) True   e) False
 f) True   g) True   h) False

4–5

 1 g vii   2 c v   3 a ii   4 b iii   5 d iv   6 e i   7 f vi

Unit 3

The inevitability of change

1 a) He teaches at London Business School.
 b) He is an expert on:
  i) organisational behaviour.
  ii) change in organisations.

2 a) True   b) False   c) False   d) False   e) True
 f) False   g) True   h) False

3 a) logical
 b) simple recipe
 c) step-by-step approaches
 d) one single way
 e) basic principles
 f) internal organisation
 g) environment

4 a) adaptability   e) readiness
 b) changeability   f) capable
 c) flexibility   g) capabilities
 d) organisational

5 Changeability – readiness to change

6

company	president	problems
McDonald's (Europe)	Denis Hennequin	declining sales and market share
Dell	not given	competitors beginning to catch up with its original low-price model

change	results
McDonald's: restaurants were redesigned to make them more appealing and food began to be sourced locally	market share and profits rose
Dell: market research was carried out	information analysed with a view to spotting emerging and future customer needs

7 Pharmaceutical

8 d, b, c, a

Managing change successfully

1 a) False b) True c) False d) False
e) True f) False g) True

2 1 c 2 e 3 a 4 b 5 f 6 d

3 a) introduce d) support
b) accommodate e) respond to
c) expand f) implement

4 a) professionalised e) vast
b) systematic f) long-term
c) traditional g) phenomenal
d) ambitious h) leading

5 Because they had lots of energy and ideas, but no realistic plan for putting the ideas into practice.

6 a, c and d

7 b

Unit 4

Collective intelligence

1 a) General Motors, IBM, Wal-Mart
b) Wikipedia, eBay, Google, YouTube

2 a) False b) False c) True d) True e) False

3 a) economies of scale, risk control
b) freedom, flexibility, motivation, creativity

4 a) creativity d) motivation
b) freedom e) flexibility
c) risk control f) economies of scale

5 In knowledge-based and innovation-driven work

6 Collective intelligence

7 b

8 Enjoyment, recognition, opportunities to socialise with others

9 a) pervasive d) quaint
b) feudal e) accelerates
c) overnight

Insiders and outsiders

1 a) AstraZeneca
b) David Powell, Audit Director for Global Operations
c) Graduate Recruitment Company
d) PFJ
e) Paul Farrer

2 a) ii b) iii c) i d) ii e) i f) ii g) iii

3 a) True b) False c) True d) False e) False
f) False g) True h) True

4 a) schemes g) work; up
b) over-subscribed h) come in from outside
c) applicants i) retention league
d) marked out j) public sector
e) rotated through k) graduate intake
f) gain broad skills

5 c

Unit 5

Internet advertising

1 a) pops up f) develop
b) skip g) harness
c) sponsor h) differentiate
d) reduce i) bombarded
e) consume

2 a) friction c) interactive
b) irritating, irrelevant d) curse

3 It's … *a lean-forward experience. The audience is watching with their hand on the mouse, ready to click away as soon as they lose interest.* (lines 53–57)

4 They stop watching during the first 10 per cent of its length. They click away.

5 Engagement. This will be achievable by more interactive advertising.

6 c

Shock advertisements

1 b

2 c

3 Because it shows a rat coming out of a man's mouth.

4–5
1 f iii 2 e v 3 a i 4 c viii 5 b vi 6 h iv
7 d ii 8 g vii

6 b

7 a) the proportion of fake medicines sold in the developed world
b) the proportion of men who buy medicines from unofficial sources
c) Pfizer's share of the UK medicines market
d) the cost, in pounds, of Pfizer's campaign
e) the cost, in dollars, of Pfizer's campaign

8 Because rat poison has been found in fake medicines.

Unit 6

Financial reporting

1–2

    1 d vi   **2** b/c i   **3** a iv   **4** e iii   **5** f v   **6** c/b ii

3 **a)** False **b)** True **c)** True **d)** False **e)** True
    f) True **g)** False **h)** False **i)** True

4 **a)** $24.7 billion   **d)** $71.5 billion
    b) $1.5 billion   **e)** +2.2%
    c) −8.4 %   **f)** $5.4 billion

5 Asda stores in the UK gained market share with an increased number of customers and increased average spend per customer.
In Japan, sales at Seiyu stores fell 0.5 per cent in relation to the previous quarter, but were higher in November and December.

Short selling

1 **a)** i **b)** iii **c)** iii **d)** ii **e)** iii **f)** ii **g)** iii

2 **a)** rubbish
    b) they're not worth anything like the price on the label
    c) fee
    d) trader
    e) a fraction less
    f) He hasn't sold a single one.
    g) get rid of
    h) suspicious
    i) there's something in it for him

3 So what's actually happened? I, the short seller, have spotted that somebody is charging a lot of money for handbags that are rubbish. Next, I've found somebody who is prepared to sell any old rubbish as long as he thinks there's something in it for him.

4 **a)** False **b)** True **c)** True **d)** Not mentioned
    e) True **f)** False **g)** True

Unit 7

The place of English

1 **a)** True **b)** False **c)** False **d)** True **e)** True
    f) False **g)** True **h)** False

2 **a)** conventional   **e)** native
    b) presence   **f)** personal
    c) intelligibility   **g)** foreign
    d) ability   **h)** comprehension

3 **a)** intelligible, comprehensible   **e)** foreign
    b) conventional   **f)** present
    c) personal   **g)** able
    d) native

4 b

5 **a)** British empire
    b) cultural baggage
    c) global language
    d) cultural yardstick
    e) continental European
    f) social personality

6 According to this manager, Thais who speak good English think they know all the secrets of the world and lose some of their cultural yardsticks or references.

7 **b)** Yes, it is shifting east.
    c) No, its current global use appears as strong as ever.
    d) Yes, it adds 20 million to the global community of English speakers every year.
    e) Not necessarily, but it's true that cross-cultural communication is a tricky thing.

Living and working abroad

1 **a)** True **b)** True **c)** False **d)** True
    e) False **f)** True

2 c

3 **a)** expatriate   **d)** childcare
    b) relocation   **e)** credit history
    c) oddities   **f)** relocation agent

4 c and f

5 **a)** difficult to obtain
    b) be officially recognised as living in the country
    c) be able to live
    d) move to the new country
    e) use the services of
    f) start crying

6 **a)** No, you will do things wrong.
    b) In a hole. This is all part of the classic curve that people follow.
    c) No, you might feel (that) you have made a bad mistake.
    d) At home again.
    e) It should help you get through it.

7 h, d, a, b, c, g, f, e

Unit 8

Therapeutic consultancy

1 **a)** Professor Binna Kandola
    b) Grubb Institute of Behavioural Studies, Tavistock Consultancy Service
    c) Dr Bruce Irvine
    d) Judith Bell
    e) Mars, Morgan Stanley
    f) Sebastian Parsons, Elysia

2 **a)** anxiety   **e)** energy
    b) paralysis   **f)** therapeutic
    c) redundancies **g)** uncertainty
    d) stress   **h)** fearful

3 **a)** redundant   **e)** paralysed
    b) uncertain   **f)** therapeutic
    c) stressful   **g)** energetic
    d) anxious, fearful

4 **a)** False **b)** True **c)** True **d)** False

5 c

6 **a)** Team leaders may just go back to the traditional management methods that they know, even if they don't work.
    b) Grubb will be helping Elysia to prepare its employees psychologically, as many of them have had bad experiences in other companies.

7 b

Human capital planning

1   **a)** scarce resource
     b) the war for talent
     c) half the battle
     d) square pegs in round holes
     e) past experience and past performance

2   c, b, d, a

3   **a)** iii   **b)** ii   **c)** i   **d)** iii   **e)** ii   **f)** iii

4   **a)** enormous   **e)** common
     b) predictive   **f)** productive
     c) financial   **g)** knowledge-intensive
     d) powerful   **h)** responsible

5   **a)** False   **b)** True   **c)** False   **d)** False   **e)** False

Unit 9

Getting into new markets

1   Hitoshi Otsuki, the Director of Panasonic's overseas operations, and Fumio Ohtsubo, Panasonic's President

2   **a)** competitive
     b) foolish
     c) mature
     d) willingness to take risks
     e) load washing machines from the front
     f) have been completely redesigned

3   **a)** iii   **b)** ii   **c)** i   **d)** ii   **e)** i   **f)** iii

4   **a)** Panasonic had a strict division system, but the divisions didn't work well together, and the products that they made were not necessarily suitable for international markets.
     b) Now it has reorganised so as to have profitability as its main objective, and this means it is more able to compete internationally.

5   **a)** False   **b)** True   **c)** True   **d)** False
     e) True   **f)** False   **g)** True   **h)** True

6   **a)** stepping stone   **e)** on top of
     b) hearing aids   **f)** goal
     c) fuel cell-based systems   **g)** launch
     d) power   **h)** generate

Business-to-business e-commerce

1   1 b   2 c   3 e   4 a   5 d   6 g   7 f

2   **a)** open-plan office
     b) preaching
     c) cheer
     d) comfortable
     e) convincing
     f) business-to-business
     g) sales force
     h) sign up a new account
     i) keep the noise down

3   **a)** False   **b)** True   **c)** True   **d)** True   **e)** False
     f) True   **g)** False   **h)** True   **i)** True   **j)** True

4   **a)** performing   **e)** reduce the negative effects
     b) internal   **f)** supplied
     c) part   **g)** found it difficult
     d) internal

5   **a)** virtual Chinese-language storefronts
     b) non-Chinese sellers
     c) shifting geographic focus
     d) global platform
     e) pure China exporting centre
     f) financial crisis

Unit 10

Ethical CVs

1   **a)** liar   **c)** false; fake
     b) embellish the truth   **d)** suspicious gap

2   1   A fake degree – a journalist
     2   A year of inactivity explained by the writing of a book – a friend of the author
     3   Lied on his CV 20 years ago and put the same lie when applying for a new job, even when he didn't need to – 'example' finance director
     4   Closed up a three-month gap spent in prison for fraud – a job candidate
     5   Falsified academic qualifications – Patrick Imbardelli, Asia boss of InterContinental Hotels
     6   A fake degree – Neil Taylor, Chief Executive of a large UK hospital group

3   Because of increasing unemployment

4   **a)** Making mistakes with dates; lying about qualifications; closing up gaps.
     b) The last two are forms of lying.
     c) Background checks or routine checks can be carried out to see if lying has occurred.

5   **a)** False   **b)** False   **c)** True   **d)** True   **e)** False

6   Expressions like *I really need the money* and date of birth

7   **a)** bothers   **d)** was made a director
     b) university   **e)** extremely good at his job
     c) shown to be

Whistleblowers

1   1 e   2 c   3 a   4 d   5 f   6 g   7 b

2   **a)** That it was expanding too fast.
     b) He was forced out; he was made redundant.
     c) To the House of Commons Treasury Committee.
     d) His former boss at HBOS resigned from his job at the FSA.
     e) They suffer for their actions and pay an enormous professional and personal price.
     f) People forget the brave actions of the whistleblower, but the whistleblower's bosses will remember what they did to them.

3   **a)** True   **b)** False   **c)** False   **d)** True

4   **a)** incompetence   **e)** intervention
     b) bitter   **f)** devastating
     c) injustices   **g)** overly
     d) advocate   **h)** discredit

5   Talk about the story, not yourself.
     Keep your cool – in other words, keep calm.
     After every discussion, e-mail a note repeating your concerns.

Unit 11

The Nordic leadership style

1 **a)** operational style
   b) household name
   c) chief executives or chairmen
   d) low-key style
   e) a struggling industrial conglomerate
   f) leading industrialist
   g) mission statement
   h) powerhouse

2 **a)** True   **b)** False   **c)** True   **d)** False   **e)** True

3 b

4 a and f

5 **b)** fondness   **f)** focus solely
   c) entrepreneur   **g)** rethought
   d) passion   **h)** profit; adoption
   e) echo   **i)** openness; protection

Leadership in difficult times

1 First (line 9), Second (line 58), Finally (line 68)

2–3
   1 e ii   2 c i   3 d vi   4 a iii   5 f v   6 b iv

4–5
   1 Rudolph Giuliani, Mayor of New York at the time of the terrorist attacks of 2001 – b
   2 Andrew Higginson, Finance Director of UK retailer Tesco – c
   3 Michael O'Leary, Chief Executive of low-cost airline Ryanair – a

6 reactive: 'the danger is that business leaders are trapped' (lines 52–53)
   proactively: 'constructively reshaping events' (line 57)

7 **a)** focused   **b)** tough   **c)** painful   **d)** dignity
   e) cohesion   **f)** organisational   **g)** closeness

8 It might prevent leaders from stepping back and seeing the bigger picture.

Unit 12

Taking on competitors

1 1 c   2 e   3 b   4 f   5 f   6 d   7 a

2 **a)** True   **b)** True   **c)** True   **d)** False
   e) False   **f)** False

3 **a)** No, the joint venture will inherit Carphone's stores.
   b) No, the Carphone Warehouse brand will continue to operate under the Carphone brand.
   c) Carphone Warehouse will extend this activity by stocking laptops in all of its 2,400 stores.
   d) Best Buy have entered into a joint venture because they want to open up a new avenue of growth.
   e) Best Buy is investing £1.1bn and this will give them a 50-per-cent share in the joint venture.
   f) Best Buy and Carphone have announced a tie-up in the form of a joint venture.
   g) Carphone Warehouse made a successful entry in the PC market last year.
   h) Best Buy plans to open stores in Mexico and Turkey, but has none at the moment.

4 f, e, d, h, g, c, a, b

5 **a)** rapidly   **f)** format
   b) meaningful   **g)** launchpad
   c) dodge   **h)** incentive
   d) acknowledge   **i)** roll-out
   e) counterpart

6 **a)** roaming   **d)** complicated
   b) keener   **e)** lie at the heart of
   c) tangible aspects **f)** tech stress

7 a, b and e

Breaking up monopolies

1 **a)** Cemex   **e)** Telmex
   b) No names given   **f)** No names given
   c) Comex   **g)** TV Azteca, Televisa
   d) Telcel

2 **a)** False   **d)** False
   b) True   **e)** False
   c) False   **f)** True

3 **a)** distortions   **d)** consideration
   b) privatise   **e)** behave
   c) competition   **f)** operate

4 **a)** behaviour   **d)** consideration
   b) operation   **e)** distortions
   c) privatisation   **f)** competition

5 **a)** Privatisation
   b) competition
   c) consideration
   d) Companies' behaviour and operations
   e) Distortions

6 **a)** afterthought   **f)** regulations
   b) improvements   **g)** regulators
   c) weakness   **h)** observers
   d) the public interest **i)** sectors
   e) academics   **j)** the regulated

7 Being able to compare products from different banks more easily and being able to take your phone number from one network to another

TEXT BANK – Key

Resource bank

TEACHER'S NOTES

Introduction

These Resource bank activities are designed to extend and develop the material in the Course Book. The Resource bank contains exercises and activities relating to:

Speaking

Each Speaking unit begins with an exercise that picks up and takes further language from the Skills section of the Course Book unit, then applies this language in one or more activities. The speaking units are best done in the classroom. You have permission to photocopy the Resource bank pages in this book. In some units, you will give each student a copy of the whole page. In others, there are role cards which need to be cut out and given to participants with particular roles. These activities are indicated in the unit-specific notes which follow.

Listening

Students listen again to the interviews from the Listening sections in the Course Book, and do further activities on comprehension and language development. These activities can be done in the classroom, but they have been designed in a way that makes it easy for students to do them on their own as homework. Make photocopies for the students. Follow up in the next lesson by getting students to talk about any difficulties that they had. You could play the recording again in the classroom to help resolve problems if necessary.

Writing

A model answer is given for the writing task at the end of each case study in the Course Book. There are then two or three extra writing activities. These can all be done as homework. Again, make photocopies for the students. After correcting the writing exercises in class, go over key points that have been causing problems.

Resource bank: Speaking

General notes

The exercise at the beginning of each Speaking unit in the Resource bank can be used to revise language from the Course Book unit, especially if you did the Skills section in another lesson. In any case, point out the connection with the Course Book Skills material. These exercises are designed to prepare students for the role plays or discussions that follow, and in many cases can be done in a few minutes as a way of focusing students on the activity that will follow.

A typical two-person role play might last five or 10 minutes, followed by three to five minutes of praise and correction. An animated group discussion might last longer, and longer than you planned: in this case, drop one of your other planned activities and do it another time, rather than try to cram it in before the end of the lesson. If you then have five or 10 minutes left over, you can always go over some language points from the lesson again, or, better still, get students to say what they were. One way of doing this is to ask them what they've written in their notebooks during the lesson.

Revising and revisiting

Feel free to do an activity more than once. After one run-through, praise strong points, then work on three or four things that need correcting or improving. Then you can get learners to change roles and do the activity again, or the parts of the activity where these points come up. Obviously, there will come a time when interest wanes, but the usual tendency in language teaching is not to revisit things enough, rather than the reverse.

Fluency and accuracy

Concentrate on different things in different activities. In some role plays and discussions, you may want to focus on *fluency*, with learners interacting as spontaneously as possible. In others, you will want to concentrate on *accuracy*, with learners working on getting specific forms correct. Rather than expect students to get everything correct, you could pick out, say, three or four forms that you want them to get right, and focus on these.

Clear instructions

Be sure to give complete instructions *before* getting students to start. In role plays, be very clear about who has which role, and give students time to absorb the information they need. Sometimes there are role cards that you hand out. The activities where this happens are indicated in the notes which follow.

Parallel and public performances (PPP)

In pairwork or small-group situations, get all groups to do the activity at the same time. Go round the class and listen. When they have finished, praise strong points and deal with three or four problems that you have heard, especially problems that more than one group has been having. Then get individual groups to give public performances so that the whole class can listen. The performers should pay particular attention to these two or three points.

One-to-one

The pair activities can be done one-to-one, with the teacher taking one of the roles. The activity can be done a second time reversing the roles and getting student to integrate your suggestions for improvement.

Unit 1 Brands
Taking part in meetings

A

- With the whole class, look again at the expressions in the Useful language box on page 11 of the Course Book and get students to read them with realistic intonation.

- Then get students to close their Course Books and work on the exercise here.

- With the whole class, ask for answers.

> **1** feel **2** do **3** your **4** think **5** about
> **6** Maybe **7** agree **8** too **9** don't **10** sure

B

- If this is the first role play you are doing, be especially careful about structuring the activity. Explain the situation, highlighting any potential difficulties, e.g. *retail banking*.

- Divide the class into pairs and hand out the role cards.

- Begin the role play in parallel pairs. Go round the room, assist where necessary and monitor the language being used. Note down strong points and points that need correction or improvement.

- When most pairs have finished, bring the class to order, praise good language points from the role play and work on half a dozen points that need improvement, getting students to say the correct forms.

- If time permits, get one of the pairs to do a public performance for the whole class, integrating the corrections.

Unit 2 Travel
Telephoning: making arrangements

A

- Before the class, photocopy and cut up the 'turns' on page 176 of this book. Make as many photocopies as there will be groups of three. Don't mix the conversations, as this will cause some surreal exchanges! (You could make additional photocopies without cutting them up, and hand them out after the activity as a 'key'.)

- Get students to look again at the language for making arrangements on the telephone on page 19 of the Course Book.

- Get students to work in groups of three on rearranging the turns.

- Get groups to read their telephone conversations in parallel. Get students to sit back to back to read the phone call or, even better, get them to use real phone extensions.

- When the groups have finished, bring the class to order and work on any intonation or pronunciation problems.

- Get one or two of the groups to read the conversation again.

B

- Point out that this activity relates to the earlier telephone conversation that Jake mentions in his call to Maria in Exercise A.

- Get the students to work in pairs on the conversation. Go round the room and monitor the language being used. Note down strong points and points that need correction or improvement.

- When pairs have finished, bring the class to order, praise strong points and work on any areas that need improvement, getting students to say the correct forms.

- If time permits, get one of the pairs to do a public performance for the whole class, integrating the corrections.

C

- Point out that this is a telephone conversation that happens a week after the one in Exercise A. This time the pair consists of Maria's receptionist and Jake Daniel.

- Tell students to work in parallel pairs again.

- Go round the room and monitor the language being used. Again, note down strong points and points that need correction or improvement, especially in the area of telephone language.

- When the pairs have finished, bring the class to order, praise strong points and work on any problems.

- Get one or two of the pairs to do a public performance for the whole class, integrating your corrections.

Unit 3 Change
Managing meetings

A

- Get students to look again at the language for managing meetings in the Useful language box on page 27 of the Course Book.

- Then get students to close their Course Books and do the exercise as a whole-class activity.

> 1 OK, let's get down **to** business.
> 2 The purpose **of** this meeting is ...
> 3 How do you **feel** about ...?
> 4 Could you **let** him finish, please?
> 5 Could you just hang **on** a moment, please?
> 6 Perhaps we could get **back** to the point.
> 7 I think we should move **on** now.
> 8 Can we **come** back to that?
> 9 Hold on, we need to look at **this/that** in more detail.
> 10 OK, let's go **over** what we've agreed.

- With the whole class, run through the answers. Explain any difficulties.

B

- Before the class, make as many photocopies of the role cards as there will be pairs, and cut them out.

- With the whole class, explain the general situation and explain any difficult vocabulary and pronunciation, e.g. *pressure* and *scheme*.

- Start the role play in parallel pairs. Go round the room and monitor the language being used. Note down strong points and points that need correction or improvement, especially in the area of language used to manage meetings.

- When pairs have finished, bring the class to order. Praise strong points that you heard and work on points that need correction or improvement, getting students to say the correct forms.

- Get one or two of the pairs to say what happened in their role play, and what the outcome was.

Unit 4 Organisation

Socialising: introductions and networking

A

- Before the class, photocopy and cut up the 'turns' on page 179 of this book. Make as many photocopies as there will be groups of three. (You could make additional photocopies without cutting them up, and hand them out after the activity as a 'key' and to use in Exercise B.)

- Remind students of the language for introductions and socialising in the Useful language box on page 41 of the Course Book and work on any difficulties.

- Explain the situation and divide the class into groups of three. Get students to work on putting the turns into the correct order.

B

- In the same groups of three as for Exercise A, get students to start their conversations in parallel.

- Go round the room and monitor the language being used. Note down strong points and points that need correction or improvement, especially in the area of language for introductions and socialising.

- When the groups have finished, bring the class to order, praise strong points and work on any problems.

- Get one or two of the groups to read the conversation again, integrating your corrections.

C

- Ensure students understand that they will now be working in pairs: Frank and Jessica. This is the continuation of their conversation after Carl has left them.

- Divide the class into pairs and get them to have parallel conversations, using the ideas given.

- Again, go round the room and monitor the language being used. Note down strong points and points that need correction or improvement, especially in the area of language used for socialising.

- When the pairs have finished, bring the class to order, praise strong points and work on any problems.

- Get one or two of the pairs to do a public performance for the whole class, integrating your corrections.

Unit 5 Advertising

Starting and structuring presentations

A

- Get students to look again at the language for starting presentations in the Useful language box on page 49 of the Course Book. Then get them to close their books.

- With the whole class, go through the exercise, getting students to point out the unnecessary words. Explain any difficulties.

---

1 On the behalf of Petersson Mobile, I'd like to welcome you. My name's Pia Lundgren.

2 It's good to see on you all.

3 I'm going to tell to you about our latest mobile devices.

4 I've divided my up presentation into three parts. Firstly, I'll tell you about our latest phones for business users.

5 Secondly, I'll discuss about consumer devices.

6 I'll finish with off an overview of some of the trends in mobile devices that have emerged in the last few months.

7 If there's anything you're not clear about, feel so free to stop me and ask any questions.

8 I'd be grateful if you could leave out any questions to the end.

B

- Tell students that they will now be working in pairs, each member of the pair making a presentation to the other.

- Get the students in each pair to choose their subjects. Explain any difficulties.

- When they are ready, start the first role play. Go round the room and monitor the language being used. Note down strong points and points that need correction or improvement, especially in relation to the language used to start and structure presentations.

- Bring the class to order. Praise strong language points and work on half a dozen points that need improving, getting students to say the correct forms.

- Then reverse the roles in the pairs and repeat the above procedure on another topic.

Unit 6 Money
Dealing with figures

A

- Remind students about the information on figures in the Useful language box on page 57 of the Course Book. Explain any remaining difficulties.
- Then with the whole class, elicit the answers to the exercise from individual students.

1 The next three Olympic Games will take place in …
… twenty-twelve, twenty-sixteen and twenty-twenty. (BrE/AmE) *or*
… two thousand and twelve, two thousand and sixteen, and two thousand and twenty. (BrE) *or*
… two thousand twelve, two thousand sixteen and two thousand twenty. (AmE)

2 Slovakia joined the European currency at the rate of thirty point one two six korunas to the euro.

3 A (*or* One) hundred degrees centigrade (*or* Celsius) is …
… two hundred and twelve degrees Fahrenheit. (BrE) *or*
… two hundred twelve degrees Fahrenheit. (AmE)

4 There are two point four seven one acres to a hectare.

5 The UK VAT rate was reduced from seventeen point five (*or* seventeen and a half) per cent to fifteen per cent in …
… two thousand and eight. (BrE) *or*
… two thousand eight. (AmE)

6 Nine-tenths of the UK population live in towns or cities.

7 The price of a business-class return air ticket from London to New York is …
… one thousand, eight hundred and eighty-six pounds and seventy-eight pence. (BrE) *or*
… one thousand, eight hundred eighty-six pounds and seventy-eight pence. (AmE)

8 An Indian lakh is a (*or* one) hundred thousand rupees, and a crore is equal to a (*or* one) hundred lakh or ten million rupees.

9 The population of Mexico City is about …
… eighteen million, one hundred and thirty-one thousand. (BrE) *or*
… eighteen million, one hundred thirty-one thousand. (AmE)

10 Lehman Brothers went bankrupt with debts of more than …
… six hundred and seventeen billion dollars. (BrE) *or*
… six hundred seventeen billion dollars. (AmE)

B

- The idea here is for students to exchange information about two countries: Bolivia and Peru.
- Tell students to work in pairs. Hand out the information.
- Start the activity. Go round the room and monitor the language being used. Note down strong points

and points that need correction or improvement, especially in relation to numbers.

- Bring the class to order. Praise strong language points and work on half a dozen points that need improving, getting students to say the correct forms.
- Then get one student to read out the information they obtained about Peru, and another the information they obtained about Bolivia.
- Check the answers with the whole class.

Unit 7 Cultures
Social English

A

- Get students to look again at the language for socialising in Exercise B on page 71 of the Course Book. Work on the intonation. Then get them to close their books.
- Students could do the exercise in pairs, reading each alternative dialogue. (They will hopefully realise that the distractors (i.e. wrong answers) are tongue in cheek (teach this expression). However, this exercise is intended to remind them of the importance of saying the right thing!
- Go through the answers with the whole class.

1 a   2 a   3 b   4 b   5 a   6 a   7 b   8 a
9 b   10 b

B

- Explain the situation. Then get one pair to do a demonstration for the whole class. Student A must write down the expression that they want to elicit from Student B (without showing it to B, of course).
- When the whole class has the idea, get pairs to do the exercise in parallel pairs. Go round the room and monitor the naturalness of the exchanges.
- Bring the class to order and get some of the pairs to demonstrate new exchanges for the whole class. (Don't get them to repeat previous exchanges, as there will be no element of mystery, of course.)

Unit 8 Human resources
Getting information on the telephone

A

- Go through the expressions in the Useful language box on page 79 of the Course Book.
- Then go through the answers with the whole class. Point out that they have to find the expression that is not possible in each case. (For 1, mention that *Good day* is very old-fashioned, and that *I wish you a good day* is impossible in this context, at the beginning of a phone call.)

1 c   2 a   3 c   4 b   5 a   6 c

B

- Before the class, make as many photocopies of the role cards as there will be pairs, and cut them out.

- With the whole class, explain the general situation and explain any difficult vocabulary. Work on the pronunciation of *apologies* and *apologise*.

- Start the role play in parallel pairs. Go round the room and monitor the language being used. Note down strong points and points that need correction or improvement, especially in the area of telephone language.

- When pairs have finished, bring the class to order. Praise strong points that you heard and work on points that need correction or improvement, getting students to say the correct forms.

Unit 9 International markets
Negotiating

A

- Point out the link with the Useful language box on page 88 of the Course Book.

- Do the first one or two with the whole class, pointing out the grammatical and other 'clues' for what the continuation will be.

- Get students to do the rest of the exercise individually or in pairs.

- Go through the answers with the whole class, concentrating on the logic of why each answer is correct. Explain any difficulties.

> **1** g **2** f **3** a **4** c **5** e **6** h **7** i **8** j
> **9** d **10** b

B

- Before the class, make as many photocopies as there are pairs.

- With the whole class, explain the situation, pointing out similarities with the negotiating situations in the Course Book unit. Explain any difficulties.

- Divide the class into pairs – the buyer and the manufacturer – and hand out the role cards.

- When the situation is clear, start the role play. Go round the room and monitor the language being used. Note down strong points and points that need correction or improvement.

- When most pairs have finished, bring the class to order. Praise good language points from the role play and work on half a dozen points that need improvement, especially in the area of the language used for negotiations, getting students to say the correct forms.

- Ask one or two of the pairs to say what happened in their negotiations.

- If time permits, get one of the pairs to do a public performance for the whole class, integrating your corrections.

(Note: this negotiation continues in Resource bank: Speaking, Unit 12.)

Unit 10 Ethics
Considering options

A

- Point out the link with the Useful language box on page 101 of the Course Book.

- Get students to do the exercise individually or in pairs.

- Go through the answers with the whole class. Explain any difficulties.

> **1** The way I see it **is** that employees will always take advantage of the company.
>
> **2** Let's look at the issue from another **angle**.
>
> **3** Let's consider another **approach**.
>
> **4** There are several ways we could **deal** with this.
>
> **5** I'm with you **up** to a point, but it might not work.
>
> **6** You could **be** right, but it's a risky strategy.
>
> **7** One consequence could **be** that they all resign.
>
> **8** The best way to **deal** with the problem is to talk to him.
>
> **9** I'll arrange **for** the employee representatives to meet us.
>
> **10** The next thing to do is **fix** up an appointment with them.

B

- With the whole class, explain the situation. Explain any difficulties, for example *mileage* and the pronunciation of *receipts*.

- Divide the class into small groups of three or four, who will have parallel discussions to talk about each option. Go round the class and assist the discussions; help with two more options if necessary. Encourage imaginative thinking!

- When most pairs have finished, bring the class to order. Praise good language points from the discussion and work on half a dozen points that need improvement, especially in the area of the language used to consider options, getting students to say the correct forms.

- Ask one or two of the groups to say what other options they came up with in their groups.

- If time, get one of the groups to do a public performance for the whole class, integrating the corrections.

Unit 11 Leadership
Presenting

- Point out the link with the Useful language box on page 109 of the Course Book.

- Get students to do the exercise individually or in pairs.

- Go through the answers with the whole class. Explain any difficulties e.g. *exponential*.

> **1** d **2** f **3** a **4** e **5** i **6** b **7** h **8** c **9** g

B

- The main purposes of this activity are to recycle the language used for presentations in the Useful language box on page 109 of the Course Book and to apply the advice given to presenters in the Course Book.

- You could get students to prepare and give these presentations in class. (If available, hand out overhead pens and transparencies so that students can prepare visual aids.) Even better, get them to prepare the presentation for a later class. (If computers and software are available, you could even get them to present visuals on PowerPoint.)

- Do one or two presentations in a lesson. Keep others for later lessons.

- When students give their presentations, get the audience to monitor if the speaker is following the advice in the Course Book.

- Monitor the language being used. Note down strong points and points that need correction or improvement.

- When the presentation has finished, praise good language points from the presentation and work on half a dozen points that need improvement, especially in the area of language used for presentations, getting the presenter to say the correct forms.

- Ask the group to comment tactfully on how far the speaker followed the advice. Get them to balance any criticism with praise of good points. (Speakers at this level may say, perhaps rightly, that they're concentrating on the English so much that they don't have time to think about gesture, body language, etc.)

Unit 12 Competition
Negotiating

- Point out the link with the Useful language box on page 117 of the Course Book.

- Get students to do the exercise individually or in pairs.

- Go through the answers with the whole class. Explain any difficulties.

> **1** I'm sorry, (but) we can't accept that!
> **2** I'm afraid the specifications for your product are rather basic.
> **3** Unfortunately, the minimum order quantity has just doubled.
> **4** To be honest, we have big production problems at the plant.
> **5** If you insisted on this delivery date, the products would probably arrive late.
> **6** Transport could be problematic.
> **7** Getting the exact colours that you want may be difficult.
> **8** We might not be able to reduce our prices any further.

B

- Point out that this is a continuation of the role play in Resource bank: Speaking, Unit 9, Exercise B, but it doesn't matter if your students haven't done it. (Ensure, however, that they understand the initial situation in that role play.)

- Underline that the situation as it is now has nothing to do with the negotiations that they might have enacted in Resource bank, Unit 9. The idea is rather to take a situation that is 'stuck' and use the right techniques (and language of course) to progress further.

- Divide the class into pairs.

- When the situation is clear, start the role play. Go round the room and monitor the language being used. Note down strong points and points that need correction or improvement.

- When most pairs have finished, bring the class to order. Praise good language points from the role play and work on half a dozen points that need improvement, especially in the area of negotiations language, getting students to say the correct forms.

- Ask one or two of the pairs to say what happened in their negotiations to 'unblock' the situation.

- If time permits, get one of the pairs to do a public performance for the whole class, integrating the corrections.

Brands

TAKING PART IN MEETINGS

A   Complete the expressions with the words from the box.

your	too	think	sure	maybe
feel	don't	do	agree	about

1   How do you .... about that ... ?   *(Asking for opinions)*

2   What .... you think?   *(Asking for opinions)*

3   What's .... view?   *(Asking for opinions)*

4   I .... we should ...   *(Making suggestions)*

5   How ....?   *(Making suggestions)*

6   .... we could ...   *(Making suggestions)*

7   I .... with you.   *(Agreeing)*

8   I think so, ...   *(Agreeing)*

9   Why .... we ... ?   *(Making suggestions)*

10   I'm not so ....   *(Disagreeing)*

B   Use the expressions in Exercise A and others from page 11 of the Course Book to role-play a meeting about this situation.

To cut costs, the Chief Executive of a bank wants to close the least profitable branches and invest more elsewhere.

Student A is the Chief Executive of the bank.

Student B is the Head of Retail Banking, with responsibility for the bank branches. They meet to discuss the Chief Executive's proposal.

Student A: Chief Executive of the bank

You want to close branches (10 per cent of the total number):

- in towns where there are too many;
- where the building could be sold to developers for other uses, for example to be transformed into bars or restaurants.

This will allow the bank to invest more in its online banking operations and other activities.

Student B: Head of Retail Banking

You are against branch closures because the bank:

- needs to be visible everywhere, even if some branches are unprofitable;
- cannot depend completely on its website. For example, customers need somewhere to pay in cheques. (They don't like paying them in by post.)
- can make good profits in branch banking – what you call 'good old-fashioned banking'.

RESOURCE BANK – Speaking

TELEPHONING: MAKING ARRANGEMENTS

A Look again at the Useful language for making arrangements on the telephone on page 19 of the Course Book. Rearrange the 'turns' that your teacher will give you into a logical telephone conversation.

B This telephone conversation is the one that Jake mentions in his call to Maria in Exercise A. Role-play the conversation. Student A is Jake Daniel. Student B is Maria Templeton.

Jake:	Introduce yourself and your organisation (Richmond Advertising).
Maria:	Say hello. Say you're very busy.
Jake:	Explain that you would like to meet to talk to her about advertising her organisation (Wolfson's Estate Agents) in local magazines across the country.
Maria:	Say again, politely, that you are very busy, and that he should call again next month, when things should be quieter.
Jake:	Apologise for phoning at an inconvenient time.
Maria:	Say that it's not a problem.
Jake:	Confirm you will phone sometime next month.
Both:	End the conversation suitably.

C This telephone conversation takes place a week after the one in Exercise A.
This conversation is between Maria's receptionist and Jake Daniel. Work in pairs.
Have the conversation, using these ideas.

Receptionist:	Give the company name – Wolfson's Estate Agents. Greet the caller. Offer to help them.
Jake:	Say you'd like to speak to Maria Templeton.
Receptionist:	Ask who's calling.
Jake:	Give your name and organisation.
Receptionist:	Tell him you're putting him through. (You try to do this, but find that Maria's on another line.) Explain this and offer to take a message.
Jake:	Explain that you should be meeting Maria Templeton at 10.30 tomorrow, but something's come up. (Give a reason.) Give your phone number and ask if Maria can call you back to arrange another time.
Receptionist:	Ask for Jake Daniel's number.
Jake:	Say it's 00 44 7979 238841. Say that this is your mobile number and she can call anytime she likes.
Receptionist:	Confirm.
Jake:	Thank the receptionist for his/her help and say goodbye.
Receptionist:	Say goodbye.

TELEPHONING: MAKING ARRANGEMENTS

'Turns' for Exercise A

Receptionist:	Good morning, Wolfson's Estate Agents. How may I help you?
Jake:	Could you put me through to Maria Templeton's extension, please? My name's Jake Daniel.
Receptionist:	Certainly. Putting you through.
Maria:	Hello. Maria Templeton speaking.
Jake:	Hello. It's Jake Daniel here, from Richmond Advertising. You remember I phoned last month about advertising in our local magazines across the country.
Maria:	Er ...
Jake:	You said you were very busy and you told me to phone again this month.
Maria:	Oh, right, I remember now.
Jake:	I'm calling because I'll be in your area next week and I'd like to make an appointment to see you, if that's OK.
Maria:	OK. What day would suit you? I'm pretty busy next week, but I could probably fit you in.
Jake:	How about Tuesday? Could you make it then?
Maria:	Let me look now. I'll check my diary. Tuesday morning would be possible. What about 10.30?
Jake:	That's fine. Thanks very much. I look forward to meeting you.
Maria:	See you on Tuesday morning.
Jake:	Right. Bye.
Maria:	Bye.

Change

MANAGING MEETINGS

A   Add the missing word to each of these expressions.

1 OK, let's get down business.	*(Starting)*
2 The purpose this meeting is …	*(Setting objectives)*
3 How do you about …?	*(Asking for reactions)*
4 Could you him finish, please?	*(Dealing with interruptions)*
5 Could you just hang a moment, please?	*(Dealing with interruptions)*
6 Perhaps we could get to the point.	*(Keeping to the point)*
7 I think we should move now.	*(Speeding up)*
8 Can we back to that?	*(Speeding up)*
9 Hold on, we need to look at in more detail.	*(Slowing down)*
10 OK, let's go what we've agreed.	*(Summarising)*

B   A mid-size (100 employees) media company in a large north European city wants more of its staff to cycle to work. Each employee would be entitled to receive €400 to buy a bicycle. Student A, the Chief Executive, is a keen cyclist and supports the scheme. Student B, the employee representative, is personally against it. Role-play the meeting.

Student A: Chief Executive

You want to introduce the scheme because it would:

- reduce pressure on the company car park.
- help to reduce traffic in the city.
- help reduce pollution.
- set an example to other companies.
- be good for the image of the company.

Student B: employee representative

You (and two-thirds of the employees) are against the scheme because:

- cycling is dangerous: there are almost no special cycle routes in the city.
- there are 250 days of rain a year in the city.
- work clothes are not suitable for cycling.
- the money could be better spent on other things. (Think of two or three things.)

Organisation

SOCIALISING: INTRODUCTIONS AND NETWORKING

A Look again at the Useful language for introductions and networking on page 41 of the Course Book. Three people are talking during a coffee break at the annual US Industrial Plastics Convention. Work in groups of three. Rearrange the 'turns' that your teacher will give you into a logical conversation.

B Act out the conversation together.

C Now work in pairs. One of you is Frank and the other Jessica. Continue the conversation.

Frank:	Ask Jessica what she does at Advanced Avionics and where she is based.
Jessica:	You work at the company's site in Houston. Say that you're involved in purchasing components. You are always looking for lighter and stronger ones.
Frank:	Say that your research department is looking at a whole range of strong plastics at the moment.
Jessica:	Express interest, and say that you recently finished your doctorate in this area.
Frank:	Express surprise, and say that you'd like to read it.
Jessica:	Say that it's on the University of Texas physics department website.
Frank:	Promise to look for it and read it. Then invite Jessica to visit your research laboratory at Performance Plastics in Seattle.
Jessica:	Say that you'll be going to see someone in Seattle next month. You'd be happy to go to Performance Plastics as well. Give the date that you'll be there, and the times that you'll be free.
Frank:	Fix a time.
Jessica:	Confirm you'll be there. Give Frank your business card and say you look forward to seeing him in Seattle.
Both:	Close the conversation suitably.

Organisation

SOCIALISING: INTRODUCTIONS AND NETWORKING

'Turns' for Exercise A

Carl:	Hi, Frank. How's everything going?
Frank:	Fine, Carl. I'm still with Performance Plastics. As you may have heard, I'm in charge of the research department now.
Carl:	Yes, I'd heard you'd got promotion. Congratulations!
Frank:	Thanks. It's quite a challenge, I can tell you!
Carl:	Frank, have you met Jessica? She's at Advanced Avionics.
Frank:	No, I don't think so. Pleased to meet you.
Jessica:	Nice to meet you. I've heard a lot of good things about Performance Plastics!
Frank:	Really? That's good to hear! We work a lot with aircraft manufacturers like yours. Let me give you my business card.
Carl:	You and Jessica have something in common. You both work in advanced plastics.
Frank:	Yes, we're very interested in replacing as many metal components as possible with plastic ones.
Carl:	I've got a meeting. I'll leave you two to it.
Frank/Jessica:	OK, see you later.

Advertising

STARTING AND STRUCTURING PRESENTATIONS

A Cross out the extra unnecessary word in each of these expressions.

1 On the behalf of Petersson Mobile, I'd like to welcome you. My name's Pia Lundgren.

2 It's good to see on you all.

3 I'm going to tell to you about our latest mobile devices.

4 I've divided my up presentation into three parts. Firstly, I'll tell you about our latest phones for business users.

5 Secondly, I'll discuss about consumer devices.

6 I'll finish with off an overview of some of the trends in mobile devices that have emerged in the last few months.

7 If there's anything you're not clear about, feel so free to stop me and ask any questions.

8 I'd be grateful if you could leave out any questions to the end.

B Work in pairs. Using correct versions of the expressions in Exercise A and others from page 49 of the Course Book, Student A makes the beginning of a presentation to Student B about one of the subjects below. Then Student B makes the beginning of a presentation to Student A about another of the subjects.

1 An estate agent talks about trends for residential property in three areas: city centres, the suburbs and the country.

2 A marketer talks about three possible user groups for a new energy drink: children playing sport, adults when they are stressed at work and older people when they feel tired.

3 A psychologist talks about responses to TV advertising among professionals, skilled workers and unskilled workers.

4 An economist talks about the current economic situation in one of the following areas: Europe, Asia, North America or South America.

DEALING WITH FIGURES

A   **Say these sentences.**

1   The next three Olympic Games will take place in 2012, 2016 and 2020.

2   Slovakia joined the European currency at the rate of 30.126 korunas to the euro.

3   100°C is 212°F.

4   There are 2.471 acres to a hectare.

5   The UK VAT rate was reduced from 17.5% to 15% in 2008.

6   $\frac{9}{10}$ of the UK population live in towns or cities.

7   The price of a business-class return air ticket from London to New York is £1,886.78.

8   An Indian lakh is 100,000 rupees, and a crore is equal to 100 lakh or 10,000,000 rupees.

9   The population of Mexico City is about 18,131,000.

10   Lehman Brothers went bankrupt with debts of more than $617bn.

B   **Work in pairs. Student A has information about Bolivia. Student B has information about Peru. Communicate this information to each other.**

Student A

	Bolivia	Peru
Area	424,164 square miles	
Population	10,027,643	
Population of largest city	835,267 (La Paz)	
GNP	£5.7bn	
GNP per head	£609	
Adult literacy	90.3%	
Doctors per thousand population	1.2	

Student B

	Bolivia	Peru
Area		496,225 square miles
Population		27,419,294
Population of largest city		8,472,935 (Lima)
GNP		£47.2bn
GNP per head		£1,711
Adult literacy		90.5%
Doctors per thousand population		1.2

RESOURCE BANK – Speaking

SOCIAL ENGLISH

A Choose the most suitable and tactful thing to say at a cocktail party, a) or b), in response to the questions 1–10.

1 Is this your first visit to the country?
   a) No, I was here a long time ago, when I was a student.
   b) No, and I had a terrible time last time I was here.

2 What do you do?
   a) I'm in luxury goods.
   b) It's none of your business.

3 How long have you been here?
   a) Two days, but it seems like two weeks.
   b) I got in on Thursday afternoon.

4 Have you been to this city before?
   a) No, and I can't believe the traffic!
   b) No, and I'm really glad to be here!

5 Is your visit for business or pleasure?
   a) A bit of both, really.
   b) Pleasure? You must be joking!

6 How do you find the climate?
   a) Very pleasant – not too hot, not too cold!
   b) How do you people put up with it?

7 How long are you staying?
   a) Three days, and I can't wait to get out of here.
   b) Three days, I leave on Sunday.

8 Where are you staying?
   a) At the Novotel on the main square.
   b) Some old place out near the airport.

9 What's the food like?
   a) Much too spicy for my taste.
   b) There's so much choice.

10 So, what do you think of things so far?
   a) It's too early to say.
   b) I'm very impressed.

B Work in pairs. Choose one of the expressions in the box, but don't tell your partner what it is. Say something that makes your partner use that expression in response.

Congratulations!	I don't mind.	I'm afraid ...	After you
Cheers!	Excuse me.	Yes, please.	That's no problem.
Make yourself at home.	Sorry.	Could you ... ?	Bad luck.
Help yourself.	It's on me.	That sounds good.	Not at all.

Example A: I've just had some great news. They've offered me the job!

B: Congratulations!

Human resources

GETTING INFORMATION ON THE TELEPHONE

A   Which of the three expressions is not possible in each case?

1
   a) Good morning, my name's Pia Lundgren.

   b) Hello, Carlos Suarez speaking.

   c) I wish you a good day. I am Boris Bronovski speaking.

2
   a) I'm phoning with the subject of the guarantee for a product that I bought from you.

   b) I'm calling about the guarantee on one of your products.

   c) The reason I'm calling is to ask about the guarantee on a product of yours.

3
   a) I was wondering if you could give me some more information?

   b) Could I ask you for the name of the person who deals with this?

   c) Might I persuade you to give me more details about this?

4
   a) Just to get this clear, you're saying the guarantee only lasts six months, not 12.

   b) Are you telling that I broke the product by dropping it?

   c) There's just one other thing, I'd like to check the address of your repair centre.

5
   a) Certain, what do you need to know about our repair service?

   b) I look forward to receiving the product, and when we do, we'll replace it.

   c) I don't think you'll be disappointed with the replacement product.

6
   a) OK, I think that's everything.

   b) Right, I think that's all I need to know.

   c) Good, we do like we said.

B   Work in pairs. Student A works in the human resources department of a company, and Student B works for an employment agency that the company uses when it needs temporary staff. Student A phones Student B to complain about some of the temporary workers that the agency has sent.

Student A: Human Resources Manager	Student B: Employment Agent
Be ready to:	Be ready to:
• talk about the problems that have occurred. (Lateness, untidy clothes, etc. Think of some other problems.)	• apologise for the problems that Student A mentions.
• accept Student B's apologies and ask for a discount of 15 per cent on their next invoice. Accept the discount that they offer.	• explain why the problems occurred and apologise. (Demand for the services of your employment agency is very high. You had to send workers that you had only just recruited.)
• ask Student B what the employment agency is doing to improve the quality of the workers that it uses.	• offer a discount on your next invoice (but not as much as Student A requests).
End suitably.	• tell Student A what you are doing to improve the quality of the workers that you send.
	End suitably.

International markets

NEGOTIATING

A **Match the two parts of these expressions.**

1 We'd like to reach a deal with you

2 We'd like the service contract to start earlier, but we

3 We'd be prepared to offer you better credit terms if

4 When you say there might be production delays,

5 That's more than we usually offer – 10 per cent

6 Sounds a good idea to me. As long as we keep

7 We are agreed on quantities, but we need to

8 I'm sorry, but I'll have to consult our Finance

9 That's it, then. I think we've covered

10 Great!

a) you increased your order.

b) We've got a deal.

c) what do you mean?

d) everything that we intended to.

e) discount is our usual maximum.

f) understand this would be difficult for you.

g) by tomorrow evening.

h) to the original delivery schedule.

i) come to an agreement on exact specifications.

j) Director about payment in dollars rather than euros.

B **The buyer for a clothing retail chain (Student A) is visiting a clothing manufacturer in south-east Asia (Student B) to discuss an order for men's shirts. Work in pairs and come to an agreement.**

Student A: Buyer

You want:

- to order 10,000 to 20,000 shirts, to your design (no variations). You expect a discount if you order more than 15,000.
- a basic price of $3 per shirt.
- half of shirts to be white, half blue.
- delivery in one month.
- payment in US dollars, 90 days after delivery. You might agree to pay in euros if the rest of the deal is good.

Student B: Manufacturer

You want:

- an order for more than 15,000 shirts. It would not be economic for you to make fewer.
- a basic price of $5 per shirt. You usually offer no discounts, whatever the order size, but you might make an exception here.
- all the shirts to be white.
- delivery in two months, but can be quicker if the design is simplified.
- payment in euros, 30 days after delivery. You might agree to be paid in US dollars if the rest of the deal is good.

CONSIDERING OPTIONS

A   Correct the one word that is incorrect in each of these expressions.

1   The way I see it be that employees will always take advantage of the company.

2   Let's look at the issue from another corner.

3   Let's consider another access.

4   There are several ways we could dealt with this.

5   I'm with you along to a point, but it might not work.

6   You could have right, but it's a risky strategy.

7   One consequence could is that they all resign.

8   The best way to treat with the problem is to talk to him.

9   I'll arrange that the employee representatives to meet us.

10   The next thing to do is point up an appointment with them.

B   Executives in a photocopier company are aware that members of the sales force are spending too much on business travel and in some cases cheating on their expenses claims.
Use the expressions for considering options to discuss the issue.

Examples of problems

- Salespeople claim for unnecessarily expensive hotels and meals, in some cases not related to client visits.

- They claim car mileage for their personal vehicles unrelated to business trips and in some cases claim for trips that they did not do.

Below are three options to solve the problem. Add two more options of your own that you can also discuss.

In pairs, discuss each option. One student describes the advantages and the other describes the disadvantages.

Options	Advantage	Disadvantage
Introduce a system of expenses per day; salespeople will no longer submit receipts.	Exact cost will be known in advance. Processing of receipts no longer required.	Cost may be higher than under the present system.
Salespeople will from now on always use the same budget hotel chain, and negotiate a discounted price with the chain.	Predictable costs, and only one invoice per month from the chain.	There is not necessarily a hotel in the chain near every client. Salespeople will complain that the hotels are too basic.
Give each member of the salesforce a credit card for company expenses.	The accounts department will not have to look at individual expense claims from each salesperson – there will be just one statement a month from the credit card company to deal with.	Spending on unauthorised items may increase.

185

PRESENTING

A Match each of the expressions (1–9) to the category (a–i) that it belongs to.

1 Let me just give you a bit of the background to how our company was founded.

a) Introducing yourself

2 That's enough on our products. Let's move on to our services.

b) Structuring the presentation

3 Hello. It's very nice to be here in Valencia ...

c) Inviting questions

4 I'm sure all of you have used our most successful product.

d) Giving background information

5 That's it for today. Thank you very much.

e) Referring to the audience's knowledge

6 What I'm going to say revolves around five basic points.

f) Changing the topic

7 Just to recap those five points very quickly, ...

g) Referring to visuals

8 So far, so good? Everyone with me?

h) Concluding

9 As you can see from this visual, the increase in sales has been exponential.

i) Ending

B Use the expressions above and those on page 109 of the Course Book to make a five-minute presentation about one of the following topics.

- The negative characteristics that make bad leaders

- A large purchase that you have made – how you decided which brand and which product in the range to buy, your experience as a customer, your feelings afterwards, etc.

- An activity that you like doing in your free time – the time required, equipment needed, the benefits, etc.

NEGOTIATING

A Change these expressions so that they are more diplomatic or speculative, using the expression(s) in brackets.

1 We can't accept that! (sorry)

2 The specifications for your product are very basic. (afraid / rather)

3 The minimum order quantity has just doubled. (unfortunately)

4 We have big production problems at the plant. (honest)

5 If you insist on this delivery date, the products will arrive late. (would / probably)

6 Transport will be problematic. (could)

7 Getting the exact colours that you want will be difficult. (may)

8 We can't reduce our prices any further. (might)

B This negotiation is a continuation of the negotiation in Resource bank: Speaking, Unit 9. This is the situation the negotiators had reached the last time that they met (yesterday).

- order quantity: 17,500
- basic price: $3.80 per shirt
- delivery: 7 weeks
- colour: half white, half blue
- payment: US dollars
- credit terms: 60 days after delivery

Imagine that the manufacturer has found that it will not be possible to fulfil the agreement that was reached yesterday. Work in pairs. Use appropriate forms of the expressions in Exercise A, as well as other expressions from page 117 of the Course Book, to discuss the situation.

The manufacturer has found that:

- it will only be able to produce 10,000 shirts in the time available
- the basic price will be $3.90 per shirt (smaller production run means higher unit cost)
- delivery will be in eight weeks after all
- all the shirts will be white, rather than the mix of colours originally agreed
- it will only accept payment in euros (worried about possible fall in value of dollar)
- credit terms are 45 days maximum.

RESOURCE BANK – Speaking

Brands

A 🔊 CD1.2 **Listen to part one of the interview and match the two parts of the expressions.**

1	real	**a)**	identity
2	physical	**b)**	traction
3	visual	**c)**	manifestation
4	design	**d)**	customer or consumer
5	target	**e)**	product
6	persuasive	**f)**	audience
7	end	**g)**	ideas and perceptions
8	target	**h)**	user

B **Now match the expressions in Exercise A to these explanatory phrases.**

i) the people to whom it is hoped to sell brands (3 expressions)

ii) the powerful ideas that people have about brands

iii) the look of the brands (images used in advertising, etc.) (2 expressions)

iv) when brands are seen in terms of the item being sold

v) brands that are powerful in the marketplace

C 🔊 CD1.3 **Listen to part two. True or false?**

1 Brands are a useful way of transmitting information.

2 This information is only about what the brand does.

3 Brands help you choose between products.

4 The physical differences between products mentioned here can be very large.

5 Chris Cleaver mentions BMW, Audi, Mercedes and Porsche.

6 Brands help you decide if the product is right for you or says the right thing about you.

D 🔊 CD1.4 **Listen to part three. In what order do you hear these adverbs?**

a) hugely

b) technically

c) primarily

d) particularly

E **Now use the adverbs from Exercise D to complete these sentences.**

1 Nokia invented the market in a way, for many people, ... people of Chris Cleaver's generation.

2 Nokia is what you might call .... the master brand.

3 Nokia wanted to satisfy the needs that that one emerging customer group has, ... younger consumers.

4 Nokia expanded .... in terms of what it offers.

UNIT 2 Travel

SHOLTO SMITH, AREA SALES DIRECTOR FOR HYATT HOTELS

A ◀) CD1.9 **Listen to part one and replace the eight mistakes in the transcript below with what Sholto Smith actually says.**

A key point is the location of our hotels, um, good connections with um subway underground networks, near the airport, um, and obviously close to an office that the guest is working in while they're staying in the hotel. Um, technology is also a key characteristic, and nowadays it's expected because obviously people have, um, good technology at home and therefore if it's also available in a hotel, that's also, um, a key feature. Um, Internet, a business centre, um, obviously translation services and that kind of facility is also, is important, and guests also expect an area where they can, er, go to a gymnasium, they can exercise, um, and also that kind of thing. These would be the most important features.

B ◀) CD1.10 **Listen to part two. Are these statements about expressions that you hear true or false?**

1 If someone is more *savvy* than before, they are cleverer, more knowledgeable, etc.

2 If a company *adds value* to a particular service, it offers the same service as before.

3 If a range of services *takes in* a particular service, it includes it.

4 If you do something *on a daily basis*, you do it once a week.

5 If you take a *shuttle service* to a particular place, you can go there but you can't come back.

6 If a hotel *drops its rates*, it lowers its prices.

C ◀) CD1.11 **Listen to part three. Which of these things are *not* mentioned?**

1 environmental policies

2 healthy eating

3 gym facilities

4 water conservation

5 better transport links

6 low-energy lighting

7 high-speed Internet

8 live entertainment

9 television on demand

10 lower-cost phone calls

RESOURCE BANK – Listening

Change

ANNE DEERING, HEAD OF TRANSFORMATION PRACTICE AT INTERNATIONAL MANAGEMENT CONSULTANTS A T KEARNEY

A ◀)) CD1.14 **Complete these statements with appropriate forms of expressions from part one.**

1 If you consider something, you take it ....

2 The appearance of something is what it ....

3 If you calculate the effect of something, you .... it.

4 Someone committed to change is .... in it.

5 If they want it done properly, they should do it ....

B ◀)) CD1.15 **Listen to part two and find expressions in relation to change to replace the expressions in italic.**

1 the *complete series of steps* involved to make change happen (7 letters)

2 *feeling tired* when there is too much change (7)

3 *not believing in* its benefits (7, 5)

4 doing it so that its benefits are *continued* (9)

5 *strong positive feelings* about it (7 and 10)

6 getting managers *all to feel the same way about it* (7)

7 providing an *example* of how to do it (4, 5)

8 getting people to keep *concentrated* on it (7)

C ◀)) CD1.16 **Complete the table with words from part three, and related words.**

verb	noun
organise	.........[1]
.........[2]	merger
.........[3]	creation
.........[4]	involvement
converse	.........[5]
.........[6]	construction

UNIT 4 Organisation

RICHARD RAWLINSON, VICE-PRESIDENT OF THE MANAGEMENT CONSULTANTS BOOZ & CO.

A 🔊 CD1.24 **Listen to part one. True or false?**

Looking at ...

1 an organisation's formal structure is enough to understand it fully.

2 decision rights involves looking at what each manager has the authority to decide.

3 these rights also means looking at who is kept informed and who approves the decisions.

4 information flows means looking at the way communications, information and data flow around the organisation, and who has access to them.

5 incentives means just looking at bonuses.

6 all of the above gives you understanding of a company's DNA.

B 🔊 CD1.25 **Listen to part two and replace the eight mistakes in the transcript below with what Richard Rawlinson actually says.**

If you want to start an analysis, we have a survey tool – it's on a website, orgdna.com, where you can respond to just a small number of questions about your organisation and then we compare that to answers from about 30,000 other executives and we can discover patterns, and that helps us to say that your organisation is like these other organisations, and so we can get some learning from similar organisations. And we call that the 'orgdna profiler'. It gives you a surface view and it's a good place to start the dialogue. But then we have to go much deeper. And we usually organise both workshops with the executives and investigations into particular aspects that seem to be particularly interesting. So, for example, we might take a single major difficult decision and look at how that was actually made, and really you often find that the reality is quite different from the theory.

C 🔊 CD1.26 **Find nouns in part three that mean the following.**

1 making products

2 selling products

3 one of a company's activities, such as 1 and 2 above

4 an area chosen by a company in relation to the way the firm is organised

5 one of the individual parts of a company

6 main office

D 🔊 CD1.26 **Complete these statements with appropriate forms of verbs from part three.**

1 If someone manages a department, they .... it.

2 If a company satisfies the needs of different markets, it .... well to them.

3 If someone understands a situation after thinking about it, they .... it ....

4 If a company organises an activity in a particular way, it .... it in that way.

5 If a company delivers goods to a particular place, it .... them there.

6 If someone in a company is responsible to another person, they .... to that person.

RESOURCE BANK – Listening

Advertising

A 🔊 CD1.31 **Listen to part one and match the two parts of these expressions.**

1 What are the key elements of

a) all most important to understand what it is that the campaign must try and achieve.

2 ... what is it that that person wants to happen as a result of

b) a product.

3 So in order to decide whether it [a campaign] is good or bad, it is first of

c) Coca-Cola or jeans.

4 Some people might say, well that's obvious [the purpose of the campaign is] – to sell ... more bottles of

d) spending money on this advertising campaign?

5 ... it [the campaign] is simply to sell more of

e) an issue.

6 Sometimes it is to change people's views of

f) a really good advertising campaign?

B 🔊 CD1.32 **Listen to part two. Find the verbs used in these contexts. (Give their infinitive forms.)**

To ...

1 *decide* exactly what a brief should be

2 *have the same ideas* about it (occurs twice)

3 *broadcast* an advertising campaign

4 *explain* the brief for the needs of different people

5 *explain* what is required to the creative people

6 *have* ideas in relation to the brief (phrasal verb)

C 🔊 CD1.32 **Listen again to part two and find these nouns and noun expressions.**

1 telling people the best things to do in the campaign (1 word)

2 showing people ideas about the campaign (1 word)

3 a discussion of different ideas about the campaign (1 word)

4 the time when you do what has been decided for the campaign (2-word expression)

5 advertisements and related activities in the campaign (2-word expression)

6 places where the advertisement is shown (such as TV, posters) (3-word expression)

D 🔊 CD1.33 **Listen to part three and look at these statements about expressions as they are used here. True or false?**

1 *youthful* is related to youth, which means 'a young person' or 'young people in general'

2 *viral* is used in a technical sense to talk about computer viruses

3 *content* is an adjective meaning 'happy'

4 *lob* can be used to talk about football, as here, or tennis

5 *outrageous* means 'forbidden'

6 *PR* means public relations

DARRELL MERCER, INVESTMENT DIRECTOR AT PSIGMA INVESTMENT MANAGEMENT

A 🔊 CD1.37 **Listen to part one and match the verbs (1–5) to the expressions (a–e) that they relate to.**

1 provide
2 have
3 achieve
4 design
5 manage

a) the strategy for the client
b) investment solutions
c) a certain level of return
d) capital
e) that strategy on an ongoing basis

B **Now match the expressions in Exercise A to their meanings (i–v).**

i) obtain income from an investment
ii) decide how a client's money is to be invested
iii) continue to invest money in the best way
iv) offer different ways of investing money
v) possess money available to invest

C 🔊 CD1.38 **Listen to part two. Darrell Mercer uses these expressions (a–f) to introduce the different asset classes. Put them into the order in which they occur.**

a) We then look at …
b) And then we have the final asset class …
c) We also look at …
d) So moving up the scale of risk we go from …
e) We look at …
f) We then look at …

D 🔊 CD1.39 **Listen to part three and find two-word expressions that mean the following.**

1 good things to invest in, in general
2 the way an economy starts growing, then grows faster, then slows down, over a period of time
3 a period when an economy is getting smaller
4 a good place to invest so that your money does not lose value
5 actions to improve one's financial situation after a difficult period
6 countries that are growing very fast and becoming much richer

UNIT **7** Cultures

JEFF TOMS, MARKETING DIRECTOR AT FARNHAM CASTLE, AN INTERNATIONAL CULTURAL TRAINING CENTRE

A ◀)) CD1.44 **Listen to how these expressions are used in part one. True or false?**

1   Someone's *perception of* something or their *perspective on* it is the way that they understand it.

2   If something *revolves around* something else, it depends on it.

3   If an experience is *frustrating*, it is satisfying.

4   Someone who is *keen* to do something wants to delay starting on it.

5   If sales people *exalt the virtues* of their products, they praise and recommend them.

6   If a business contact *entertains* you, they sing and dance for you.

B ◀)) CD1.45 **Listen to part two and find nouns and noun phrases with these meanings.**

1   tasks

2   all the valuable things that someone is able to do, considered together (two-word expression)

3   referring to what someone is like

4   what people think will or should happen

5   two different words to describe the degree to which someone is able to change their behaviour in different situations

6   a set of rules that control the way that something will be done

C ◀)) CD1.46 **Listen to this extract from part three and replace the seven mistakes in the transcript below with what Jeff Toms actually says.**

I think also one of the key traits of the successful international businessperson is to be non-judgemental. For instance, if you come from an Asian culture, er, to try and do business with, er, a Western culture, er, for certain the way that people do things will be very different – er, the hierarchy, the structure, the decision-making procedures, the seniority and the influence of the people you're doing business with – will be fundamentally different. Er, you may not agree, you may not like the way that business is done in another culture; but the way that people do business in that culture is as a result of many, many years of, of evolution and so you have to be accepting, er, that it may be not to your liking and it may be different, but it is not mistaken.

RESOURCE BANK – Listening

194

© Pearson Education Limited 2010 **PHOTOCOPIABLE**

Human resources

A ◀)) CD2.6 **Listen to part one. Put these events into the order they are mentioned.**

a) We work through a CV, perhaps give tips and hints as to how best to present that.

b) We also work with them on how they present themselves.

c) Candidates apply online for roles that we advertise.

d) Candidates have the opportunity to come in and meet with a Hays consultant.

e) Candidates also have the opportunity to get advice from that website, as well as to how they should structure their application.

f) The Hays consultant works with them to gain an understanding of what type of role they're looking for.

B ◀)) CD2.7 **Listen to part two. Complete the table with words from part two, and related words.**

noun	verb
recommendation	.........^{1}
.........^{2}	interview
.........^{3}	advise
appearance	.........^{4}
employer	.........^{5}
.........^{6}	clip
proof	.........^{7}
demonstration	.........^{8}

C ◀)) CD2.8 **Listen to part three. In what order do you hear these adverbs?**

a) absolutely   b) equally   c) generally   d) globally

e) probably   f) recently   g) truly

D **Now match the adverbs in Exercise C to their meanings in the context they are used in part three.**

- all over the world
- at the same time
- in general
- in the last few years
- it's likely that
- really
- totally

RESOURCE BANK – Listening

International markets

ANDY SIMMONS, A PARTNER AT THE GAP PARTNERSHIP AND AN EXPERT ON NEGOTIATING

A 🔊 CD2.18 **Listen to part one. Choose the correct definition (a or b) for the nouns (1–7) as they are used in the recording.**

1 environment
   a) the air, water and land on earth   b) the place, conditions, etc. in which something happens

2 feedback
   a) advice, criticism, etc. about how useful something is
   b) a very unpleasant high noise caused when a microphone is in the wrong place

3 vehicle
   a) something that is used to achieve a particular result
   b) a car, bus, truck, etc.

4 format
   a) the form in which information, etc. is communicated
   b) used to talk about videos, CDs, etc. in relation to the equipment they can be played on

5 workshop
   a) a room where tools and machines are used for making or repairing things
   b) a meeting of people who try to learn something by practising it

6 habit
   a) something that you do regularly, often without thinking
   b) a long piece of clothing used by some religious groups

7 degree
   a) a course of study at a university, and the related qualification
   b) the level or amount of something

B 🔊 CD2.19 **Listen to part two and find adjectives and expressions used as adjectives that mean the following.**

1 where each side wants to do better than the other

2 where there is a lot of argument and disagreement

3 where only one side can get what they want

4 where both sides work together

5 where both sides get what they want

6 suitable for the situation

7 very ready

C 🔊 CD2.20 **Listen to this extract from part three and replace the seven mistakes in the transcript below with what Andy Simmons actually says.**

… effective negotiators are able to watch for when there is more room for negotiation. What I mean by that is, the ability to be able to look out and hear what we call 'soft revealing give-aways'. These are the small bits of language around proposals that will tell you that the person you are dealing with, the person on the other side of the table, has more negotiation room. And these are words like 'I'm looking for … approximately … in the region of … around about … I'd like … I'm hoping for … currently … right now … er, probably'. Er, these are words that negotiators spot to help them understand just how flexible the other side is. And so language itself is very important and the control of that language; but also the ability to listen. Because the more information you have, the more powerful you become, because knowledge is power.

DAVID HILLYARD, DIRECTOR OF PROGRAMMES AT EARTHWATCH

A ◀)) CD2.26 Listen to part one of the interview and match the verbs (1–7) with the expressions (a–g) to which they relate.

1	cope	a)	real data
2	support	b)	scientific data
3	provide	c)	in their environment
4	degrade	d)	a hundred projects
5	design	e)	the environment
6	join	f)	research projects
7	collect	g)	researchers in the field

B Now match the verbs and expressions in Exercise A to their meanings (i–vii).

i) gather information

ii) damage the air, water, etc.

iii) deal with difficult conditions

iv) provide help with administration, organisation, etc. for the different activities

v) decide how a research activity should work, how it should be organised, etc.

vi) go to work with other people already at work

vii) supply real and objective information

C ◀)) CD2.27 Put this information from part two in the order in which you hear it.

a) Leading companies can then influence other companies to follow.

b) Most people in the world work for a company.

c) Many companies are able to set leading examples, to innovate and to find new solutions to the environmental problems.

d) Leading companies can influence government.

e) EarthWatch works with many companies to promote good practice.

f) Companies produce the goods and services that we buy and use.

g) Companies can inspire and motivate their employees to do something for the environment.

h) Businesses need to change the way they operate in order to help and reduce their effect on the environment.

D ◀)) CD2.28 Correct these statements with correct forms of expressions from part three.

1 Two organisations that work together are in partnerhood, which is a type of collaborism.

2 Protecting the environment is referred to as conversation.

3 The chance to do something is an occasion to do it.

4 People who do research are researchists.

5 Datums is a plural word used to talk about scientific information.

6 People who work on a project are evolved in it.

7 Someone who promotes the environment is referred to here as an embassy worker.

RESOURCE BANK – Listening

ELIZABETH JACKSON, MANAGING DIRECTOR OF DIRECTORBANK, AN EXECUTIVE RECRUITMENT COMPANY

A 🔊 CD2.32 **Complete the table with expressions from part one, and related forms.**

adjective	noun
courageous	.........¹
.........²	indecisiveness
respectful	.........³
emotionally intelligent	.........⁴
.........⁵	sensitivity
cold	.........⁶

B Match the adjectives in Exercise A to their meanings.

1 unable or unwilling to make decisions

2 able to understand others' feelings

3 cool and unemotional

4 brave

5 showing that other people are important, not treating them rudely, etc.

6 with a high level of understanding of one's own and others' feelings

C 🔊 CD2.33 **Listen to part two. What do the underlined words below refer to?**

1 They seem to have a natural ability to lead people.

2 There is plenty of both types of this, to show that leadership is a natural talent, but that it can be learnt.

3 Some leaders have it – this quality that people admire and that makes people want to follow them.

4 These can be learnt, but leaders who have them from birth have an advantage over those who don't.

5 The fact that most US astronauts were first-born might be due to this – just chance.

6 Most people can improve it, but the natural leaders will usually win.

D 🔊 CD2.34 **Look at the statements about expressions used in part three. True or false?**

1 If you are *privileged* to do something, you have the advantage of doing something that many people have not.

2 If you *pave the way* for someone else, your success makes it easier for them to be successful.

3 If you have *tremendous tenacity*, you give up easily.

4 If you *fight like a cornered rat*, you fight very hard.

5 If you *strike a chord* with people, they dislike you.

6 If you have *innate ability* for something, you learnt how to do it.

7 If you *work ahead of the pack*, you understand situations and do things before others do.

8 If you *work outside the box*, you do things in normal ways.

A 🔊 CD2.36 **Listen to part one. True or false?**

1   The Competition Commission is a private company.

2   It only looks at mergers between companies.

3   One of the industries that Rory Taylor mentions is car manufacturing.

4   The investigation into the ownership of UK airports is getting a lot of attention.

5   BAA owns seven airports.

6   The way that airports are owned is referred to as their 'ownership organisation'.

7   The investigation is looking at bringing more competition into airport ownership.

B 🔊 CD2.37 **Listen to part two and complete these statements about markets.**

1   The d........................ of a market are the way that it works.

2   Rory Taylor refers to competitors as s........................, p........................ or, more informally, p........................ .

3   A c........................ market is one where there are few competitors. The related noun is c........................ .

4   A c........................ market is one where suppliers are reacting with each other as they normally should.

5   A s........................ market is one where competitors are not reacting with each other as they normally should.

C 🔊 CD2.38 **Listen to this extract from part three and replace the seven mistakes in the transcript below with what Rory Taylor actually says.**

We could contrast that with another investigation that we did, completed about two years ago, into what's known as liquid petroleum gas for domestic users. Basically, this is for customers who are not supplied for gas through pipes – they live in distant areas, and therefore they need the gas, which is also known as propane, propane, delivered to their house and put in a tank. Again this is a market with only four major players in it, concentrated in the same way seemingly like the groceries industry, but we found a far more static market. Er, we found that customers were not changing between the companies, the companies were not competing with each other, erm, and as a result we were finding higher prices, less innovation and less choice.

RESOURCE BANK LISTENING KEY

Unit 1

A – B

1 b v **2** e iv **3** a iii **4** c iii **5** d i **6** g ii **7** h i **8** f i

C

1 True

2 False (The information is also about what the brand is like and how it appeals to you and connects with you.)

3 True

4 False (There is very little physical difference between the products.)

5 False (He mentions the first three brands, but not Porsche.)

6 True

D

d, a, b, c

E

1 d **2** b **3** c **4** a

Unit 2

A

A key point <u>would be</u> the location of our hotels, um, good <u>links</u> with um subway underground networks, <u>close to</u> the airport, um, and obviously close to an office that the guest <u>would be</u> working in while they're staying in the hotel. Um, technology is also a key <u>feature</u>, and nowadays it's expected because obviously people have, um, <u>great</u> technology at home and therefore if it's also available in a hotel, that's also, um, a key feature. Um, Internet, a business centre, um, obviously translation services and that kind of facility is also, is <u>paramount</u>, and guests also expect an area where they can, er, go to a gymnasium, they can exercise, um, and also that kind of thing. These would be the <u>key</u> features.

B

1 True

2 False (The company adds an additional benefit or service.)

3 True

4 False (You do it every day.)

5 False (A shuttle service goes both to and from a place.)

6 True

C

5 and 8

Unit 3

A

1 into account

2 looks like

3 measure

4 engaged

5 themselves

B

1 process

2 fatigue

3 cynical about

4 sustained

5 passion, enthusiasm

6 aligned

7 role model

8 focused

C

1 organisation

2 merge

3 create

4 involve

5 conversation

6 construct

Unit 4

A

1   False (It's very important to go beyond that.)
2   True
3   True
4   True
5   False (It's also about promotion and other rewards.)
6   True

B

If you want to start an analysis, we have a survey tool –
it's on a website, orgdna.com, where you can <u>answer</u> just
a small number of questions about your organisation
and then we compare that to answers from about <u>40,000</u>
other executives and we can <u>recognise</u> patterns, and that
helps us to say that your organisation is like these other
organisations, and so we can get some learning from
<u>comparable</u> organisations. And we call that the 'orgdna
profiler'. It gives you a <u>superficial</u> view and it's a good
place to start the <u>conversation</u>. But then we have to go
much deeper. And we usually organise both workshops
with the executives and <u>probes</u> into particular aspects
that seem to be particularly interesting. So, for example,
we might take a single major <u>controversial</u> decision and
look at how that was actually made, and really you often
find that the reality is quite different from the theory.

C

1   manufacturing
2   marketing
3   function
4   geography
5   business unit
6   headquarters

D

1   run
2   responds
3   figure; out
4   operates
5   ships
6   report

Unit 5

A

1 f   2 d   3 a   4 c   5 b   6 e

B

1   identify
2   agree
3   air
4   articulate
5   brief
6   come up with

C

1   recommendations
2   presentation
3   debate
4   execution phase
5   creative material
6   channels of distribution

D

1   True
2   False (Here it is used to talk about an idea that
    spreads over the Internet, by word of mouth, etc.)
3   False (It's a noun used to talk about what something
    contains.)
4   True
5   False (It's used here to talk about something that's so
    good it's shocking.)
6   True

Unit 6

A – **B**

1 b iv   **2** d v   **3** c i   **4** a ii   **5** e iii

C

d, a, f (or f, a), c, e, b

D

1 attractive areas   **4** safe haven
2 economic cycle   **5** recovery play
3 economic depression **6** emerging markets

Unit 7

A

1 True
2 True
3 False (A frustrating experience is one where you do not get what you want.)
4 False (Someone who is keen to do something wants to do it immediately.)
5 True
6 False (If a business contact entertains you, they might take you to a restaurant, invite you to their home, etc.)

B

1 assignments   **4** expectations
2 skill set   **5** adaptability, flexibility
3 traits   **6** parameters

C

I think also one of the key <u>features</u> of the successful international businessperson is to be non-judgemental. For instance, if <u>you're coming</u> from an Asian culture, er, to try and do business with, er, a Western culture, er, for certain the way that people do things will be <u>fundamentally</u> different – er, the hierarchy, the structure, the decision-making <u>process</u>, the seniority and the influence of the people you're doing business with – will be fundamentally different. Er, you may not agree, you may not <u>approve of</u> the way that business is done in another culture; but the way that people do business in that culture is as a result of many, many years of, of <u>development</u> and so you have to be accepting, er, that it may be not to your liking and it may be different, but it is not <u>wrong</u>.

Unit 8

A

d, f, b, a, c, e

B

1 recommend   **5** employ
2 interview   **6** clippings
3 advice   **7** prove
4 appear   **8** demonstrate

C – **D**

e – it's likely that
f – in the last few years
g – really
b – at the same time
d – all over the world
a – totally
c – in general

Unit 9

A

1 b   **2** a   **3** a   **4** a   **5** b   **6** a   **7** b

B

1 competitive   **5** win–win
2 high-conflict **6** appropriate
3 win–lose   **7** well prepared
4 co-operative

C

… effective negotiators are able to watch for when there is more <u>scope</u> for negotiation. What I mean by that is, the ability to be able to look out and <u>listen for</u> what we call 'soft <u>exposing</u> give-aways'. These are the small bits of language around proposals that will tell you that <u>your counterpart</u>, the person on the other side of the table, has more negotiation room. And these are words like 'I'm looking for … <u>roughly</u> … in the region of … around about … I'd like … I'm hoping for … currently … right now … er, probably'. Er, these are words that negotiators spot to help them understand just how <u>movable</u> the other side is. And so language itself is very important and the control of that language; but also the ability to listen. Because the more information you have, the more powerful you become, because <u>information</u> is power.

Unit 10

A – **B**

1 c iii **2** d iv **3** b i **4** e ii **5** f v **6** g vi **7** a vii

C

f, h, c, b, g, e, a, d

D

1 Two organisations that work together are in *partnership*, which is a type of *collaboration*.

2 Protecting the environment is referred to as *conservation*.

3 The chance to do something is an *opportunity* to do it.

4 People who do research are *researchers*.

5 *Data* is a plural word used to talk about scientific information.

6 People who work on a project are *involved* in it.

7 Someone who promotes the environment is referred to here as an *ambassador*.

Unit 11

A

1 courage
2 indecisive
3 respect
4 emotional intelligence
5 sensitive
6 coldness

B

1 indecisive
2 sensitive
3 cold
4 courageous
5 respectful
6 emotionally intelligent

C

1 natural born leaders
2 evidence
3 charisma
4 leadership skills
5 coincidence
6 their skill set

D

1 True

2 True

3 False (You keep doing it until you succeed, and don't give up.)

4 True

5 False (They like you.)

6 False (You were born with it.)

7 True

8 False (You do things in unusual ways.)

Unit 12

A

1 False (It's a public body.)

2 False (It also looks at matters in regulated industries.)

3 False (He mentions water, energy and communications, but not cars.)

4 True

5 True

6 False (The correct expression is 'ownership structure'.)

7 True

B

1 dynamics

2 suppliers; providers; players

3 concentrated; concentration

4 competitive

5 static

C

We could contrast that with another <u>enquiry</u> that we did, completed about two years ago, into what's known as liquid petroleum gas for domestic users. <u>Essentially</u>, this is for customers who are not supplied for <u>energy</u> through pipes – they live in <u>remote</u> areas, and therefore they need the gas, which is also known as propane, propane, delivered to their house and put in a tank. Again this is a market with only four major players in it, concentrated in the same way <u>in nominal terms</u> like the groceries industry, but we found a far more static market. Er, we found that customers were not <u>switching</u> between the companies, the companies were not competing with each other, erm, and <u>consequently</u> we were finding higher prices, less innovation and less choice.

CASE STUDY WRITING TASK: MODEL ANSWER

Dear David

As you know, we've recently been having intensive discussions within the Hudson organization about the future of our brand, in particular whether to go upmarket or downmarket. At a meeting of our key people recently, we decided to take the upmarket route. We want to develop the Hudson label as an exclusive brand, keep the 'Made in America' tag, sell at higher prices, and use product placement and high-profile celebrities to advertise our products.

We also want to stretch the Hudson brand and use it on high-quality watches and jewelry, in an agreement with a Swiss manufacturer.

I would like to arrange a meeting with you and your key associates to discuss these issues further and to decide how to move forward. Would next Wednesday, May 13, at 10:30, here at my office in Newark, be suitable for you?

Looking forward to hearing from you.

Best wishes

Carly Angelo
CEO, Hudson Corporation

A Look at the model answer above. Write an e-mail in reply, from David Wright, Head of European Marketing Associates, to Carly Angelo, Hudson Corporation, including these points.

- You are glad that Hudson has come to a decision in relation to its future marketing strategy.

- You look forward to discussing a detailed plan of action on how to put the selected strategies into action.

- Confirm that you can come to the meeting on the day suggested, but in the afternoon if possible. Say which two of your associates you will be bringing with you, and their areas of expertise.

End suitably.

B It's six months later. Write the press release issued by the public relations (PR) firm that Hudson has hired to announce its new activities. (See the Writing file, Course Book page 126, for the format of press releases.) Don't forget to include:

- who the press release is intended for

- an attractive subject line.

Begin the main part of the text:

Hudson Corporation is pleased to announce ...

End with the name and details of a contact person at the PR firm.

CASE STUDY WRITING TASK: MODEL ANSWER

Dear Tom

I was sorry to hear about the problems that your executives have been experiencing during the trips that we have organized for them. I have taken up the problems with the various companies concerned, and can report the following:

- The Excelsior Hotel has apologized for your executive's bad experience and will offer a free night's stay the next time your company uses the hotel.

- The car rental firm has refused to admit that there was a problem, so we will be terminating our agreement with them. We have negotiated a new agreement with another car rental firm, with better cars, bigger discounts, etc. You should save at least 10 per cent on bookings we make for you with this new company.

- On the lost luggage, the airline concerned confirms that it has been reorganizing its baggage complaints department following the merger with another airline. It says that it can now offer $250 compensation for each bag that it mislaid. This will be paid to us and credited to your account with us in the next few months.

- The airline has admitted responsibility for the chaos surrounding its delayed flight to Moscow. As compensation, it has agreed to upgrade your managers from business class to first class at no cost for the next 12 months on all bookings made through us.

I hope this information is useful, and will encourage you to continue to use our services.

Sincerely*

Lynn McNulty
Account Manager

* This is used in the US, rather than 'Yours sincerely'.

A Look again at the hotel facilities in Listening, Exercise A on page 16 of the Course Book. Your company, Eco Consultants, has booked you into the Harbour Panorama hotel, part of another chain, in Sydney, Australia, for this year's International Green Business Conference. Write a fax to the hotel (see the Writing file, Course Book page 128, for the format of faxes), asking them to confirm the availability of the following:

- shuttle bus to the conference venue (frequency, duration of journey?)
- gymnasium and swimming pool (size, indoor or outdoor?)
- business centre with translation facilities (time needed, cost?).

End suitably.

B You work in an airport car rental office that has to close early because of a shortage of staff. Write the notice to customers that you put on the door of the office. (See the Writing file, Course Book page 131, for the format of notices.) Include the following:

- name of company
- reason for early closing
- when the office will reopen
- where customers should go to pick up their cars (city centre office – give the address).

Offer apologies.

End with your name and position.

Change

CASE STUDY WRITING TASK: MODEL ANSWER

Minutes of the management meeting

Date	13 May
Venue	Asia Entertainment meeting room, Hong Kong
Present	Scott Henderson (Chief Executive), Robert Crawford (Vice-President) and Australian managers
	Asia Entertainment senior executives, and Cindy Chow (Human Resources Director)

	Action	By
1 Reapplying for positions		
Human resources department (HRD) managers will reassure employees and explain the procedures for this after meetings with employee representatives.	CC	20 May
2 Redundancy and compensation		
HRD will put together attractive packages and submit them to relevant staff as soon as possible, to minimise uncertainty.	CC	25 May
3 Company language		
Decker agreed to provide English-language courses at the company's expense. Decker's VP will select a language training provider.	RC	1 June
4 Computer system		
Decker's Chief Executive will lead a task force of managers from both companies in upgrading the company's website and internal network. Will also organise training in how to use the new network.	SH	15 June
5 Management style		
New guidelines will be issued to improve communications, and make clear a policy of making management jobs open to both Chinese and Australian nationals.	SH	30 June
6 Food in staff restaurant		
We will ask the restaurant manager to make more Asian food available.	RC	20 May

A Look again at the business situations in Starting up, Exercise C, on page 22 of the Course Book. Imagine that you are in one of the situations. Write an e-mail to a friend about it, asking for his/her advice.

- Explain the background to the situation.

- Describe your feelings and reactions.

- Ask your friend for advice on what to do.

End suitably.

B Look again at the completed business brief on Vietnam on page 26 of the Course Book. Write a summary of it in less than 110 words.
(See the Writing file, Course Book page 131, for more information on summaries.)

Organisation

CASE STUDY WRITING TASK: MODEL ANSWER

To:	donald.sumner@instep.com
From:	meredith.quincy@instep.com

Donald – This is to let you know the outcome of discussions at our European head office in Paris last week about the possible move to Beauchamp.

Views of managers were very divided on moving to Beauchamp, but following discussions with them, I feel we can go ahead and make the move. (As you can imagine, some were unhappy at the idea of leaving Paris, but many – more than I expected – could see the personal benefits for them and their families.)

However, the company's needs are the most important thing, of course, and the benefits, including the tax incentives offered by Beauchamp town council, are too good to walk away from.

We can make an official announcement very soon. I will ask our European HR Manager in Paris, Sylvie Juliénas, to draw up an action plan/schedule for the move in the next few weeks.

Meredith

A You are Sylvie Juliénas, Instep's European HR Manager. Draw up an action plan for the move of Instep's European subsidiary to Beauchamp, based on the following information. (See the Writing file, Course Book page 129, for the format of action plans.)

- We have to give notice of our intention to leave our existing offices to the building's management company by the end of January (six months' notice required).

- The new Beauchamp offices will be ready by late March.

- Staff from all departments except Accounts and HR will move out to Beauchamp in early April.

- HR staff will move in mid-June.

- The Accounts department will be the last to move, by late July.

- All staff will leave our Paris office by 31 July. All remaining equipment and office furniture to be moved out by then.

B You are Paolo Marchese, the Italian manager at Instep's European subsidiary. In discussing the move with others at Instep, you said, 'I am absolutely against it. It will upset families and cause a lot of problems for some staff. I will have to sell my apartment if we move. I only bought it last year, so I will probably lose a lot of money – I don't think I will get any compensation for that, do you?'

Write a letter to Sylvie Juliénas, HR Manager at Instep's European subsidiary, saying that you are against company's move. Give your reasons – the one above, giving details, and one other. (See the Writing file, Course Book page 126, for the format of letters.)

RESOURCE BANK – Writing

Advertising

Panther Air: Advertising campaign concept

Key messages

Convey the special features of the service – exclusivity, safety, quality and service.

USPs

- Avoid the delay of queuing for scheduled flights at check-in and security desk, luxurious levels of in-flight service. (Drive straight to plane and go through special Panther-dedicated security procedures. Panther recruits cabin staff with service background in luxury hotels, not other airlines.)

- Competitive prices compared to similar services

Target audience

Senior company directors, particularly in those companies who cannot afford to buy their own executive jet.

Campaign

- <u>TV commercials</u> on business news programmes.

  Key slogan: 'Travel in considerable style at a reasonable price'

  Campaign to be filmed with real passengers on a Panther flight (get their permission in advance)

  Get a celebrity with a 'rich' voice to do the voiceover, to be written to emphasise the key messages and USPs above. (Emphasise especially the cabin staff recruitment policy.) Classical music background.

- <u>Advertisements</u> in business magazines – still photos from the TV campaign to suggest luxury, comfort, etc. Same slogan as above. Minimum of text. The main message should come through pictures and slogan.

A You are the CEO of a UK-based multinational. You saw Panther's ad in a business magazine. Send an e-mail to your PA (personal assistant), Sue, asking her to contact Panther in order to find out more about their services. Explain where you saw the ad and ask her to find about:

- whether they can provide flights for four people (you and three other directors) from Manchester to Baltimore in the US, arriving in the morning, local time, and returning the same evening, on 31 May;

- how much this would cost;

- if they can arrange for you and your colleagues to be picked up from your homes around Manchester by chauffeur-driven cars and, if so, whether these cars can drop you directly by the steps of the plane.

Thank her and end suitably.

B A recently founded snack-food company has been growing fast, thanks to word-of-mouth advertising alone. You have just been appointed as its first ever marketing executive and you call a meeting with managers in other departments to discuss possible marketing plans. You want to discuss money available, possible marketing activities (not just advertising) and their potential effect on sales, production levels required if demand really takes off, etc.

Write an agenda for the meeting. (See the Writing file, Course Book page 128, for the format of agendas.)

Money

To:	rebecca.rae@xfproducts.co.uk
From:	david.bannister@ventcap.com
Re:	Our investment in New Formula XF anti-wrinkle cream

Dear Rebecca

It was very nice to meet you on the programme yesterday. Congratulations again on your very impressive pitch!

This is to confirm the terms of our investment: we will invest $350,000 in order to manufacture, launch and market the product, in return for an equity stake of 55 per cent. In return, we will provide you with the expertise to develop a proper business plan, with sales and profit projections, along with technical help in moving to a larger-scale production process. We will review the terms of our joint project in 12 months.

I will send you a contract by courier with these terms in the next few days.

We will be in touch soon to set up our first meeting for the joint project.

Best regards,

David Bannister

Ventcap Inc.

A   It is 18 months later. New Formula XF anti-wrinkle cream has been a big success, and David Bannister has suggested further investment to build a second manufacturing plant. You are Rebecca Rae. Since David Bannister invested in your company, you have recruited three managers to take responsibility for different areas. Write a report for them to read under these headings. (See the Writing file, Course Book page 130, for the format of reports.)

- **Executive summary**
- **Introduction/background** to XF, before and after David Bannister became involved
- **Developments** during the last 18 months, including sales figures in general terms
- **Conclusion/recommendation** about David Bannister's future involvement, and other possible sources of finance in order to develop the product further

B   To your report above, you add an appendix with a graph for sales figures for New Formula XF anti-wrinkle cream over the last 18 months. Draw a graph for the sales for each month over this period (you can make up the figures), and then describe it using some of the language for describing trends on page 56 of the Course Book.

CASE STUDY WRITING TASK: MODEL ANSWER

Culture

For me, the most interesting information in this unit has been about the way that people use time, and about the related issue of building relationships.

Time

From the unit, we see that this isn't just about punctuality for meetings. It's also about the time you spend outside the meetings themselves. You have to think about time you can spend in the evening with contacts in restaurants and time meeting people who are not directly involved in the business you have come to discuss.

Relationship building

This seems to be important in a wide range of cultures. A lot of businesspeople around the world want to get to know the person that they're going to be dealing with, before they start doing business. If you watch someone in social situations, you can find out a lot about them!

A When Rosana goes to Russia (Course Book page 73), she receives a fax at her hotel on her last day there from Ludmila, her business contact in St Petersburg. The fax is an invitation to Ludmila's house in the country outside the city the next day. Rosana wants to leave St Petersburg that evening (Friday) to fly back home.

Write the fax that Rosana sends to Ludmila in reply, thanking her for the invitation, but refusing it politely, giving your reasons. (See the Writing file, Course Book page 128, for the format of faxes.)

B A course of ten weekly intercultural training sessions (two hours each) has been organised in your company for staff who receive visits from foreign suppliers. Write a notice for the notice board in the staff coffee room. (See the Writing file, Course Book page 131, for the format of notices.) Include with the following information:

- the name of the course;
- the benefits of attending;
- the training approach (a lot of role play and 'hands-on' activities);
- who will be running the course;
- where and when it will be held.

CASE STUDY WRITING TASK: MODEL ANSWER

Fast Fitness Inc.,

80 Front Street, New York, NY 10003–1324
Tel. 212-872 3700, Fax 212-872 3750
www.fastfitness.com
e-mail: zb@fastfitness.com

Mr. Paulo Goncalves,
Rua de Lisboa 421,
São Paulo 01028,
Brazil

December 9th

Dear Mr. Goncalves,

Re: General Manager, São Paulo

Thank you for coming to the interview for the post of General Manager of
our chain of health and leisure clubs in São Paulo. We are delighted to offer
you the job, commencing January 2nd.

We believe that your high profile as a martial-arts actor in Brazil will be an
important asset in promoting the chain.

Please let us know as soon as possible by e-mail if you will be accepting
this offer. I will then courier you a contract for you to sign.

Sincerely,

Zoe Bondachuk

Zoe Bondachuk
CEO, Fast Fitness Inc.

A You are Paulo Goncalves. Write an e-mail in reply to the letter above. (See the Writing file, Course Book page 127, for the format of e-mails.)

- Confirm that you accept the job.
- Say that you look forward to receiving the contract.

End suitably.

B You are Zoe Bondachuk. Write the standard letter that you send to the unsuccessful candidates, including appropriate forms of these expressions.

- glad to meet
- interesting discussions
- very strong candidates
- unfortunately
- every success in the future

RESOURCE BANK – Writing

International markets

CASE STUDY WRITING TASK: MODEL ANSWER

To:	roberto.gonzalez@pampasleather.ar
From:	brad.schulz@wca.com

Roberto – It was great meeting you here in Seattle. I hope you had a smooth trip back to Buenos Aires. This is to confirm that we would like to order all three models, as long as they are all made in Argentina – no outsourcing. Following our discussions, we would like to make this first order with these quantities and prices:

Clubman: 200 @ $320   Nightrider: 1,200 @ $250   The Look: 900 @ $140

Prices to include all delivery costs to the port of Los Angeles.

As discussed, we will pay by bank transfer 30% immediately and 70% two months after receiving the goods. For such a large order, we would expect an introductory discount of at least 5%, but as you promised to give our order high priority, we would be willing in this case to accept 3%.

Delivery must be within five days of the agreed date, otherwise there will be penalties. These penalties will be mentioned in the final contract.

Following what we said on guarantees, we would accept a guarantee of three years for all three models.

I hope all of the above is now acceptable for you and, if this order goes ahead, I'm sure we can build on it and form a long-term relationship with your company.

Best wishes

Brad Schulz
CEO, West Coast Apparel Inc.

A It is five years later, and Pampas's products are selling very well in WCA's outlets in the US. Now Brad Schulz and Roberto González have signed a joint-venture agreement to sell Pampas clothing in Europe, through a new chain of stores called Luxury Leather to be financed by the two companies (50 per cent each).

Write the press release issued by the public relations (PR) firm that they hire to announce their new activities. (See the Writing file, Course Book page 126, for the format of press releases.) Don't forget to include:

- who the press release is intended for

- an attractive subject line.

Begin the main part of the text:

WCA and the Pampas Leather Company are pleased to announce ...

(Make up any other information you wish.)

End with the name and details of a contact person at the PR firm.

B Choose one of the two articles in Reading on pages 84–85 of the Course Book, and write a summary of it in less than 100 words. (See the Writing file, Course Book page 131, for more information on summaries.)

CASE STUDY WRITING TASK: MODEL ANSWER

Management meeting

held on March 12

New drug for river blindness

It was decided to go ahead with the development of this drug, even if its future profitability is not clear. The general feeling was that the positive PR that could come out of this drug will help to compensate for its development costs. Following the negative publicity of the last few years, we need to improve our image, and this will be a good way of achieving this aim.

Test results on PX200, our new drug for treating heart disease

Some patients have experienced severe breathing difficulties after taking the drug and other unpleasant side effects, but most have received significant benefits. Our research people tell us that the potential for this drug is enormous once the difficulties are resolved, which they say should be quite soon. In view of this, it was agreed that we should withhold the test results for the time being, as there should be more positive results to announce before long.

New dieting product

The feeling of the meeting was that we should avoid another PR disaster at all costs. We will therefore stop testing this drug on animals and use the new computer-based techniques that the research department is developing. If we can make a success of this drug, it will be extremely profitable.

A You are UP's Marketing Manager for the new dieting product. You know it will be ready in sufficient quantities in late September. (It is now January.) Draw up an action plan for its release, based on the points below, giving additional information, and timings. (See the Writing file, Course Book page 129, for the format of action plans.)

- Press release, announcing the new drug, saying that it will be provided to government health authorities and aid organisations at below cost.

- Arrange interviews between UP researchers and magazine and newspaper journalists (general press and those specialising in developing countries).

- Meet with government officials and aid organisations to discuss how they can distribute and use the product in Africa.

- Official launch.

B Write your CV/résumé in English (as ethically as possible!) under these headings.

- Career goals
- Qualifications
- Experience
- Interests
- Personal details

RESOURCE BANK – Writing

Leadership

CASE STUDY WRITING TASK: MODEL ANSWER

To:	nadine.browning@jpsconsultants.com
From:	silvio.perugia@linasports.it

Dear Nadine

We have now interviewed three members of the Lina Sports board. They are all candidates to take over from our CEO, Franco Rossi. Each candidate has very different ideas about the future direction of the company.

The first strategy was presented by Laura Alba. She wants a takeover by the French retailer Universelle. We would rely less on football and athletics sportswear and offer more clothing and other products for sports such as golf, rugby and ice hockey.

Claudio Bruni gave the second possible strategy. He wants us to buy smaller specialist companies and develop their activities. He also wants to reduce our use of sportspeople to endorse our products. He would use them instead to advise us on product development.

Veronica Castello's strategy, the third alternative, was to sell high-end footwear and clothing by famous international designers. These products would have high profit margins. She also wants to sell wider ranges of customised shoes, bags and sports accessories.

Most of the other directors in the meeting thought that the first alternative was the best, as strategies 2 and 3 are too risky in the current difficult economic climate. I would welcome your opinion on this strategy.

Looking forward to hearing from you.

Best wishes
Silvio Perugia

A It is one month later. Franco Rossi is now Lina Sports's Chairman and Laura Alba its CEO. They arrange a meeting to discuss the possible takeover by Universelle with its Chairman and CEO. You are Franco Rossi. Draw up an agenda with headings for all the things that you will need to discuss at the meeting with Universelle before the takeover can go ahead. (See the Writing file, Course Book page 128, for the format of agendas.)

B Look again at the Vocabulary section in the Course Book, page 104. Write a short report (100 words) on a leader that you admire, using some of the words there, as well as others of your own.

CASE STUDY WRITING TASK: MODEL ANSWER

To:	raj.patel@rashidsinghenterprises.in
From:	carolina.aguilar@fashionhouse.com

Dear Mr Patel

It was a pleasure to meet you in Mumbai last week. If you can agree to the following as the outcome of our negotiation, we will place our order immediately.

- Goods: 1,000 necklaces @ $115 and 1,000 bracelets @ $95 to be shipped immediately, and 2,000 more of each at the same prices by November 15. 3,000 earrings (i.e. 1,500 pairs at $50 per pair) to be shipped by November 30

- Delivery: As the orders are very urgent, we would like delivery by air – charges to be paid by us.

- Trade discount of 2.25% off your list prices. (We hope you will be able to offer a bigger discount on future orders.)

- Returned goods: we will return any unsold goods within one month, and the amount will be credited to our account against future orders. We agreed that there will be no refunds for unsold goods.

- Guarantee: one year for bracelets and earrings, and you kindly offered us a three-year guarantee for necklaces.

- Payment: I agreed to discuss this with our accounts people. They say that we can currently offer a 10-per-cent deposit when the order is placed, with the remainder 60 days after delivery. (I'm sorry we can't offer better terms, but this is now company policy, and we are not able to vary it.)

Looking forward to hearing from you, and, hopefully, to doing business with you.

Best wishes

Carolina Aguilar
Buyer, Fashion House Inc.

A Reluctantly, Raj Patel agreed to the payment terms in the e-mail above. It is now mid-March, and all the goods were delivered on time by November 30 last year, but Fashion House has still not paid any of the invoices sent by Rashid Singh Enterprises, despite several reminders.

The Head of Accounts at Rashid has sent e-mails to the salespeople, telling them not to accept any more orders from Fashion House, but the salespeople have been deleting the e-mails without reading them.

You are the Head of Accounts at Rashid Singh. Write a notice for the sales office notice board, informing salespeople about the situation and telling them not to accept any more orders from Fashion House. (See the Writing file, Course Book page 131, for the format of notices.)

B Look again at the completed minutes of a meeting in the Language review section on page 116 of the Course Book. Write the corresponding action minutes for the same meeting. You can add your own information where necessary. (See the Writing file, Course Book page 129, for the format of action minutes.)